Policy Design in the Age of Digital Adoption

Explore how PolicyOps can drive Policy as Code
adoption in an organization's digital transformation

Ricardo Ferreira

BIRMINGHAM—MUMBAI

Policy Design in the Age of Digital Adoption

Copyright © 2022 Packt Publishing

Group Product Manager: Rahul Nair

Publishing Product Manager: Yogesh Deokar

Senior Editor: Arun Nadar

Content Development Editor: Yasir Ali Khan

Technical Editor: Nithik Cheruvakodan

Copy Editor: Safis Editing

Project Coordinator: Shagun Saini

Proofreader: Safis Editing

Indexer: Hemangini Bari

Production Designer: Joshua Misquitta

Senior Marketing Coordinator: Sanjana Gupta

Marketing Coordinator: Nimisha Dua

First published: April 2022
Production reference: 1110422

Published by Packt Publishing Ltd.
Livery Place
35 Livery Street
Birmingham
B3 2PB, UK.

ISBN 978-1-80181-174-3

www.packt.com

"The best return for 1 year is to grow rice. The best return for 10 years is to grow trees. The best return for a lifetime is to educate people."
– Guan Zhong

137.036

Contributors

About the author

Ricardo Ferreira, MSc, believes in democratizing technology. Currently as an EMEA CISO at Fortinet, he serves as an advisor to help organizations and CxOs establish their security posture at scale.

With over 15 years of experience working on disruptive technology such as Cloud, Artificial Intelligence, and DevOps, he has had various roles, always connected to innovation in Cisco, Rackspace, HSBC, and EY. He has worked with some of the largest financial institutions to adopt Cloud platforms ensuring compliance, risk, and regulatory needs.

He is an active member of the cyber security industry, advancing standards and guidelines at **Cloud Native Computing Foundation** (**CNCF**) and **Cloud Security Alliance** (**CSA**).

"A big thank you to my wife, Claudia, and our lovely daughter. Life would not be the same without you both." 137.036

About the reviewers

Derek Held is a cloud security engineer with over a decade of experience in the information technology industry. He started his career at a help desk while attending Washington State University and, over the years, sharpened his focus on security. Today, he helps organizations using cloud-first and cloud-native strategies to establish security automation, protect operations, and become industry leaders in security. He firmly believes in the mantra that security needs to be a business enabler. Derek has a bachelor's degree in business administration with a major in management information systems from Washington State University and is currently pursuing a master's in engineering and technology management from his alma mater.

Jesse Loudon is a principal consultant and Microsoft Azure MVP with over a decade of experience in consulting and delivery, including working closely with companies on the ASX 100. With a passion for managing cloud infrastructure and Policy as Code, he is a regular contributor to the open source community as a maintainer of several public repositories and a strong advocate of helping to drive cloud adoption to new heights through the use of repeatable and reusable assets. Jesse currently resides in Sydney, Australia, with his wife and their young daughter and can occasionally be found on the beach doing DevBeachOps.

> *"I'd like to thank my amazing wife, Emma, and our incredible daughter, Cynthia, for their amazing support and patience with me over the years as I've often been engaged with doing community-related activities such as book reviews, coding, blogging, and meetup presentations outside of normal working hours, which has meant less time for family. You guys mean the world to me and you have my heartfelt gratitude for helping me follow my passion."*

Shivasheesh Tripathi is a solution architect at TCS, carrying more than 13 years of experience across multiple technology segments – DevOps, the cloud, CI/CD, automation, SecOps, and cloud transformation. He holds a degree in electronics engineering, with specialized certifications in Azure Security, Terraform, and GitOps. He has been supporting key organizations (finance, high-tech, and the like) on key initiatives and transformations, including DevOps, the cloud, Infrastructure as Code, Policy as Code, and CI/CD platforms. Outside work, he loves cricket, writing poems, and learning next-gen tech.

"To my partner, for always being there for me, and supporting me when I needed it the most.

To my kid, who is my oxygen and motivates me every day to keep striving.

To my parents, who raised me to become who I am today. I do not have words to express what you mean to me.

To my brother and sister for always keeping a special family bond together.

To my friends, thank you for every single moment that we have spent together.

And to the Packt Publishing team for the opportunity to help with this wonderful book."

Ken Adler is a fellow at Indeed.com, specializing in production identity and authorization Policy as Code. Previously, he was a principal consultant at Thoughtworks, focusing on security in digital platforms and digital transformation. Ken is a pioneer member of the Internet Society and lives in the San Francisco Bay Area.

Table of Contents

3

Policy as Code a Business Enabler

Section 2: Framework

4

Framework for Digital Policies

5

Policy for Cloud-Native Environments

6

Policy Design for Hybrid Environments

7

Building a Culture of PolicyOps

Section 3: Tooling

8
Policy Engines

9
A Primer on Open Policy Agent

10

Policy as Code Tool Evaluation

11

Cloud Providers Policy Constructs

Preface

The increase of digital enablement is a critical priority for countries and business organizations. With an estimate of US$2.8 trillion of spending in digital transformation globally by 2025, it is crucial to support and have the tools to make these efforts as smooth as possible.

Currently, most digital transformations are aspirational; only a small percentage goes beyond pilot mode, as evidenced by the latest reports by McKinsey and Harvard Business Review. This book leans on the best practices of design thinking and public policy design to bring frameworks and best practices to design and implement digital policies at scale into an organization to significantly improve its digital transformation effort.

It focuses on the intersection of people, technology, and processes. Throughout the book, we focus on people. We elevate the people aspect dimension with PolicyOps and how it brings the dimensions of automation, native digital platforms, and people to build instruments that foster a culture of inclusivity and experimentation.

We discuss and review the state of art in Policy as Code, **policy engines** (**PEs**), giving a focus to Open Policy Agent, and how to use it effectively to build guardrails, authorization (coercive instruments) across digital services. We focus on instruments adapted for hybrid environments and the native cloud providers' policy capabilities.

Finally, we talk about frameworks and how to link policies to business processes using **information technology service management** (**ITSM**) tools present in any modern organization.

These concepts allow you to build policies that work across the fundamental tenets of the organization, by using the robust frameworks discussed in the book coupled with PEs such as Open Policy Agent to accelerate digital adoption.

Who this book is for

Decision-makers, such as **Chief Information Officers (CIOs)** and **Chief Information Security Officers (CISOs)**, responsible for affecting change horizontally, **enterprise architects**, and **DevOps engineers** will benefit from this book.

This book is intended to help professionals design, implement, and measure policies in their organizations. A basic understanding of concepts such as cloud-native technologies, Infrastructure as Code, DevOps, and automation is expected to work through the book.

What this book covers

Chapter 1, *Introduction to Policy Design*, the introductory chapter, presents you with an overview of policies, the different types of instruments, and the most common frameworks used in policy design.

Chapter 2, *Operationalizing Policy for Highly Regulated Industries*, dives deep into highly regulated industries, talking about regulatory frameworks and controls and different access control mechanisms.

Chapter 3, *Policy as Code as a Business Enabler*, introduces Policy as Code and how it can benefit an organization, especially to bring automation and agility to traditional risk and compliance teams that haven't fully embraced the digital organization.

Chapter 4, *Framework for Digital Policies*, introduces a framework that can be used to design policies. The framework is based on **Observe, Orient, Decide, Act (OODA)** loops and discusses how challenges can be identified and policies designed, implemented, and measured.

Chapter 5, *Policy for Cloud-Native Environments*, covers cloud-native environments, discussing the paradigms found in these platforms, such as containers, serverless, and policies associated with these environments.

Chapter 6, *Policy Design for Hybrid Environments*, goes beyond cloud-native to talk about the challenges of hybrid environments, how you must consider the challenges of having heterogeneous systems, and how to establish a policy overlay across them.

Chapter 7, *Building a Culture of PolicyOps*, establishes the main purpose of PolicyOps, including how organizations can use this function to build digital goals and policies.

Chapter 8, *Policy Engines*, focuses on PEs. We cover engines such as Sentinel, K-Rail, and jsPolicy. This chapter covers small examples of each of those engines and how and when to use them.

Chapter 9, *A Primer on Open Policy Agent*, covers the most popular PE, **Open Policy Agent**. In this chapter, we discuss the engine, its language, Rego, and how to make the best use of Policy as Code, highlighting different use cases.

Chapter 10, *Policy as Code Tool Evaluation*, is one of the most important chapters of the book as it uses radar charts to help you evaluate PE capabilities or any other aspect the organization digital maturity. The concepts here can be applied way beyond measuring toolset capabilities.

Chapter 11, *Cloud Providers Policy Constructs*, focuses on the major public cloud providers' native policy capabilities and how to use them to build Policy as Code constructs.

Chapter 12, *Integrating Policy as Code with Enterprise Workflows*, provides an approximation of the real world as we discuss major ITSM frameworks, such as ITIL and COBIT, and how they need to be integrated with an automated policy enforcement posture across the organization.

Chapter 13, *Real-World Scenarios and Architectures*, discusses different scenarios using the framework from *Chapter 4*, *Framework for Digital Policies*, based on the OODA loop to identify the organizational challenge to design and implement policies.

To get the most out of this book

A familiarity with YAML and a basic understanding of coding are helpful but not required to follow along. There are concepts that do not require any expertise beyond familiarity with information technology.

Software/hardware covered in the book	Operating system requirements
YAML	Windows, macOS, or Linux
JavaScript	

Download the color images

We also provide a PDF file that has color images of the screenshots and diagrams used in this book. You can download it here: `https://static.packt-cdn.com/downloads/9781801811743_ColorImages.pdf`.

Conventions used

There are a number of text conventions used throughout this book.

`Code in text`: Indicates code words in text, database table names, folder names, filenames, file extensions, pathnames, dummy URLs, user input, and Twitter handles. Here is an example: "The preceding snippet ensures there are not any infringements in the data localization, as we specify the region with `"aws:RequestedRegion"`: `"eu-central-1"`."

A block of code is set as follows:

```
policy "preventEC2unaprovedinstances" {
    source = "./mypolicyinsentinel.sentinel"
    enforcement_level = "advisory"
}
```

When we wish to draw your attention to a particular part of a code block, the relevant lines or items are set in bold:

```
    - name: "pod_image_pull_policy"
      enabled: True
      report_only: False
```

Any command-line input or output is written as follows:

```
rsff@xps:~$ ./opa
-bash: ./opa: Permission denied
```

Bold: Indicates a new term, an important word, or words that you see onscreen. For instance, words in menus or dialog boxes appear in **bold**. Here is an example: "Select **System info** from the **Administration** panel."

> **Tips or Important Notes**
> Appear like this.

Get in touch

Feedback from our readers is always welcome.

General feedback: If you have questions about any aspect of this book, email us at customercare@packtpub.com and mention the book title in the subject of your message.

Errata: Although we have taken every care to ensure the accuracy of our content, mistakes do happen. If you have found a mistake in this book, we would be grateful if you would report this to us. Please visit www.packtpub.com/support/errata and fill in the form.

Piracy: If you come across any illegal copies of our works in any form on the internet, we would be grateful if you would provide us with the location address or website name. Please contact us at copyright@packt.com with a link to the material.

If you are interested in becoming an author: If there is a topic that you have expertise in and you are interested in either writing or contributing to a book, please visit authors.packtpub.com.

Share your thoughts

Once you've read *Policy design in the age of digital adoption*, we'd love to hear your thoughts! Scan the QR code below to go straight to the Amazon review page for this book and share your feedback.

https://packt.link/r/1-801-81174-1

Your review is important to us and the tech community and will help us make sure we're delivering excellent quality content.

Section 1: Foundation

In this section, you will understand the why and the what of policies, current challenges organizations face, and what is needed to make Policy as Code a reality in an organization.

This section contains the following chapters:

- *Chapter 1, Introduction to the Policy Design*
- *Chapter 2, Operationalizing Policy for Highly Regulated Industries*
- *Chapter 3, Policy as Code as a Business Enabler*

1
Introduction to Policy Design

This chapter starts the journey of understanding policies, their use, their importance, and how they are effectively used.

This chapter discusses the foundation of **policy design**, what constitutes a policy, how it is sketched together, and why policies are used. We will discuss design theory and how to create sound policies while demonstrating the most common instruments used to develop policies and their life cycles.

Once these elements are established, parallels from public policy to the digital organizational context later in the book will be more straightforward, as well as understanding how policies can help organizations in their digital journey by enabling faster digital adoption across the organization.

By the end of this chapter, you will understand how the field of public policy and associated tools can be transposed for digital adoption in an organization. This is typically achieved by a layer of governance that encompasses people, processes, and technology by creating coherent policies using **persuasive system design** (**PSD**), nudging, and incentives for more effective digital governance.

In summary, this chapter highlights how the field of policy design can be used to create a proactive governance model that goes way beyond enforcing and authorization, to increase digital adoption throughout an organization.

In this chapter, we are going to cover the following main topics:

- The why, what, and how of policies
- From design theory to policy implementation
- Policy design – key issues, tools, designs over time, effectiveness
- The business value of digital policies

The why, what, and how of policies

Let's look at a definition for policy. Cambridge Dictionary states the following: "A set of ideas or a plan of what to do in particular situations that has been agreed to officially by a group of people, a business organization, a government, or a political party." If we summarized it in a few words, it would be *a set of guidelines to gain a positive outcome.*

In our world, we live and abide by policies implemented by the government, our work environment (by our corporate policy), and our daily lives, for example, by an individual policy (such as a healthcare plan).

This section will discuss why policies are essential, especially in the globalized world we live in, and what business benefits we can derive by implementing and using them.

We will discuss the elements of a policy and show how the different elements can be combined to achieve a goal. You will also realize the pervasive nature of policies, how governments use public policies, how organizations implement corporate policies, and even the use of artificial intelligence in some algorithms, such as reinforced learning.

Why policies

Let's look at an example of a health policy enacted by the EU to reduce smoking and premature deaths.

Tobacco consumption is the single largest avoidable health risk and the most significant cause of premature death in the EU, responsible for nearly 700,000 deaths every year. Around 50% of smokers die prematurely (on average 14 years earlier).

Despite considerable progress made in recent years, the number of smokers in the EU is still high – 26% of the overall population and 29% of young Europeans aged 15-24 smoke.

The complete policy can be consulted at `https://ec.europa.eu/health/tobacco/overview_en`.

The initial paragraph unpacks the why. The program's objectives are to protect its citizens from dying prematurely. The overarching goal is health.

Another example from the EU is education policies, for example, the **European policy cooperation (ET 2020 framework)**, which is a strategic framework for cooperation in education and training (ET 2020). This and other education policies can be accessed here: `https://ec.europa.eu/education/policies/about-education-policies_ka`.

The policy goals are to develop education programs to tackle skills, aging societies, and technological developments.

These policies have laid out their *goals* and the *elements* of what will be used (for example, **publicity**, **regulation**, and **tax rules**).

They can ensure compliance to a certain standard or streamline processes to provide a map for accepted behaviors. They can influence the desired outcome so that a specific positive goal is achieved. In sum, policies are everywhere in our day-to-day lives as they make up the basis of our society and a mechanism to influence positive results.

What is a policy?

As we saw previously, policies are designed to help an entity (governments, organizations, or groups) create guidelines to achieve a goal.

Suppose we follow the literature on the latest research in policy creation. In that case, the taxonomy in broad terms is divided into two main parts: the *policy's goal*, what we are trying to achieve, and *policy tools*, how we achieve those goals, which we will go into more detail about later.

Usually, the policy aim will involve establishing the following:

- **The goal**: What are the general ideas behind the policy?
- **The objectives**: What is the policy going to address?
- **The setting**: What are the environmental nuances where the policy is going to be applied?

Let's take the example of the tobacco health policy that we saw earlier.

The program's objectives would be to protect its citizens from the effects of tobacco and dissuade younger people from picking up the habit.

The goal would be linked to positive health and economic outcomes as well as a financial goal related to the prevention of disease, which left unchecked would lead to increased costs to national health systems.

The setting is related to how the EU operates regarding cross-border trading. The setting would consider the international cooperation and the usage of the European Anti-Fraud Office.

This example explains the components that go into the policy and their concerted usage for a specific goal.

The how of policies

As we have seen, a policy starts with an aim that needs to be well defined to create the *goals*, *objectives*, and *settings*. In this section, we will focus on how policies are created effectively by using instruments to achieve the strategy's goals. This helps determine the strategy of the policy as well as the elements that go into it:

- The instrument **logic** specifies the preference of the instrument, that is, whether it's going to be a coercive instrument (enforcement, authorization), a suasion instrument (nudging, incentives), a statistical instrument (data presented in a digestible impactful way), or a financial instrument (bonus, subsidies).

- The **mechanics** of the instruments, such as the specific type of instrument, for example, training incentives or publicity campaigns.

- The instrument **nuances** specify how the instrument will be used as part of regulations, guidelines, standards, and so on.

Using the tobacco health policy as an example, the instrument **logic** you could use to achieve the goal could be as follows:

- **Coercion**: By restricting areas where people can smoke (smoke-free environments)
- **Suasion**: Using advertising on packaging and labeling with strong images (people dying in hospitals from lung cancer)

The mechanics would be the use of regulations for trade and increased tax. Since it's a regulated product, the tool nuances would use labeling mandated by the guidelines.

It would also be beneficial to be reminded that there are other instruments to achieve policy objectives, which can be seen in the following:

- **Coercive instruments**: These are used to make sure the rules are abided by. We can think about laws, mandatory regulations, or standards. They exist to make sure a determined code is followed with penalties if not. For example, speeding on a motorway would be against the regulations and would have a penalty to dissuade that type of behavior.

- **Financial instruments**: These are used to provide incentives for a determined behavior aligned with a policy goal. An organization might use bonuses based on targets on earnings to increase sales in a specific service or product. A particular policy of the government to improve a particular sector might give tax breaks or subsidies, for example, in green sectors nowadays.

- **Social instruments**: Staff and volunteers can be used to influence outcomes. A policy to reduce wildfires might engage volunteers to do sensibilization activities in local populations or use paid staff to clean areas with increased hazard potential.

- **Statistical instruments**: One of the oldest resources to influence behaviors is statistical instruments, the art of presenting impactful data. An organization might use environmental statistical instruments to change behaviors to reduce water wastage by showing how much water can be saved. A policy to reduce mobile phone usage while driving might use statistical instruments such as billboards with crucial information highlighting fatal accident statistics.

The following table gives an overview of the policy tools associated with each type of governing resource. It highlights how the different tools can be used at each point of the policy goal:

Policy	Policy Level	Program Level	Measurement Level
Goal	Policy goals What are the ideas governing policy development? (Health, economic, digital adoption)	Program objectives What does the policy address? (Adopting the cloud, reducing digital costs, upskilling the workforce)	Operational settings What are the specifications? (Considerations about current workforce knowledge, **Cloud Service Providers** (**CSPs**) bias)
Tools	Instrument logic What are the preferred instruments? (Suasion, coercion)	Program mechanisms What specific instruments are going to be used? (Add-on to browser, authorization mechanisms)	Tool calibration Are there any specifics for the instruments? (Standards, regulations, certifications)

Table 1.1 – Policy taxonomy (adapted from Howlett and Rayner)

A good policy requires a mix of elements. This is where design choices are essential. Later on, we will see that the tenets of good policy design are around the three Cs, **coherence**, **consistency**, and **congruency**. We can follow a structured approach by using existing design frameworks to make it easier for us, which the next section will discuss.

From design theory to policy implementation

As we have seen, policies can become very complex, as they usually require a mix of goals and instruments, making them prone to becoming inconsistent or lacking coherence by mixing too many diverging instruments.

This section will highlight how several frameworks from **design thinking** and PSD can create policies that consider different groups' viewpoints to make them robust and sound.

Design thinking theory

Design thinking started when creativity and empathy were required in the problem-solving aspect. The field matured once Herbert A. Simon created an iterative process that considered the experiences of different stakeholders. The same technique is required in policy creation as policy-makers need to have a broad range of perspectives to create effective policies.

Design thinking also makes sure that silos, hierarchies, and bureaucracies are torn down. Those of you with a more technical background might be able to see hints of the DevOps philosophy; this is not accidental. In design thinking, cross-collaboration is crucial as one of its aspects relies on empathically understanding different groups.

Let's say an organization wants to improve its cloud support and services to the business units. Usually, a project intended to start such an effort would begin by seeking out where in the organization teams, business units, and individuals have these capabilities more embedded than others and start asking questions such as the following:

- Where are the highest areas of cloud detraction at the moment?

- What factors seem to foster digital resistance?

- How is this digital illiteracy going to cause problems a few years from now?

- What types of problems would the lack of cloud adoption lead to?

- What are some success stories within the organization concerning cloud adoption?

This set of questions specific to cloud adoption can be adapted to start the design thinking process across different areas to improve digital adoption (goal) across business units that don't have the necessary level of maturity. If we unpack the questions into pillars, it would be summarized as considering the **environmental factors**, **stakeholder involvement**, **mapping**, and **assessment**. These pillars can be combined to understand better the targets, development, and use of digital policies.

Design thinking process

Design thinking is a conceptual framework that can be visually represented as follows:

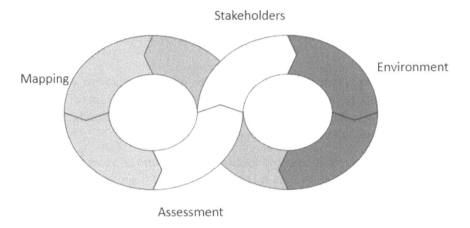

Figure 1.1 – Design thinking phases

The following are summarized descriptions of each of the phases.

Environmental factors

This strategy explores an individual's and group's behaviors in different contexts; it tries to identify trends that might influence future outcomes by understanding various factors, such as inputs, technologies, or multiple fields.

This strategy can be used to create a data-driven approach to highlight potential opportunities, weaknesses, or methods that augment our current understanding.

A good analogy for this strategy is to see it as a fishermen's net where the range is broad to catch different and unrelated viewpoints.

Stakeholder involvement

In design thinking, the stakeholder phase relies on people and their behaviors to understand the issue at hand. While the previous strategy was more concerned with a broad range, we funnel it further to engage with the different individuals at this stage.

Stakeholder involvement is about identifying and understanding the user's needs to create more efficiency, which can be achieved by observing the user interacting with a service. In this strategy phase, it's also imperative to ask open-ended questions of a diverse group of people, leading to deeper involvement and a broader understanding of the process.

This strategy is one of the most time consuming as it requires many interviews and questions between several stakeholders and target groups.

Mapping

This strategy is one of the most important as it is where we start to derive insights. In the previous strategy phase, we were concerned with getting data from the most varied sources. In contrast, here we begin to correlate, building insights.

Mind maps and similar concepts can be used to link different ideas. This is extremely useful in policy because it allows mapping to be used by various stakeholders to understand how they relate to each other.

For example, if an organization wanted to improve customer satisfaction, it would be helpful to know what steps are involved when a customer interacts with a service, the clicks they do to understand the portal, and in the case of e-commerce, the act of navigating the application or website until they commit to a buy. Like Steve Jobs used to say, understand the customers and work backward. Visually mapping these experiences helps identify areas, services, and processes that can be streamlined, resulting in a more efficient experience for the customer.

There's also **Wardley mapping**, a framework to enable strategic thinking that can fit in this strategy. More information can be found at `https://medium.com/wardleymaps`.

Assessment

In this strategy phase, the connection between the issues has been established. The insights gave rise to valuable information, which can be categorized, labeled, and understood. This information can inform the environmental factors and create a feedback loop, as seen in *Figure 1.1*.

Persuasive system design

PSD is a framework based on information systems designed to influence and shape attitudes, beliefs, intentions, or behavior without coercion or deception. This is different from the instruments that we talked about earlier, especially the coercive instruments. In PSD, it's about voluntary reinforcement, shaping attitudes and behaviors.

Persuasive systems might use either computer-human persuasion or any other mediated persuasion technique. Computers do not have intentions of their own, so generally, people create algorithms that contains the developers and data bias (`https://www.vox.com/recode/2020/2/18/21121286/algorithms-bias-discrimination-facial-recognition-transparency`).

The creation of PSD follows a very structured approach, as seen in the following diagram:

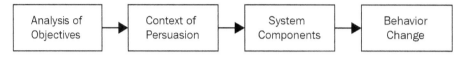

Figure 1.2 – PSD phases

Using the diagram as an anchor, we can see the initial phase is **analysis of objectives**. Here, we establish goals and choose the design. We also establish the types of persuasion, such as direct or indirect. Remember that this is an incremental process, it will be tailored to the user, and questions can be used to calibrate during this initial phase.

These types of designs can be found at `http://ui-patterns.com/patterns/perception-and-memory/list`.

Next, we need to understand the **persuasion context**, the wanted outcome, the user context, and the user's environment.

This will allow us to tailor the system; for example, doing a PSD for mobile or desktop environments is very different, hence understanding the environment where the user will interact needs to be assessed. The *context of the persuasion phase* will also design the message and how it will be delivered.

The **system components** phase is where the individual components will be assembled to support the previous methods, for example, using suggestions, rewards, and visual attractiveness. This can also be defined as **persuasive appeal** or **persuasive inquiry**.

Finally, these phases contribute to the goal, which is the **behavior change** that the system was designed around.

Let's look for real-world examples of PSD, such as gamification, including Waze for driving, Robinhood for trading, and Facebook for social media. Gamification has considerable success in shaping user behavior, which in the case of policies can be used as a suasion instrument to shape users' behaviors.

An overlay framework for designing policies

If we look around the technology world, policy development has typically been done by bureaucrats or lawyers, which, aside from rare exceptions, has rarely brought design thinking into policy creation. The reverse is also true. Go through any significant cloud provider governance paper and you will see that most of it has been created by technical folks without the lenses from other groups.

The purpose is to develop a framework that abstracts the pieces discussed earlier, design thinking and PSD, and lays the foundation to start thinking about policies and instruments in a structured approach to design effective policies.

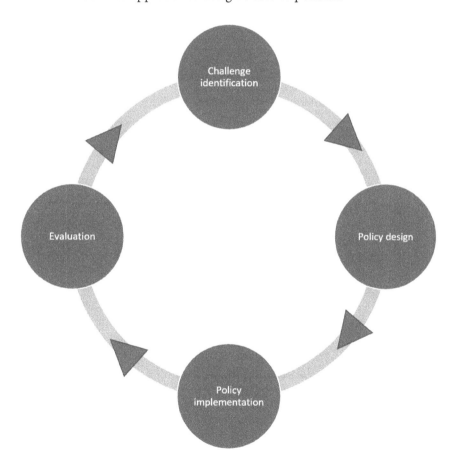

Figure 1.3 – OODA loop for policy design

Inspired by the Observe, Orient, Decide, Act (OODA) loop, the preceding diagram is a high-level framework that can be applied to digital policy design, which will be expanded on and used as the basis for *Chapter 4, Framework for Digital Policies*, where we will use this framework to abstract the frameworks discussed in this chapter.

Policy design – key issues, tools, designs over time, and effectiveness

As seen in the previous section, applying creative techniques and persuasive designs to get diverse viewpoints and influence is essential to formulate policies beyond authority.

This section will discuss what tools are available to achieve these goals; we will talk about conflicts and how to manage them, the fundamentals of measuring the effectiveness of policies, and the building blocks to develop robust policies.

This section will give tools that, coupled with the previous processes, allow you to start thinking about the challenges a policy can tackle using a systematic approach.

Suasion tools

With the digital psychology advancements in recent years, especially in social media and behavioral insights (Cambridge Analytica) with a lot of controversies surrounding some elections and how data from users was leveraged to influence the vote, nudging is becoming a valuable tool in policies; this new method, combined with the old marketing premises, makes for effective suasion tools that can be used to steer individuals toward a choice.

Nudging

Standing on the shoulders of Tversky and Kahneman's work on in irrationality, Richard Thaler began to look into this in more detail. He created what we know as **nudge theory**; we can define it as a way to influence choice without limiting choice or making more costly alternatives in terms of social sanctions. They are called nudges because there are flaws in how individuals process decision-making, and nudges can use those flaws.

Ana Caraban et al.'s *Technology-Mediated Nudging in Human-Computer Interaction* is an important research paper that focuses on using nudges via technology.

Some real-world examples might be as follows:

- **Positioning**: In supermarkets, premium products are placed at eye level, while kids' products, such as cereals with cute characters, are placed a bit lower down so that kids see the product and ask their parents for it.

- **Opt-out policies**: Implicit deny in authorization systems is the default to increase security. In mobile games and applications, a usual pattern is to ask for a subscription to increase revenue, the process of canceling a subscription being more complex than signing up.

- **Suggesting alternatives**: Commonly used in car rental upselling, as the suggestion can be an improved model for a minimal price. The same can be used in policies for cost savings, suggesting smaller virtual machines when working on development environments to reduce costs.

Nudging tries to influence a person's behavior with subtle changes to guide users toward a choice or behavior. Nudging can be a potent suasion tool, especially for adopting new digital technologies.

Marketing

Another tool that can be used for suasion is social marketing. We can use marketing concepts to influence behaviors that will benefit the organization, individuals, or business units in this approach.

You might think that traditional marketing is geared toward promotions, price, and placement. Still, more recently, it has been used in social media, which is becoming more recognized for its suasion aspects. Let's look at the center of excellence for social marketing. The **National Social Marketing Centre** (**NSMC**) has established benchmark criteria, a set of elements included in successful marketing campaigns.

I have adapted them for you to use as a reference; do not think about them as a checklist but as intertwined concepts.

Refer to `https://thensmc.com/`.

The following table, adapted from the NSMC, shows the key elements that are used in the most successful social marketing efforts, which can be used when developing suasion tools:

Strategy	Description
Behavior	This is the goal focused on changing specific behaviors.
Customer focus	Understand target needs, behavior, and issues they face by using data and research methods.
Theory	Uses behavioral theories to understand and inform the campaign.
Insight	Create actionable insights that will lead to campaign development.
Exchange	Cost analysis between the old behavior and the new behavior.
Competition	Understand what competes for the user's attention and time.
Segmentation	Identify the target segments and groups and classify them to enable tailored interventions.
Delivery mix	Use mixed methods to bring behavioral changes.

Table 1.2 – Marketing key elements (adapted from NSMC)

If we put these elements in a more visual form, as shown in *Figure 1.4*, **feedback loops** are present throughout the pieces. All of them feed into the **delivery mix**, which we can say is the output of the different layers:

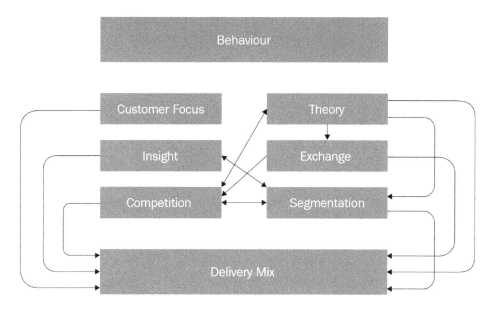

Figure 1.4 – Marketing key elements visual feedback loop

The use of behavioral insights and behavioral analytics in policy are increasing. Nudging, in particular, has been receiving tremendous attention as it allows you to improve the existing instruments and understand suitable targets and methods to send the message. For the long term, the marketing benchmark described is also an excellent place to start. It enables policies to be grounded in mechanisms that have worked to the marketing advantage and complement the other tools in this chapter.

Authority tools

In this section, we will be talking about authority tools that are part of coercive instruments. These tools are usually conveyed in the form of mandatory requirements, regulations, certifications, or laws.

This is not an exhaustive list, but an introduction to some concepts around authority tools will be necessary during the policy design phase.

Authorization

Authorization refers to the process of giving an entity, be it a person, group, or supergroup, the ability to do an action. We will focus on authorization models more deeply in the following chapters. Still, it is essential to understand how we can leverage authorization as an instrument to design policies.

If we think about it, authorization is probably the most ancient and powerful used tool, from regulations, licenses, and permits to certificates, accreditation, and more. It is used because it can serve several purposes:

- Recognizes sources of power
- Legitimates sources of power
- Mitigates information asymmetries

Authorization mechanisms are still the most effective way to create an environment of trust, especially in the digital realm. Finally, authorization is essential in risk management; any preventative framework seeks to minimize risk and ensures that those who engage in risky activities are trained, skilled, and authorized.

Regulation

As per the **Organization for Economic Co-operation and Development** (**OECD**), the definition of regulation, as seen at `https://www.oecd.org/gov/regulatory-policy/`, is as follows:

Regulatory policy is about achieving government's objectives through the use of regulations, laws, and other instruments to deliver better economic and social outcomes and thus enhance the life of citizens and business.

Regulations usually are made through an independent body for a specific sector, for example, in the case of banking in the UK, it is the **Financial Conduct Authority** (**FCA**) that creates regulations on how UK financial services should conduct themselves and what guidelines to adopt, and also to investigate, ban, and freeze assets of organizations and individuals. There is also the **European Banking Authority** (**EBA**), which is the European counterpart.

A regulation that is quite famous nowadays is the **General Data Protection Regulation** (**GDPR**), which requires an organization that processes EU citizen data to process and maintain that data in a specific way, with fines and penalties for organizations that don't respect it.

In *Chapter 2, Operationalizing Policy for Highly Regulated Industries,* we will be covering regulations in more depth for the different sectors.

Licenses

Licensing is one of the many tools that governments and organizations use as a form of authority to provide access in specified terms and conditions. In the open source world, there are more than 100 licenses (`https://opensource.org/licenses/alphabetical`); all these types of licenses can be used as a form of authority to provide the following:

- Customer protection
- Information asymmetries
- Recovering costs
- Integrity

For example, the license for an encryption algorithm, OCB, limits its usage for military applications:

2.2 Restrictions

2.2.1 The preceding license does not apply to and no license is granted for any Military Use of the Licensed Patents.

Certifications

Certification is a system of formal recognition that an event has happened; for example, birth, death, education, or professional achievements are examples of authoritative declarations. These can be used to convey authority and expertise.

For example, a certification from Google, Cloud Digital Leader, can be used as proof that the person passed an exam that allows them to articulate Google Cloud products' capabilities and how they can benefit an organization.

A more mundane example is using a certified electrician to check your house's electrical wiring. The certification proves that the electrician underwent a course and has met the requirements to pass the exam and become certified.

Financial tools

Governments often use financial tools in traditional policy design, such as subsidies, grants, tax concessions, or a mix, as we have seen previously. Financial tools can be a powerful incentive, primarily in organizations creating policies around digital adoption.

It's essential to understand how the different groups in their journey and equitably use financial tools to produce positive outcomes for all groups.

The following figure shows the difference between equity and equality:

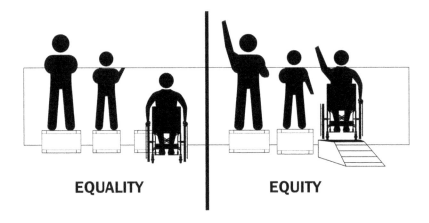

Figure 1.5 – Equality versus equity

For financial tools to be effective, it is essential to understand that different teams and business units will require different levels of support. As shown in the preceding figure, it is essential to be aware of those nuances and create policies that equitably use financial instruments.

Conflict management

Policy design is a process that, due to its nature, encourages or penalizes groups in a system, effectively exposing, strengthening, or destabilizing existing relationships. Be mindful when designing policies, as in any good process design, of the need to collect feedback and incorporate it when necessary. Clarifying interest, generating good alternatives, and clear communication should be used to address conflicts.

Understanding the three Cs for effective policy design

As we have seen in the earlier sections, a policy comprises several instruments with multiple analysis levels in between. As such, assessing the effectiveness of a policy requires a layered approach. First, we need to understand the interactions between the tools and how policies can be mixed.

Asking questions from within the organization would allow a policy designer to construct policy mixes that are effective, taking into consideration *Table 1.1*.

Those questions could be as follows:

- What tools does an organization have?

- How can these be classified?

- Have they been applied in the past?

- Has there been a usage pattern?

- How can we improve on past patterns?

These questions allow someone to break down the elements and understand previous and future potential interactions.

We can decompose the various components, *goals*, *instruments*, and *calibrations/settings*. These are the elements that will make up the policy.

If we refer back to *Table 1.1*, we can see the overall interaction and the components and position of the policies.

We should notice that typically, there are two types of designs:

- **Theory inspired**, generally used in areas that haven't had past policies, for example, nanotechnology or the cloud, which require a built-from-the-ground approach. It requires policy actors to be highly technical in the field to minimize the risk of poor design emerging.

- Secondly, **real-world-inspired** policies, built on top of established ones, are more common than theory-inspired policies.

Both these policies during their life cycle can suffer changes characterized by the following:

- **Layering**: New elements are added to the policy without removing the previous ones, usually leading to incoherence between the goals or inconsistency between the instruments.

- **Conversion**: This happens when most of the elements are kept to serve another goal; while consistency can be achieved by not changing the instruments, incongruency is introduced as old instruments mix with new goals.

- **Drift**: This happens when the policy elements are still maintained even though the policy's environment has changed.

Usually, a combination of several policies might be in place. As such, it is essential to understand whether one will replace an existing policy or create another layer in the policy.

Good policy design will involve a mix of instruments to address the required governance context and policy matching within an environment. In other cases, it will require the reshaping of an existing policy.

The basic principle of a sound policy design, regardless of the context, is to ensure that **consistency**, **congruency**, and **coherency** are achieved.

The following figure represents the three Cs and how each C ties to the goals or instruments:

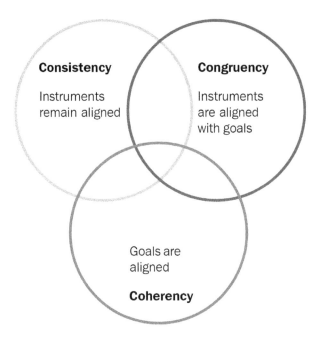

Consistency

Instruments remain aligned

Congruency

Instruments are aligned with goals

Goals are aligned

Coherency

Figure 1.6 – The three Cs of policy

This section highlighted how you could use the instruments presented within this chapter to achieve a policy goal. It discussed the types of policies that you might encounter and how to design for new or already established policies considering the effective combination of **goals**, **instruments**, **settings**, and **calibrations** coherently, consistently, and congruently.

The business value of digital policies

As we have seen throughout this chapter, instruments, tools, and processes typically used in public policy design can be adapted for digital policies. Organizations in their digital journey need to embrace the cloud, analytics, or artificial intelligence. Having a robust governance model is key, as traditionally, there has been a lack of effective governance for this new digital world, resulting in almost one-third of companies failing in their digital transformation efforts (`https://www.bcg.com/en-pt/publications/2020/increasing-odds-of-success-in-digital-transformation`).

This part will briefly cover a high-level overview of the most significant enablers of using policies and their instruments in an organization to advance the state of digitization.

Effective digital programs

According to the existing literature, one of the most common failures in digital transformation focuses on misalignment with the business. This would be attributable to an *incongruent policy* in the policy design world, where the instruments were not aligned with the goals.

This chapter highlights that cross-collaboration is key to building effective policies, especially in new technological fields. It requires in-depth technical know-how coupled with broader stakeholder buy-in to design effective policies.

Some of the aspects of successful digital transformations are as follows:

- **Adaptive governance**: Most of the programs in digital transformations use and focus on old methods; there is no effort spent on creating policies that use and leverage novel methods such as PSD and design thinking in the governance structure to bring everyone from the CxO to the individual contributor together.

- **Orthogonal feedback loops**: **Key Performance Indicators** (**KPIs**) and metrics with the necessary data availability and quality are closely monitored and fed across all areas of the business undergoing transformation.

- **Technologist-driven but business-integrated**: As we have seen in this chapter, in areas where new policies are going to be established, that is, *theory-inspired policies*, it will require actors to be highly technical in the field to minimize the risk of poor design emerging.

The frameworks, instruments, and methods discussed here with a public policy lens can be transposed to create effective digital policy programs. As you will see in the later chapters, most of the existing policies nowadays in the digital realm use coercive instruments, such as authorization.

We are starting to see some regulations, guidelines, and standards come up, such as the ENISA Cloud Certification scheme (`https://www.enisa.europa.eu/news/enisa-news/cloud-certification-scheme`), and ISO is creating standards on artificial intelligence (`https://www.iso.org/committee/6794475.html`). These regulations are still in the early days but will be the basis of the regulations for EU innovative tech in the coming years.

Governance agility

Governance traditionally has not been linked to how it can help the organization adapt to its environment and surrounding factors. An excellent example is the pandemic of 2020, which disrupted the governance structure regarding ways of working. Layering was introduced to safeguard existing governance processes, but it led to *inconsistency*.

Digital exhaustion caused by video calls is now being discussed by the governments of several countries on regulating working laws. Organizations are trying to create hybrid working environments as more than 40 percent of employees want to leave for a more flexible workplace (`https://www.bloomberg.com/news/articles/2021-03-22/bosses-are-clueless-that-workers-are-miserable-and-looking-to-leave`).

These external factors pushed many organizations to adapt quickly, and we will see the results of using instruments misaligned with goals resulting in *incongruent policies*. Although these external factors have brought challenges, they can be an opportunity for organizations to take a step back and reshape their policies.

Adaptive governance enables resilience and takes the organization a step ahead by increasing agility and creating solid feedback loops to adapt to unforeseen external factors.

Summary

This chapter explained the purpose of policies, their elements, and how to design them. We introduced some of the best frameworks in the field to create policies that take a holistic approach to the organization.

The field of policy design is complex, but we gave a high-level view of the basic concepts and processes that can be used, such as design theory, policy effectiveness, and the link to the digital transformation effort. These concepts and elements are fundamental; as we have seen, a policy will usually need to mix elements to achieve a specific goal.

We covered several types of instruments, suasion, coercive, and financial, and I hope that it is clear that for effective policies, we should try to use several instruments applied to where they make the most sense. As you will see, most policies use coercive instruments, such as authorization, but it is essential to understand that other instruments can and should be used.

This chapter also highlighted that to build digital policies, we should use effective frameworks that focus on design thinking theory or marketing best practices as it is essential to get diverse viewpoints from actors and target users by using empathy and creativity to design effective policies.

We also highlighted the need to design from scratch or reuse policies considering the three Cs for consistent, congruent, and coherent policies. Finally, we expanded on the role that policies have in the digital governance structure. Organizations will benefit from having adaptive governance that will help them respond to external factors and give them an edge with digital transformations.

We hope this chapter has given you the foundational know-how to understand the policies on which we will expand in subsequent chapters. In the next chapter, we will be looking more in depth at coercive instruments, regulations, and standards. For example, we will look at GDPR, how different sectors use regulations, and how policies can integrate with those requirements.

We will also expand on access controls, their types, and their integration with cloud vendors, and finally, we will discuss control catalogs to achieve policy needs.

2

Operationalizing Policy for Highly Regulated Industries

In this chapter, you will understand the role policy plays in regulated industries. We will discuss the different types of sectors and the regulations these industries use, focusing mainly on regulations and guidelines implemented in digital technologies such as the cloud, AI, and big data.

We will discuss access control models as they form the basis for authorization policies by limiting access to users and groups. Since we will be talking about regulated industries, we will look at regulatory frameworks and the controls used to achieve them, including GDPR and NIST 800-53, highlighting their significant points.

We will touch on the regulated industry's existing policies and regulatory frameworks, make sense of the fragmented landscape, and understand authorization policy models covering multi-cloud, container, and serverless platforms.

Finally, we'll cover frameworks and control catalogs used to achieve policies. These instruments are coercive but are the most commonly used and are essential for grasping the design of effective digital policies.

In this chapter, we are going to cover the following main topics:

- Highly regulated industries and their policy needs
- Policy through catalog controls
- Access controls for enforcing policies

Highly regulated industries and their policy needs

The previous chapter highlighted that policies are used to achieve a specific goal and establish governance using different instruments. Regulation is a type of **coercive instrument** defined to help achieve compliance and model behaviors. Regulation can also be a law, for example, **General Data Protection Regulation** (**GDPR**), or in other cases, acts of parliament. In the EU, due to the *primacy of European Union law*, a legal principle establishes the precedence of European Union law over conflicting national laws of EU member states.

This leads us to the regulatory bodies of several key industries, such as finance, healthcare, government, and more. These bodies create regulations that all organizations in specific sectors must abide by, usually coming in two types:

- **Guidelines**: A *piece of advice* used to provide direction and information; for example, the UK's **Financial Conduct Authority** (**FCA**) published the FG 16/5 Guidance for firms outsourcing to the *cloud*.

- **Regulations**: A *mandatory ruleset*; for example, (EU) Regulation 2015/2303 regarding risk concentration explains what needs to be done by the sector entities and the penalties for not following them.

This section discusses the regulatory landscape from a technological perspective for several regulated sectors. It explains what frameworks the different sectors need to use and the challenges within these regulations.

Financial Services Industry (FSI)

The **Financial Services Industry** (**FSI**) has been one of the sectors that regulators, both regional and broader ones such as the **European Banking Authority** (**EBA**), the **Financial Industry Regulatory Authority** (**FINRA**), and the **Securities and Exchange Commission** (**SEC**), have been pushing for the last couple of years to adopt guidelines regarding disruptive technology. With the advent of digitization, the FSI has been trying to modernize, especially in the light of challenges such as fintech being more agile and gaining market share. Senior stakeholders in the FSI are worried that they lack the necessary fintech skills to be competitive: `https://www.pwc.com/gx/en/industries/financial-services/assets/pwc-global-fintech-report-2019.pdf`.

Despite the lack of innovation, regulators and banks have been trying to establish guidelines and recommendations in new technologies, examples of which are listed here:

- **Financial Conduct Authority** (**FCA**) on AI: `https://www.fca.org.uk/publication/research/research-note-on-machine-learning-in-uk-financial-services.pdf`.

- European Banking Authority (EBA) on cloud outsourcing: `https://www.eba.europa.eu/regulation-and-policy/internal-governance/recommendations-on-outsourcing-to-cloud-service-providers`.

- Monetary Authority of Singapore (MAS) on the cloud: `https://www.mas.gov.sg/development/fintech/technologies---cloud`.

While these publications are good news and show that the FSI is keen to adopt the latest technology trends, it also means that there is *inconsistency* in the instruments from a policy perspective. For example, you can see fragmentation regarding cloud adoption in the following figure:

Supervisory authority regulations, expectations and statements
applying to cloud computing   Table 4

Frameworks	Outsourcing		Governance and risk management		Information security	
	General	Cloud-specific	General	Cloud-specific	General	Cloud-specific
EIOPA						
BaFin						
MAS [37]						
FINMA						
FCA						
PRA						
OSFI						
SAMA						
* Currently under review						
General framework		General framework		General framework with a specific section on the cloud		

Figure 2.1 – Cloud regulations and guidelines across regulators

Figure 2.1 highlights the complexity, bringing challenges for organizations mainly because they operate without geographical borders. Still, the policies need to respect the regulator's policies across their jurisdiction. For a more comprehensive view, please take a look at `https://www.bis.org/fsi/publ/insights13.pdf`.

There have been some efforts in this regard; for example, the **European Union Agency for Cybersecurity (ENISA)** has been trying to address the regulatory landscape in the EU by creating a unified cloud cybersecurity framework: `https://www.enisa.europa.eu/news/enisa-news/cloud-certification-scheme`.

While cloud providers have created their own set of frameworks and guidelines specifically for FSI, as shown in the following list, it still leaves organizations in the same spot regarding multijurisdictional policy and compliance:

- **Google Cloud Platform**: https://cloud.google.com/files/financial-services-compliance-overview.pdf.

- **Amazon Web Services**: https://aws.amazon.com/blogs/architecture/aws-well-architected-for-financial-services/.

- **Azure**: `https://azure.microsoft.com/en-au/blog/azure-solutions-for-financial-services-regulatory-boundaries/`.

While having these best practices from the **Cloud Service Providers** (**CSPs**) is good, there's also a need for dedicated resources that understand the environmental nuances and create orthogonal policies across the business, as we saw in the first chapter.

We will expand these concepts regarding *PolicyOps* in a *Chapter 7, Building a Culture of PolicyOps*.

Healthcare

The healthcare industry had a slow start in terms of technology adoption, but jumped ahead 10 years ago. Recent market studies have placed the sector with significant growth in the digital space, especially the cloud, with a CAGR of approximately 14%. It is one of the sectors that has made enormous strides regarding the use of AI in diagnostics, prevention, and treatments. One good example is the use of AI to create and distribute COVID-19 vaccines: `https://www.techrepublic.com/article/how-ai-is-being-used-for-covid-19-vaccine-creation-and-distribution/`.

Due to the sensitivity of medical records, one of the challenges facing this sector is processing data containing **Personally Identifiable Information** (**PII**) and **Protected Health Information** (**PHI**) data to derive insights, which is one of the reasons why regulators such as the European Commission have already proposed a regulation on AI, which can be consulted here: `https://ec.europa.eu/newsroom/dae/items/709090`. This new proposal would complement the existing Medical Device Regulation (MDR). In terms of regulations, they can be defined at a national level enforced by each country, and then more broadly as regards the EU/US, with the main ones being the following:

- The **Health Insurance Portability and Accountability Act** (**HIPAA**) is a regulation in US law designed to protect medical records and other personal health information.

- **Health Information Technology for Economic and Clinical Health** (**HITECH**) builds on the HIPAA, was enacted to provide an extension to electronic records, increases the penalties in the case of non-compliance, and enforces notification breaches.

- The EU **Network and Information Security Directive** (**NIS Directive**), despite being a cybersecurity directive, relates to healthcare as each country needs to have a national **Computer Security Incident Response Team** (**CSIRT**), perform regular security assessments, engage in cross-collaboration within the CSIRTs and other groups, and supervise critical sectors such as health and finance.

- The **Medical Device Regulation** (**MDR**) expanded on the existing Medical Device Directive (MDD) from 1993 to bring more scrutiny to medical data and medical devices.

There is also GDPR, which we will cover in more depth in this chapter. It works along similar lines to the preceding regulations and directives. Despite not being healthcare-centric, it regulates how data should be managed, be it medical or personal.

Similar to the FSI sector, as innovation becomes the norm, more clarity, guidance, and rules are needed in the healthcare sector to avoid fragmented regulations, thereby facilitating navigation of medical sector regulations, especially regarding AI and big data, which is gaining traction in this sector.

Policy through catalog controls

As seen in this chapter, highly regulated industries need to follow their country laws, regulator-established guidelines, and sector regulations. Some frameworks can help these industries become compliant with a specific regulation or law.

The frameworks, controls, and regulations selected in this section focus on technology such as the **cloud**, **AI**, **payments**, and **big data** to give you an understanding of the frameworks and catalogs for technology policy.

National Institute of Standards and Technology

The **National Institute of Standards and Technology** (**NIST**) is a non-regulatory agency that promotes science, investigation, and standards. NIST has several frameworks, standards, and catalogs.

From a framework perspective, NIST's **Cyber Security Framework** (**CSF**) was designed by NIST and is used globally. They have also created security and privacy control catalogs, of which catalog 800-53 is probably the most well-known.

NIST CSF

The NIST CSF was developed in response to President Obama signing Executive Order 13636, in response to the ongoing cybersecurity hacking of US companies. The CSF provides a framework based on five central pillars:

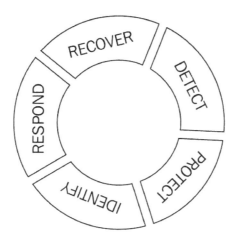

Figure 2.2 – NIST pillars

These five pillars convey risk concepts throughout the organization, allowing one to map the current state and a roadmap on what needs improvement. While the framework operates at a high level, it is key because it creates a common vocabulary across the organization, from the CxO to the engineering teams, becoming a critical enabler of security across groups.

More information on NIST can be found here: `https://www.nist.gov/cyberframework/new-framework`.

NIST 800-53v5

This control catalog from NIST establishes an information security standard. The goals of these controls are to protect resources, operations, users, and organizations from cybersecurity events, human error, and disasters. The controls are flexible and can be applied to any organization.

The majority of cloud providers have implemented these controls and provided proof of it: `https://cloud.google.com/security/compliance/nist800-53`.

FedRAMP is a cloud security management program for US federal agencies looking to consume cloud service offerings in a way that safeguards the security and protection of federal information. Typically, CSPs need to obtain an attestation of their services as they map their controls against NIST 800-53 controls to establish the low, medium, and high FedRAMP baselines.

Open Security Controls Assessment Language

NIST, collaborating with the industry, developed the **Open Security Controls Assessment Language** (**OSCAL**), a machine-readable format based on XML, JSON, and YAML. This allows the representation of control catalogs, security baselines, system security plans, and assessment plans to be automated and integrated within development teams.

As seen in this chapter, there are challenges with regulatory standards, particularly their fragmentation across jurisdictions. Another aspect is the evolving nature of regulations, making them hard to track, manage, and understand their overlap in terms of scope.

This is where OSCAL comes in, as it simplifies system security and privacy posture assurance. As these tasks are resource-intensive, sometimes, many organizations do not have complete visibility of the security and privacy posture due to budget constraints.

OSCAL provides a standardized way to streamline the documentation, implementation, and assessment of security controls, for example, NIST 800-53 or GDPR, and show the overlap between them.

The automation and data standardization reduce complexity and costs to allow continuous compliance within best practices and alignment with the necessary regulations.

More information on OSCAL can be found here: `https://pages.nist.gov/OSCAL/documentation/`.

OSCAL brings innovation to a traditional security and compliance environment where Word and Excel are the norm and enables organizations to move to a **Policy as Code** approach based on open and standard data structures such as XML and JSON.

It allows extensibility and integration with other business areas as the security controls can both be read by a human and a machine. It also develops a deeper integration within business units by providing APIs for **Compliance as a Service** (**CaaS**) to build the next generation of policy tools.

International Organization for Standardization

Much like NIST, the **International Organization for Standardization** (**ISO**) has been developing globally recognized standards in relation to standardization, research, and education since 1947. From the most common management standard, *ISO 9000*, which is recognized globally, the ISO has also drawn up standards regarding the cloud, AI, and big data, which we will talk about next.

ISO/IEC 27017

This standard expands on ISO 27001/2 and adds more controls to cover the cloud adequately. Much like NIST 800-53 controls, it allows CSPs and users to achieve a safer cloud environment, thereby reducing security problems.

ISO/IEC TR 20547-1:2020

Information technology – Big data reference architecture – Part 1: Framework and application process

This standard provides a big data framework and reference architecture so that organizations can use it as a basis for their problem domain; it describes architectures, the underlying technology, and big data concerns.

ISO/IEC TR 24029-1:2021

Artificial Intelligence (AI) – Assessment of the robustness of neural networks – Part 1: Overview

This standard provides direction in an area with a lot of ambiguity due to the nature of the neural networks and their non-linear nature. It provides information on statistical methods, formal methods, and empirical methods to assess the robustness of neural networks.

Cloud Security Alliance

The **Cloud Security Alliance** (**CSA**) offers cloud security-specific research, education, certification, events, and best practices. Since it's led by industry and volunteers, most of its research is derived from practitioners, which is an important part.

STAR

Security, Trust, Assurance, and Risk (**STAR**) is a publicly accessible registry with the **Cloud Controls Matrix** (**CCM**) results provided by popular cloud computing offerings.

It can be accessed here: `https://cloudsecurityalliance.org/star/registry/`.

Cloud Controls Matrix v4

Much like NIST 800-53 and ISO 27001/2, the CCM is a framework with controls that are aligned with CSA best practices covering the following tenets:

- Cloud computing concepts and architectures
- Governance and enterprise risk management

- Legal issues, contracts, and electronic discovery

- Compliance and audit management

- Information governance

- Management plane and business continuity

- Infrastructure security

- Virtualization and containers

- Incident response

- Application security

- Data security and encryption

- Identity, entitlement, and access management

- Security as a service

- Related cloud technologies

CCM v4 and its controls can be downloaded from here: `https://cloudsecurityalliance.org/download/artifacts/cloud-controls-matrix-v4/`.

General Data Protection Regulation

General Data Protection Regulation (**GDPR**) regulates how organizations that operate in the EU can use, process, and store personal data. GDPR replaced the 1995 data protection directive. Despite being drafted in the EU, it can fine organizations across the globe, as long as they reference EU personal data.

The major components of GDPR are as follows:

- GDPR principles

- Rights of the data subject

- Controller and processor

- Transfers of personal data to third countries or international organizations

There are two types of penalty; the first, for less severe infringements, entails a maximum fine of 10 million euros, or 2% of global revenue, while the second, covering more severe violations, rises to a maximum of 20 million euros, or 4% of global revenue.

Over the last three years since the enaction of the GDPR, the top fines have been as follows:

- Google (50 million euros)
- H&M (35.3 million euros)
- Telecom Italia (27.8 million euros)
- British Airways (20 million euros)

The list of organizations affected, together with the specific articles they violated, can be referenced here: `https://www.enforcementtracker.com/`.

The key GDPR articles to familiarize yourself with are as follows:

- GDPR Article 17: The right to erasure (the right to be forgotten), which, from a policy perspective, would mean that a data lineage must be in place to track and delete data as it flows within an organization.

- GDPR Article 25: This article speaks to implementing authorization policies within the organization based on IAM and the access control models we described in this section.

- GDPR Article 17/32: This range of articles is the most influential from a technological perspective. It covers the rights of the data subject, controller and processor responsibilities, and processing activities that need to be taken into account when assessing compliance with GDPR.

- GDPR Article 46: This article refers to data residency and transfers, and how data should be transferred to third countries, which is especially important in cloud providers, big data systems, and so on, as data gets shuffled globally for redundancy and insights.

EU Cloud Code of Conduct (CoC)

The EU Data Protection Code of Conduct for Cloud Service Providers is a voluntary framework on which CSPs can voluntarily adhere to the code of conduct by means of self-assessment or third-party certification. The CoC covers GDPR compliance and requirements.

This code of conduct is very relevant, especially in view of recent news of cloud providers being probed by the EU under the Schrems II case.

The replacement for the data transfer mechanism between the EU and US (**EU-US Privacy Shield**) is being analyzed and doubts have emerged regarding its privacy and legality (`https://techcrunch.com/2021/05/27/eu-bodies-use-of-us-cloud-services-from-aws-microsoft-being-probed-by-blocs-privacy-chief/`).

More information on the EU Cloud Code of Conduct can be found here: `https://eucoc.cloud/en/home/`.

Health Insurance Portability and Accountability Act (HIPAA)

The HIPAA of 1996 is a regulation that sought to simplify the rules necessary for electronic health care data security and privacy.

The regulation has three major points:

- Technical safeguards: These concern the technology that is used to protect the PHI.

- Physical safeguards: These focus on physical access to PHI irrespective of its location. It covers PHI stored in a data center or the cloud.

- Administrative safeguards: These are the policies and guidelines that bring the security and privacy elements together. These are the HIPAA compliance list elements and are usually part of the remit of a security or privacy officer. Nowadays, this compliance checklist is also part of the Policy as Code movement and can be seen as part of PolicyOps.

In terms of penalties, fines can range from 100 to 50,000 US dollars per violation, with a maximum of 1.5 million dollars per year, which is considerably less than the GDPR fines.

The list of settlements can be consulted here: `https://www.hhs.gov/hipaa/for-professionals/compliance-enforcement/agreements/index.html`.

Some of these certifications need to be validated by a trained auditor; in other cases, a self-assessment questionnaire can be used, depending on the needs of the organization.

This section introduced some standards, regulations, and guidelines that can be used to create security policies in the organization. Most of these policies will use coercive instruments. Still, it's up to PolicyOps to design effective policies, use suasion instruments in the first instance, or coercive instruments in the second instance, along with guardrails. This can help accelerate digital enablement programs.

Access controls for enforcing policies

If we look at the instruments required to enforce policies, coercion is the most effective and common. As such, it is essential to understand access control mechanisms when designing and implementing digital policies. In this section, we will talk about them and how they can be used. We will start with some of the security principles and how access control models can help achieve some of those principles.

Security principles

There are some security principles related to access controls that we are going to highlight in this section. These principles are required to prevent access control faults, such as privilege leaking, privilege blocking, or privilege conflict.

The following are some of the most common principles that we should be mindful of when using access control models.

Segregation of Duties

One of the basic building blocks of risk and creating organizational controls is the **Segregation of Duties** (**SoD**). This principle is used to prevent errors and fraud by splitting tasks and assigning them to multiple users. For example, a nuclear launch requires numerous people to sign it off; a more mundane example happens in payroll, where usually, the employee responsible for doing the accounting is not the same person who issues the checks.

Least privilege

Another essential principle is the **principle of least privilege** (**PoLP**), meaning only the required permissions are given to a user, group, or system. For example, suppose the purpose of a sole user is to activate backups. In that case, they will not need to install software, delete programs, or change records. Their only requirements are the ability to run the backup system. A real-world example is a typical workplace, where the marketing department should not have access to the financial records of the employees. This same example can be applied when constructing applications. A marketing application should only be sandboxed to the permissions required; it should not require other permissions.

Data abstraction (DA)

The principle of **abstraction** allows us to model complex security models. As we identify and break down components to assign them roles, we achieve a simplified security view of the domain.

Access controls

The traditional mechanisms of **Identity and Access Management** (**IAM**) are based on *access control*, which, after identifying the proper permissions, are attached to policies for authorizing users, groups, or supergroups.

Next, we will discuss some access control models.

Role-Based Access Control

Role-Based Access Control (**RBAC**) is an access control model in which authorization is provided depending on the person's role. Imagine having the same permissions as accountants; this would lead to serious security issues.

RBAC provides fine-grained access to those who need access to a resource determined by **authorization policies**. Since this model is based on roles, this method can be used to aggregate roles flexibly, as the permission to access a specified resource is based on duties, not personal preferences.

RBAC is a simple model that can achieve three security principles: **Segregation of Duties** (**SoD**), **principle of Least Privilege** (**PoLP**), and **security data abstraction**.

By *role assignment*, an actor can only be granted access if they have an active assigned role. It can be leveraged to split functions across actors, thereby achieving SoD.

Role authorization, in which the actor will only be allowed to access the resources according to the role assigned, achieves PoLP as the role contains only the necessary amount of privilege to perform the job.

Security data abstraction is built into access control models such as RBAC as they allow the abstraction of security. In the case of RBAC, it enables abstraction with roles.

The following diagram shows a visual representation of RBAC:

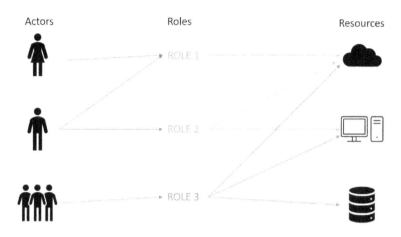

Figure 2.3 – RBAC actors, roles, and resources

In the diagram, actors can be individuals or groups, as shown on the left side. These actors can have multiple roles; for example, the second actor can have ROLE 1, access to the cloud, and ROLE 2, with access to the computer systems. The group in the diagram has ROLE 3, which grants access to all resources.

The diagram highlights the simplicity of the model in using roles to access different resources.

The benefits of RBAC are as follows:

- **Simplicity**: Users are bound to roles, not to individual documents or systems, making the creation, management, and auditing of policies simple.

- **Management**: Since users and groups are associated with roles, altering policies and permissions related to a role is straightforward and simplifies management operations.

- **Cost**: RBAC is simple to implement and operate, making it a cost-effective access control mechanism.

On the other hand, there are also some shortcomings:

- **Role proliferation**: As the organization grows, users accumulate roles as they change positions or acquire more responsibilities. Very often, these roles don't get pruned, and hard-to-spot security issues arise.

- **Scalability**: During the initial assessment and deployment, RBAC does its job. Once growth starts to happen, ambiguity appears as a result of organizational charts or updates to job definitions, and RBAC starts to become challenging as one-off solutions to address specific permissions are implemented.

- **Lack of context**: RBAC does not consider contextual information such as device type, user location, and time. A user accessing proprietary information at random outside working hours should be treated as suspicious. RBAC is unable to stop those types of activities that require context.

Overall, RBAC is a model with a very well-established userbase. Since it's based on lattice-based access control, it can be expanded to take into consideration an organization's needs; for example, using responsibilities to mimic a hierarchy, as shown in the following diagram:

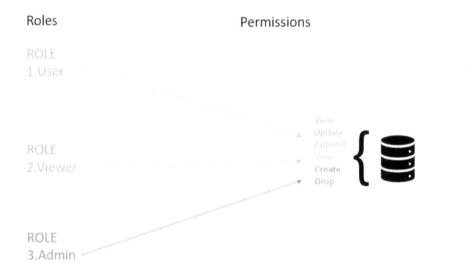

Figure 2.4 – RBAC with hierarchical roles

In *Figure 2.4*, we can see permissions differ based on the hierarchies of the role, such that the **User** role has access to the DB system and can view, update, and append records to the DB. **Viewer** can only view records. Finally, **Admin** is a role with the ability to create and drop tables.

While RBAC has its shortcomings, it is still in use, but with the shift to microservices, multi-cloud, and serverless, more modern access controls such as ABAC are being sought, which we will expand on next.

Attribute-Based Access Control

Attribute-Based Access Control (**ABAC**) can be seen as an improvement of RBAC that extends the roles by providing policies and attributes. These attributes enable context to be added to the authorization decision. The attributes can be as follows:

- **User attributes**: These can be roles, organizations, departments, and clearance types.

- **Environment attributes**: These can include time, location, and device type.

- **Resource attributes**: These include the owner, naming, data classification, and resource timestamps.

For example, in the payroll department, the user in the RBAC model will always have access to a system record, whereas with ABAC, there can be decisions based on environment attributes, such as only allowing access during working hours and from approved devices.

In the following figure, we can see the operation of the ABAC model:

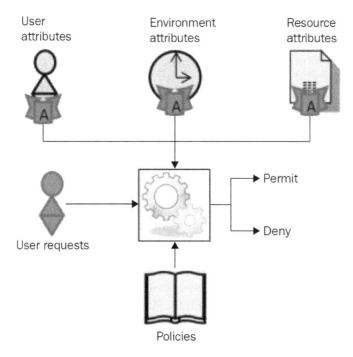

Figure 2.5 – ABAC overview

As shown in *Figure 2.5*, ABAC works by having an *engine* that takes the different attributes and gives authorization decisions based on those factors. This certainly has advantages compared to RBAC, which can be summarized as follows:

- **Abstraction**: Access control separated from business logic.
- **Centralization**: Policies are centrally maintained.
- **Flexibility**: ABAC can be used against APIs, systems, and microservices.
- **Context-aware**: ABAC can consider the location, devices, and other contextual attributes when making decisions relating to authorization.

On the flip side, ABAC also presents the following challenges:

- **Complexity**: Due to a variety of attributes, implementing and using ABAC can result in added complexity, especially when compared to the simpler RBAC model.
- **Performance**: As a result of its architecture, the *engine,* also known as the **Policy Decision Point** (**PDP**), depending on its configuration and how it communicates with internal or external sources with varying latency, can introduce performance issues.
- **Auditability**: Understanding the policy engine and queries result is difficult, especially when many policies and attributes are present. To successfully audit the system requires all possible combinations of attributes, policies, and permissions to be considered.

ABAC is more modern than RBAC and is the default that companies are adopting nowadays to control access to modern applications, APIs, and data lakes. Since it allows organizations to be compliant with complex regulations using complex attributes, it helps organizations bridge business and policy enforcement.

Next Generation Access Control

Next Generation Access Control (**NGAC**) uses graphs to model the authorization, allowing the representation of any system you want in a graph, mimicking your organizational structure, and adhering to your organization's semantics.

NGAC is composed of entities representing the resources you want to control access to, their relationship, and how users interact with the system.

There are different types of entities: users, objects, user attributes, object attributes, and policies. The following graph represents an organization with users, folders, files, and two policies. The edges define the permission actors will have on the resources.

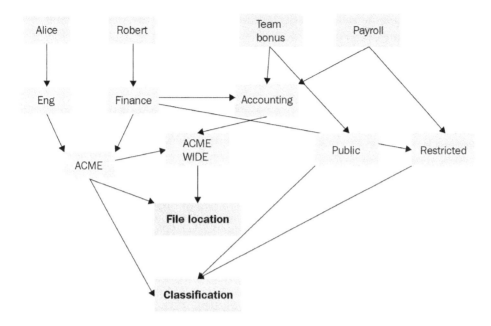

Figure 2.6 – NGAC graph policies overview

We can see that there are two files, **Team bonus** and **Payroll** in the **ACME WIDE** location under **Accounting**. Both these *edge nodes* (files) link to the classification edges **Public** and **Restricted**, and similarly, to **File location** (**ACME WIDE**, **Accounting**)

The policy classes in this diagram are **Classification** and **File location**.

Robert has access to both the **Team bonus** and **Payroll** files as he is part of the **Finance** team, which has access (*green arrow*) linked to the policies.

Although Alice has a direct path to both files, her group, **Eng**, part of **ACME**, is only connected with the **Public** part of the **Classification** policy, allowing her just access to the **Team bonus** file.

While NGAC architecture is complex compared to RBAC and ABAC, you can consult NIST 800-178 to have a more in-depth understanding (`https://csrc.nist.gov/publications/detail/sp/800-178/final`).

NGAC is becoming more attached to the latest infrastructure requirements, such as microservices, multi-cloud, containers, and serverless needs, and its benefits are as follows:

- **Scaling**: NGAC shines when processing complex access decisions as it scales linearly. At the same time, ABAC becomes exponential. In a vast amount of rules, it will make a huge difference.

- **Flexibility**: Similar to ABAC, it can take into context user, environment, and resource attributes.

- **Cloud-tailored**: NGAC is a cloud-first citizen considering service mesh needs, multi-cloud, containers, serverless, and other modern infrastructure paradigms.

This section presented some access control models, of which RBAC is the simplest, with good performance, but does not scale. ABAC is very flexible, but its performance and audit are a bottleneck. The newest in the family, NGAC, attempts to solve the other models' challenges by creating overlay access policies on top of a graph representation of the organization provided by the user.

These models can help us establish policies, such as data localization policies, in which data from the EU can't go into the US. Some of the models discussed can use context attributes for complex policy enforcement.

Summary

As we have seen in this chapter, regulated industries must make sure they are compliant with the specific jurisdictional regulator, which can be a challenge due to the fragmented regulatory ecosystem, despite some attempts to unify and create overlays across states, which is still a work in progress. We discussed several frameworks, regulations, and standards that can be used as part of a policy to enable digital adoption.

We showed the most common access control models, what the industry is moving toward, and how these mechanisms help in enforcing policies. We highlighted NGAC, a natural fit with the advent of containers and serverless distributed across different cloud providers, especially in highly regulated industries with their risk concentration needs.

Finally, we talked about the different types of policy frameworks. We discussed one of the most important nowadays, GDPR, and the subsequent frameworks that have been created to enable compliance, such as the Cloud Code of Conduct. OSCAL, which is a big game-changer for Policy as Code, is also worthy of a mention. While it is still in its early days, its potential is immense, and it's getting a lot of support from the community and industry.

This chapter discussed regulations, compliance, frameworks, and controls, which focused on coercive controls. Although it contrasts somewhat with the first chapter, it allows you to understand the most common instruments you need to create effective policies.

The next chapter will see how policies can enable business agility and how bringing policies to a digital paradigm can benefit the organization.

3
Policy as Code a Business Enabler

I've seen great technical solutions throughout my career that didn't correspond to the needs of the business; either there was a lack of alignment of technical features with business requirements, or the solution was chosen without consideration for the requirements.

This chapter tries to help you avoid that pitfall by enabling you to understand the needs of the business and how to position Policy as Code for business units or executives. The previous two chapters explained how policy should be designed and some frameworks that could help us structure the several phases. Then, we navigated regulatory compliance and how organizations must comply with external regulators. Nonetheless, organizations use internal policies and processes to fulfill those regulatory needs using old-fashioned methods such as Excel or Word documents, preventing agility as intense manual techniques are used and not achieving compliance by design due to the lack of automation in static documents, impeding the digital maturity in **lines of business** (**LoBs**).

This chapter will cover Policy as Code for improving an organization's goals and identify key aspects such as agility, innovation, and compliance. We will discuss the benefits that Policy as Code can bring to an organization.

In this chapter, we are going to cover the following main topics:

- Policies at speed – Policy as Code
- Governance agility – automating policies
- Business benefits of policy as code

Policies at speed – Policy as Code

I think everyone can agree that the pandemic of the last couple of years has strained many organizations. Still, the ones that quickly got back on track and had less disruption were the agile ones. These organizations were not afraid to challenge the status quo, and as a result adapted very quickly to external events.

This can remind us that speed matters and can represent a significant advantage to an organization.

Speed as a business enabler

For example, let's look at great leaders from the past. Shackleton, during his expedition, was able to save his crew by trading speed over comfort during his trip to the South Pole, where they got stuck. He chose to be as agile as possible in that harsh environment. He knew that speed was essential and was the best option for saving himself and his crew.

The same has already happened in companies that adopted digital transformation to become quicker and more innovative, especially during the COVID-19 pandemic.

One aspect is the utilization of digital platforms, such as cloud computing. It brings an operating model that leverages speed, scalability, and agility. These platforms allow leaders to benefit from economies of scale for their business value.

Let's look at the latest IT innovations. We can all agree that virtualization and open source were significant catalysts. They allowed organizations to run a business application with fewer costs and a fraction of the original investment. There is another paradigm shift with the cloud, which is slightly different, as it requires an investment in capabilities, and the benefits start to be realized in the medium to long term through a faster go-to-market, advanced predictive analytics, and innovation.

These benefits come at a reduced risk, with a much faster deployment cycle, typically in days instead of months.

This is something the book tries to help with, since creating policies for digital adoption requires a paradigm shift in terms of how we perceive these platforms and how we change the organization to this new operating model. An excellent example is to shift from project to product funding.

These new digital platforms, including the cloud, big data, and AI, help organizations to transform by adopting a more modular approach. The traditional reactive ticket-driven operation moves into a more proactive self-service organization that leverages APIs between business units, achieving self-service and using Policy as Code to support the organization in its digital journey.

One of the popular paradigms that formalizes an improved digital operating mode has been DevOps, the embodiment of collaboration. Our next section will discuss its relation to agility and how it can be a force multiplier by leveraging Policy as Code.

The rise of DevOps

Since we are talking about business enablement and how speed can be one of the biggest differentiators for organizational success, the popularity of DevOps has risen quite considerably in the last few years, as demonstrated in *Figure 3.1* from Google Trends:

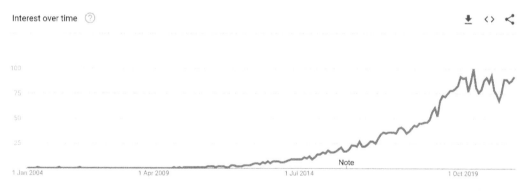

Figure 3.1 – DevOps work trend Google searches

DevOps is a set of non-prescriptive practices that leverage small teams, fast and safe deployments to production, a shift to the left in security, a learning culture, and a blameless culture. The most significant change/challenge for organizations adopting DevOps is to adopt substantial behavioral and cultural changes rather than technical changes.

DevOps tries to create high-performing teams by creating a culture of collaboration. This results in multi-stakeholder groups working in alignment with each other to create value for the organization by removing traditionally existing friction between teams.

DevOps encourages continuous delivery, where testing and operations happen simultaneously, reducing lead time and facilitating a faster go-to-market. Continuous delivery is one of the significant aspects of DevOps that drives agility within the organization.

This new agility in DevOps can be summarized in three points:

- **Goals and measuring**: Setting goals and having measurements is one of the critical aspects of any technology transformation effort, especially in DevOps. With metrics, you can leverage an experiment's data and quickly change course when things are not working: the fail-fast approach.

- **Shorter feedback loops**: Shorter feedback loops mean that intercommunication among teams and business units happens very quickly. This allows defects to be spotted and fixed in the early stages of product development.

- **Experimentation**: New features and novel technologies are adopted with an experimentation culture, allowing teams the psychological safety to experiment with new proof of concepts. This is crucial as it attracts fresh talent. Typically, these professionals will want to work on novel problem domains.

An excellent book on the subject, `https://itrevolution.com/the-devops-handbook/`, talks at length about how these concepts can be achieved in an organization. The **DevOps Research and Assessment** (**DORA**) metrics, `https://www.devops-research.com/research.html#reports`, contains reports and a quick tool for comparing specific capabilities and seeing how they compare to industry peers and those areas where you can improve performance to become a top performer. You can see a diagram with all the key areas here:

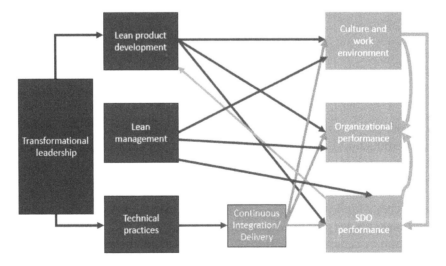

Figure 3.2 – DevOps influence map adapted from DORA

From *Figure 3.2*, we can see some outcomes marked in green, such as **Culture and work environment**, which is job satisfaction and the climate for learning and a culture of psychological safety.

Some of these learnings were identified during Project Aristotle, a study to identify the main attributes of highly effective teams at Google: `https://rework.withgoogle.com/print/guides/5721312655835136/`.

Organizational performance comprises commercial and non-commercial aspects, such as how the product is perceived externally in terms of marketing success. Internally with the velocity of releases, the amount of effort per sprints, and so on. Externally measuring the market share, number of satisfied customers, the profitability, and so on.

Software delivery and operational (SDO) performance are the performance metrics and operations availability. This output is highly interconnected, not just with management practices (gray) but also with the outcomes (green).

We can see that technical practices defined by **transformative leadership** (blue) create the basis for those outputs. **Continuous Integration/Delivery (CI/CD)** is force multiplied by the technical methods, such as continuous integration, security shift left, and monitoring and observability.

Lean product development makes work visible inside organizations. It defines working patterns such as working in small batches and constantly using feedback loops for customer feedback, which is directly related to commercial success in terms of organizational performance and the SDO.

More information on this aspect can be consulted on the DORA website: `https://www.devops-research.com/research.html`. To summarize, there must also be a cultural component change in addition to technical abilities. DevOps and **Site Reliability Engineering (SRE)** popularized these concepts and leverage everything as code. DevOps and SRE can be defined as follows:

> *"What happens when a software engineer is tasked with what used to be called operations."*

Having the infrastructure, operations, security, controls, and policy defined as code makes embedding these practices into the software life cycle frictionless, generating agility that an organization can use to differentiate itself from its competitors.

Enabling these policies as code and treating them as part of the software development life cycle brings continuous delivery, and we will expand on this topic in the next section.

Everything as code

As we saw previously, using **Everything as Code** (**EaC**) for things such as infrastructure, security, operations, controls, compliance, and policy helps us to achieve agility as those constructs are embedded in code, entailing several advantages:

- **Auditability**: Since the code is stored in a **Source Code Management** (**SCM**) system, it can be tracked for changes, workflows can be created around it for modifications, and alerts can be made.

- **Repeatability**: In modern paradigms, modularity and repeatability are critical as they allow infrastructure, policies, and controls to be reused across different environments. This is important for organizations that use a multi-cloud strategy by applying infrastructure, policies, and controls across a diverse landscape.

- **Cross-collaboration**: Since there should be a central source of truth aligned to each product, business objective, and so on, various teams from application development, security, and compliance can all contribute to the same code base, achieve living documentation, and reduce errors, misinterpretation, and suchlike. This paradigm imposes collaboration and shared understanding, allowing different stakeholders to speak a unified language.

EaC brings considerable benefits when implemented alongside transformational leadership, agility in technical practices, and lean management to achieve the required organizational performance.

In the following sections, we will discuss specific implementations of EaC and how they are commonly used.

Infrastructure as Code

As we have seen in this section, using EaC has substantial advantages. The most significant use case is to use machine-readable code to define IaaS, PaaS, SaaS, and hardware services, also known as **Infrastructure as Code** (**IaC**)

IaC is one of the most popular uses of machine-readable code, with Terraform being the most popular tool. It uses a language called **HashiCorp Configuration Language** (**HCL**). Its primary use case is the bootstrapping of resources and their configuration for heterogeneous cloud environments, allowing teams to set up their infrastructure resources in cloud and on-premises environments.

We can see a Terraform example for provisioning a virtual machine here:

```
Resource "google_service_account" "default" {
  account_id    = "service_account_id"
  display_name = "Service Account"
}
resource "google_compute_instance" "default" {
  name          = "test"
  machine_type = "e2-medium"
  zone          = "europe-central2-a"

  tags = ["foo", "bar"]

  boot_disk {
    initialize_params {
      image = "debian-cloud/debian-9"
    }
  }

  // Local SSD disk
  scratch_disk {
    interface = "SCSI"
  }

  network_interface {
    network = "default"
    access_config {
    }
  }
  metadata = {
    foo = "bar"
  }
  metadata_startup_script = "echo terraform > /test.txt"
  service_account {
    email  = google_service_account.default.email
    scopes = ["cloud-platform"]
```

```
        }
    }
```

As you can see from the example, it specifies the virtual machine definition in several parts – its name, location, and type. The rest of the configuration deals with its peripherals, disks, tags, networking, and service accounts.

More information can be consulted on the Terraform web page, and it has examples for most cloud providers: `https://learn.hashicorp.com/terraform`.

Another important aspect of IaC is the property of being idempotent, meaning that repeated runs will not change. This brings some interesting properties, including the following:

- **State-based**: What you define in Terraform is what is deployed.

- **Change control**: The only resources that change are the added or removed resources, which are especially important as you have to manage hundreds or thousands of resources.

This means that IaC can be used as governance and resource state control due to being defined as code, allowing business compliance needs to be met and enabling non-compliance issues to be quickly reverted or patched.

Now that you know how IaC works, let's move on to exploring compliance as code.

Compliance as code

Like EaC and IaC, **Compliance as Code** (**CaC**) is when we write compliance policies into a code format to integrate with the software development life cycle.

This paradigm is essential as most professionals from risk and compliance traditionally are not exposed to software practices, creating friction when engaging with other cloud-native teams. CaC can bring all teams together by applying the DevOps principle of collaboration, using a shared repository that can be consulted by the rest of the organization, increasing transparency, and so on.

One example is the highly regulated industries we talked about in *Chapter 2, Operationalizing Policy for Highly Regulated Industries*. These industries require compliance with specific regulations or standards embedded within the SDLC. This prevents mishaps from happening right at the start of the coding effort, thereby reducing the probability of launching a product with defects, leading to fines and penalties due to infringing regulatory compliance requirements.

CaC can automate the implementation, verification, monitoring, and reporting for regulatory standards via machine-readable code.

An example can be seen here using **Chef INSPEC**™:

```
Control 'azure_resource_group_example' do
  title 'Check if the Azure Resource Group matches
expectations'
  impact 1.0
  describe azure_resource_group(name: 'Inspec-Azure-Example')
do
    # Check if the Resource Group is located in the correct
region in this case Europe
    its('location') { should cmp 'westeurope' }
    # Check if the Resource Group has tags
    it { should have_tags }
    # Check if the number of public Ips is none
    its('public_ip_count') { should eq 0 }
  end
end
```

For example, the preceding code can be used to enforce compliance with a specific pattern and teams inside an organization:

- The resource groups must be located in the correct regions for data residency requirements as per the compliance team mandate.
- It should have tags for correct identification by the security and risk team.
- It should not have a public IP, as mandated by the network, and security team.

As you can see, this can be a game-changer for compliance and, more importantly, for bringing all teams together. Having multiple stakeholders cross-collaborating with only one source of truth about the environment improves auditing, agility, and compliance. These checks can be done in almost real time across business units. Let's now move on to understanding Policy as Code.

Policy as Code

We will be focusing on **Policy as Code** (**PaC**) in greater depth in later chapters. This section will introduce and cover the key differentiators from other forms of machine-readable EaC.

As we adopt new technologies and environments, it's crucial to create digital governance that leverages repeatability, automation, and self-service. PaC enables teams to shift from manually managing policy definitions to managing in an automated and scalable fashion, like the other forms of EaC in this section.

Let's have a look at some examples of PaC snippets from leading frameworks, involving an example policy that sends an alert when tags/labels do not have the proper cost center:

- Open Policy Agent:

```
package kubernetes.validating.existence
deny[msg] {
      not input.request.object.metadata.labels.costcenter
      msg := "Every resource must have a cost center
label"
}
deny[msg] {
      value := input.request.object.metadata.labels.
costcenter
      not startswith(value, "costc-")
      msg := sprintf("Costcenter code must start with
`costc-`; found `%v`", [value])
}
```

In the preceding example, we create a policy that forces resources to have a cost center, especially in large organizations where there needs to be accountability regarding projects, LoBs, or teams. Alerting and forcing resources to have a cost center associated with them improves cost management and visibility into spending and usage.

- Sentinel:

```
import "tfplan-functions" as plan

mandatory_labels = ["name", "owner", "costc" ]
allGCEInstances = plan.find_resources("google_compute_
instance")
violatingGCEInstances = plan.filter_attribute_not_
contains_list(allGCEInstances,"labels", mandatory_labels,
true)
# Main rule
main = rule {
```

```
        length(violatingGCEInstances["messages"]) is 0
    }
```

Another example of creating a cost center policy in another PaC tool, Sentinel, was seen in the preceding code snippet.

These two examples highlight a policy that enforces the resources to have a cost code associated, a critical use for organization to track the spending of projects and products.

As we have seen in the preceding sections, EaC has different applications for infrastructure, compliance, controls, policy, or even detection (detection as code).

The following diagram provides a visual explanation of how EaC fosters agility, enforces collaboration, and enables paradigms such as DevOps.

PaC is the governance layer that can automate the governance structure for digital adoption, providing verification, monitoring, and reporting via machine-readable code.

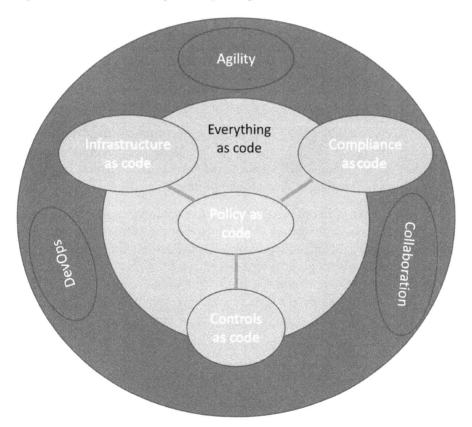

Figure 3.3 – EaC framework

While there might be overlap among the different EaC tools, PaC should be the governing framework used to define the high-level structure for goals through the organization's policies so that CaC, IaC, and others complement each other for the established policy goal.

EaC has many uses, and we have seen some high-level examples of how they can be used to construct infrastructure, compliance, and policies. This takes us to the next section, where we will be focusing on the governance aspect.

Governance agility – automating policies

I think we can all agree that governance is one of the most critical aspects of an organization. It establishes accountability and decision making while, at the same time, providing a path for everyone to have input and be able to contribute new ideas.

Sound governance will allow an organization to thrive as it establishes the building blocks of the organization, thereby reducing tactical decision making and effectively establishing the following:

- Guiding principles that enable stakeholders to have a consolidated expression of the organization's high-level business goals and values
- Objectives that define what success would look like, and the metrics associated with it

As discussed in this chapter, being agile is essential for organizations to adapt and create differentiated value that can be taken to market quickly. These two examples highlight a policy that enforces the resources to have a cost code associated, a critical use for organization to track the spending of projects and products.

The role of a **Cloud Center of Excellence** (**CCoE**) is to establish best practices to help different LoBs adopt the cloud. By having PaC as a tenet of the CCoE, we can define the controls, blueprints, templates, and adoption goals using suasion, financial, and coercive instruments. Since the CCoE is a governance layer, it can influence the best practices of teams and help define their coercive and suasion instruments. For example, the CCoE would be able to explain to the different LoBs the benefits and challenges regarding coercive instrument requirements, policy engines, or CSP controls such as AWS SCP.

Next, we will touch on the challenges in digital governance, the role of the CCoE, and how we can use the automation of policies to drive governance.

The challenges of digital governance

Establishing governance and setting up policies for the success of digital endeavors can be overwhelming with all the choices and frameworks available. That's why it's essential to adopt best practices of DevOps and EaC to have a structure that drives the organization into a more efficient operating model, with transparency and a more engaged workforce, especially when adopting new technological paradigms such as the cloud.

Be mindful that digital governance and digital policies are informed by the broader organizational context, such as fiscal policy, IT policy, or external market policies. Feedback loops should be in place to ensure external factors and other policies are taken into account.

The Cloud Center of Excellence

As with any transformation effort, it's essential to set up the necessary governance structures. Using a **Cloud Center of Excellence (CCoE)**, also known as a **Cloud Business Office (CBO)**, is a common approach to driving cloud adoption within an organization.

To ensure that the transformation is successful, organizations must have the right technology, processes, and, more importantly, people with the right skills. The CCoE supports this by ensuring cohesion between people, processes, and technology.

A CCoE is a centralized governance structure that sits orthogonally across the organization and acts as the enabler for the rest of the business. Be mindful that a CCoE is heavily based on enterprise architecture, where the main responsibilities include the following:

- Setting cloud policies
- Establishing blueprints
- Creating a novel **Proof of Concept (PoC)**
- Guiding CSP selection

These activities must be aligned across diverse business teams, including risk, security, legal, and **Security Operations Center (SOC)**, as to bring the stakeholders together early on.

The CCoE is not a structure with operational duties. Its functions should not be outsourced, as this will be the engine behind the organization's transformation. *Figure 3.4* is an example of how a CCoE can be integrated into an insurance organization. The concept is still applicable to any organization.

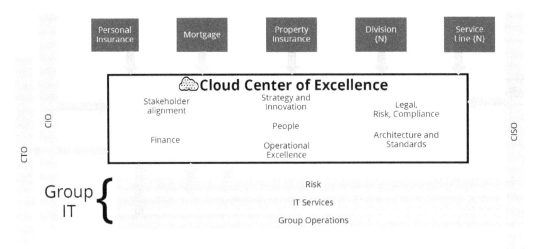

Figure 3.4 – Highly regulated CCoE integration example

As we can see, the CCoE sits at the center, soliciting contributions from across the business, for example, the personal insurance business unit or the mortgage business unit.

More importantly, it's also the place where new relationships between the CxOs can flourish, especially between the CIO, who is driving this transformational agenda, and the CISO, who should balance the risk appetite of the organization with the proper amount of autonomy in order not to choke innovation within the organization.

Since the CCoE is responsible for change across the business, several anti-patterns should be avoided and are indicative of the success the organization will have:

- **Legacy culture**: The organization has a deeply ingrained legacy culture and thinks it can reap the benefits of digitization by just migrating or accessing low-hanging fruit. In this case, there needs to be a policy effort to change the perception of digitization and its benefits to the various teams.

- **Legacy infrastructure**: The organization's current business processes are built on legacy infrastructure, and their digitization effort is only focused on peripheral changes, not addressing the core business process, which would involve changes to their core business processes.

As we will discuss in *Chapter 4*, *Framework for Digital Policies*, both top-down and bottom-up approaches are required to get everyone on board and change the core business processes with new technology.

- **Siloed approach**: The organization has legacy teams inaccessible by the CCoE and cannot push changes and best practices to the groups.

    The CCoE should have stakeholders and champions from the functional units to integrate the teams with the overall effort.

These are the most common challenges in organizations and why digitization efforts mostly fail.

The positive efforts have one thing in common; the CCoE acts as a hub with satellites across the organization to make sure there is support across the organization in terms of know-how, best practices, and upskilling.

Depending on the organization's needs, another entity can help drive cloud adoption alongside the CCoE. For example, a cloud policy council can help shape and enforce cloud-related policies to drive organizational transformations, with some of the frameworks and processes discussed in this book.

Now that we have understood the role of a CCoE and its impact on undergoing a digital transformation effort, let's discuss the business benefits of having a governance structure adopt EaC best practices.

Business benefits of PaC

PaC shares many benefits with EaC, CaC, IaC, and so on, but can encompass these paradigms and provide an abstraction layer where policies are designed to use suasion instruments as a first step prior to enforcement.

The most important topics are as follows:

- **Cross-collaboration**: This brings different stakeholders together, especially from a policy design perspective, as seen in *Chapter 1*, *Introduction to Policy Design*. In highly technical fields, experts need to work in tandem with diversified organizational stakeholders, hence why the frameworks are based on design thinking theory.

- **Cost reduction**: Policies as code can bring teams together, consolidating inefficient cycles. They can also be a significant force in adopting new technology, thereby saving organizations a lot of money in terms of remediation programs and OPEX.

- **Time to market**: As organizations adopt SDLC practices in relation to the governance structure, monitoring becomes more transparent, allowing quicker product iteration. More importantly, PaC serves as the overarching layer to make sure IaC and CaC are aligned with the policies established by the CCoE and stakeholders, allowing products to be launched with policy, compliance, and technical checks in place.

- **Agility**: With PaC, the suasion and coercion instruments can improve the organization's time to market, innovation, and standardization across business units, balancing the right amount of enforcement with proper guardrails.

- **Innovation**: PaC helps organizations to embrace new digital paradigms, such as the principles of DevOps, collaboration, continuous delivery, and a digital culture that will treat governance as a first-class digital citizen in the organizational landscape.

As such, embedding the practices that we talked about in this chapter to define PaC allows an organization to have a governance layer that will deliver on the benefits of the paradigm of DevOps, increasing collaboration among groups, reducing work duplication, and making the organization more nimble. These benefits will allow the organization to be more competitive and better equipped to adopt and tackle digital innovation.

Summary

As we have seen in this chapter, agility is one of the most defining aspects of successful organizations. We have seen in recent years that organizations that have thrived were the ones that quickly adapted to external circumstances.

One of the more prominent paradigms is DevOps, which gave rise to different applications of its principles, such as SRE, MLOps, GitOps, and NoOps. However, one of the most defining features of DevOps and its derivatives is continuous delivery and cross-collaboration. Hence, automation and EaC are essential pillars in achieving the DevOps paradigm.

PaC is a natural extension for organizations going through a digital transformation that want to have a paradigm aligned with cloud-native best practices. It is essential to make sure these policies are designed to take a holistic view of the organization and stakeholders by leveraging the frameworks discussed in *Chapter 1*, *Introduction to Policy Design*, such as design thinking and **Persuasive System Design** (**PSD**).

This paradigm can also be helpful in the highly regulated industries that we touched on in *Chapter 2, Operationalizing Policy for Highly Regulated Industries*, as the compliance teams are usually disconnected from the technical teams, and vice versa. This paradigm can bring those teams closer, demonstrate continuing compliance, and, more importantly, achieve the digital goals proposed by the organization.

The concept of PaC can strengthen an organization by granting it the necessary building blocks, including coercive instruments such as policy engines, control mechanisms, and access controls. PSD and design thinking can help define the necessary suasion instruments. These concepts lean on automation to bring competitive agility and create differentiated value by achieving the goals specified in the digital organizational policy.

The next chapter will cover a framework that simplifies the lessons learned so far in this book to assess, design, implement, and measure the policies you design.

Section 2:
Framework

This section presents a high-level overview of an agnostic framework that you will be able to use to build policies for cloud and hybrid environments. The section also covers the expansion of the framework and how to build a culture of PolicyOps.

This section contains the following chapters:

- *Chapter 4, Framework for Digital Policies*
- *Chapter 5, Policy for Cloud-Native Environments*
- *Chapter 6, Policy Design for Hybrid Environments*
- *Chapter 7, Building a Culture of PolicyOps*

4
Framework for Digital Policies

As we have seen in previous chapters, embracing modern paradigms for digital transformation, such as **DevOps**, **the cloud**, and **automation**, is necessary.

PolicyOps embodies some of the DevOps principles by enabling automation, repeatability, and transparency in policies, and as discussed in the previous chapter it allows the organization to align its business objectives with digital policies.

This chapter will detail a framework that can be used to create policies from their inception to their creation and demise. This framework is an abstraction on top of the topics we covered in the first chapter. The goal is to simplify and allow anyone to use the framework through a simple four-step methodology.

This chapter will help you to understand each phase by expanding on each of them. It will also feature real-world examples related to cost, security, and compliance to help solidify an understanding of the framework and how it can be applied.

As such, in this chapter, we will be covering the following topics:

- Framework components
- Exploring the framework stages

Framework components

As we talked about in the first chapter, it is essential when designing policies, especially in technical environments, to have broad and diverse viewpoints as well as domain expertise. This was the biggest reason we introduced design thinking theory, **Persuasive System Design** (**PSD**), and the marketing best practices.

We will abstract some building blocks from the frameworks discussed in the first chapter and simplify them into four main phases.

This section will expand on this overlay framework and the activities that should happen at each phase. Later in this chapter, we will be using the framework to address some real-world examples.

Framework overview

This chapter will simplify the activities involved in identifying, creating, and evaluating policies, as shown in the following figure:

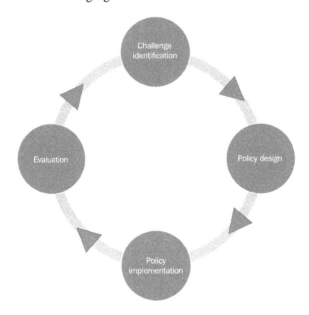

Figure 4.1 – OODA loop for digital policy design

The overlay framework, inspired by the **Observe, Orient, Decide, Act** (**OODA**) loop, can be applied to digital policy design. The OODA loop was built on the principle of agility to reduce the individual or organization reaction time.

The decision-making process is broken down into distinct but interrelated loops: observe, orient, decide, and act.

Policy design shares similarities with engineering and other fields and is dependent on humans, tools, and value extraction. At the same time, it factors in specificities regarding complex problems, goals, and conflicts of value and interests.

This four-step procedure consists of gathering and addressing goals, considering timing, value, and priority. It also considers the environmental context, the creation of feedback loops at all stages, and how to incorporate the policy actors and stakeholders into each phase audience.

The design and implementation phases select the appropriate approach to address the value and factors from the policy outcome, applying the proper approach to fit the policy's stipulation and comparing the alternatives and delivery of those arrangements.

Finally, we measure and ensure the policies are aligned through their life cycle to avoid incongruence and ensure the goals are achieved.

We will expand on each phase in more depth in the next section.

Challenge identification

This phase is where the initial challenges are identified and aligned with the goal that the policy will help achieve.

This phase is where frameworks such as design thinking theory, PSD, or marketing techniques have different viewpoints from stakeholders and actors that are impacted by the goals and instruments.

This phase is the actual planning before we start doing the policy design phase. It takes into consideration environmental factors and how the policy may be impacted by external factors, such as the regulatory landscape, culture, or organizational context.

For the planning to be effective, besides the environmental factors, there is also a need to involve the necessary stakeholders and create an effective *unified language* that can be used across all stakeholders to facilitate sharing information and results. For example, the NIST **Cybersecurity Framework** (**CSF**) addresses this by creating a common simple language for security issues. More information can be found here: `https://www.nist.gov/industry-impacts/cybersecurity-framework`.

The CSF can inspire you on how to create a common language for your stakeholders depending on the policy goal.

It's also essential to make sure this effort is mapped and shared across the stakeholders, for example, using a map to highlight the current state and where the policy will take you.

I recommend familiarizing yourself with **Wardley maps,** a fantastic tool that visually represents strategy, to help you understand the current state and where you want to go.

More information can be found here: `https://learnwardleymapping.com/`.

The following is an example of a Wardley map:

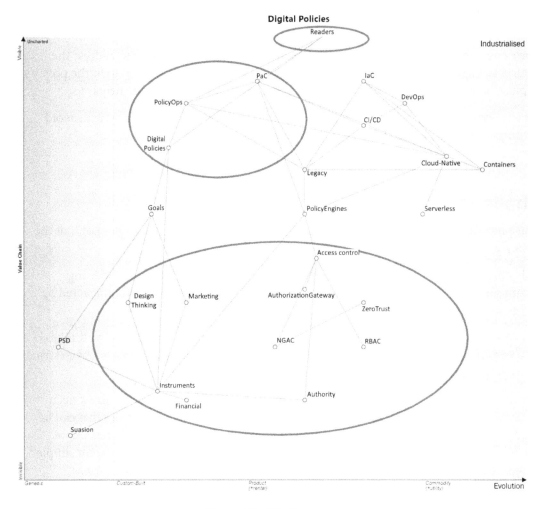

Figure 4.2 – Wardley map

The preceding map represents this book. We can see three main components:

- The *user* (**Readers**) will learn the concepts of several needs, **Policy as Code (PaC),** PolicyOps, and digital policies.

- The *needs* highlighted in this book are digital policies related to PolicyOps and PaC.

- *Activities* support the needs of instruments, access controls, and environments.

Because this is a map of the current state and future state, we can use dotted lines to show the areas we want to evolve:

- PaC

- PolicyOps

- Digital policies

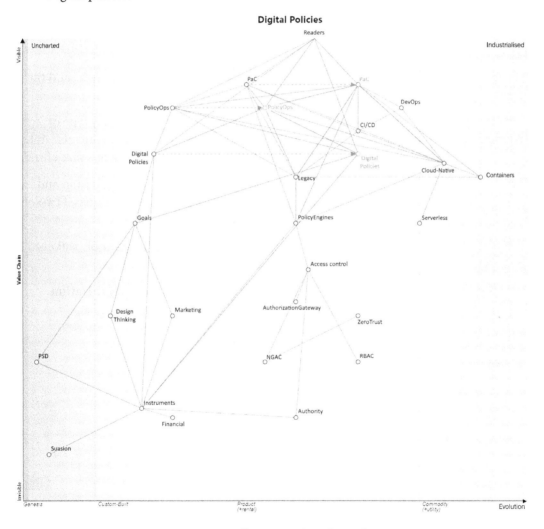

Figure 4.3 – Wardley map with evolution lines

As you can see, this type of mapping is helpful to convey strategy and design roadmaps, especially if you have different stakeholders.

You can find more examples of Wardley mapping here: `https://erik-schon.medium.com/the-art-of-strategy-811c00a96fad`.

In straightforward terms, the challenge identification phase identifies policies that consider the complex external factors in establishing achievable, realistic goals.

As we discussed previously, it's important to create common language frameworks so that everyone involved is speaking in the same terms. This phase should create an assessment that will be used throughout the life cycle of the policy.

Policy design

This phase is where the policy design happens, the choice of instruments is made, and the alignment with the goal identified in the previous phase is set.

During this phase, it is vital to consider the *assessment* to choose the necessary type of instruments correctly. Be mindful that sometimes there will be a mix of instruments while still being consistent; as long as they work together to support a policy strategy, that's fine.

For example, as we will see in the following cost policy example, we can use suasion and coercive instruments. While this increases the complexity, it can lead to synergies if two or more tools are more effective than used alone.

This mix of tools must also be factored in the *evaluation* phase, as different tools will need to be measured differently.

A sample of instruments using the **Nodality**, **Authority**, **Treasure**, and **Organization** (**NATO**) can be seen, as follows:

Positive-use instruments:

- **Nodality**: Education, advertising, training
- **Authority**: Advisory groups, agreements, regulations
- **Treasure**: Funding, grants, incentives
- **Organization**: Evaluations, hearings, processes

Negative-use instruments:

- **Nodality**: Misinformation, propaganda
- **Authority**: Banning
- **Treasure**: Budget cuts
- **Organization**: Information suppression

While this is not a comprehensive list, it shows how positive or negative instruments might be used.

This phase will create the architecture of the policy goal we are trying to achieve and the instruments used to fulfill the policy goal.

Policy implementation

In this phase, after an alignment with service delivery, the instruments are applied throughout the organization.

As seen in *Chapter 1*, *Introduction to Policy Design*, we need to be mindful of the policymakers and the policy takers, also called the **policy actors**.

Using the basic model of implementation categorization outlined as follows can help us understand how to best tackle the implementation:

- **Organization voluntarism**: Creates a communication campaign that empathically communicates the instruments and institutionalizes the policy among the actors.
- **Corporate regulation**: The policy is added to the organization's regulations, with training and other media to remind actors of the regulations.
- **Subsidization**: Financial instruments are used to influence the actors, sometimes with coercion or authority instruments.
- **Oversight**: Information is distributed among the actors supported by organization resources to provide mobilization.

There are several ways to implement the policy instruments. There needs to be an alignment that would have been discovered as part of the challenge identification from the stakeholder involvement and external factors.

We will also discuss policy engines in *Chapter 8*, *Policy Engines Design*, which can be used as authority instruments.

Evaluation

In this phase, we monitor the efficacy of the instruments, how and whether the goal is being met, and whether the instruments and goals are aligned.

As you might remember from *Chapter 1*, *Introduction to Policy Design*, we discussed the **3 Cs**:

- **Congruency**: Making sure the instruments are aligned with the goals.
- **Consistency**: The instruments are aligned with the goals.
- **Coherency**: The goals are aligned.

Thus, it is essential to have this principle in the *evaluation* phase and ensure that the policies have a cadence review to address the changing policy environment. Organizations are complex, and sometimes policies need to adapt to the circumstances. Still, it is essential to make sure that policies are appropriately patched without introducing *inconsistency*.

As we discussed in previous chapters, a mix of policies is typically used. It is essential to understand their synergies, as they might have a different efficacy from standalone instruments. Hence, we suggest that the evaluation takes a theoretical assumption with empirical observations.

Ideally, we would have empirical observations with a controlled setting using control groups, but that would be costly, and, in some cases, very difficult, due to the social nature of policy interventions.

As such, the following framework for *evaluation* is proposed:

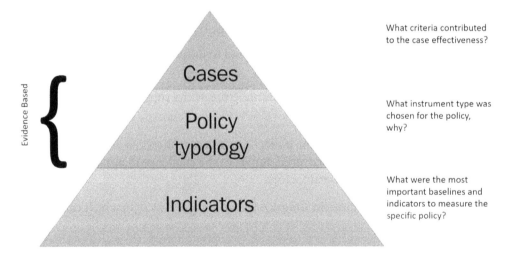

Figure 4.4 – Evaluation framework, top-down and bottom-up approaches

As shown in the preceding figure, the framework can be used from both ends, taking a dual approach:

- A top-down theory evaluation focused on answering effectiveness by analyzing the criteria that contributed to the efficacy, as seen on the top of the pyramid regarding the cases, following are some top-down example questions
- A bottom-up outcome evaluation focused on measuring indicators and baselines on the bottom in the indicators

You can use the following list of evaluation criteria adapted from the field and literature:

Top-down questions:

- What effect did the policy have on the actors?
- Were there side effects of applying the policy?
- Was the baseline defined in the second stage?
- Was the baseline explained during the implementation?
- Is the policy respecting the 3 Cs?
- What is the effect of this policy on your organization groups?
- Was the policy implemented in the agreed timelines?
- What were the costs of implementing this policy?
- Does the policy make sense in the current context?
- How involved were the stakeholders during the identification/design/implementation?
- Are the stakeholders happy with the policy?

For the bottom-up evaluation, since it is based on gauges, we need to understand that indicators need to be able to provide insight, being independent of other forces, be it cultural, structural, political, and so on.

For example, measuring the policy adoption would not capture the preferences of lines of business for another instrument. One organization might have to follow country regulations regarding adopting technology during a digital transformation program. In contrast, another organization might have financial incentives.

In each of these cases, the goal is to enable digital transformation in the organization, but the governance structure, different budgets, and other factors are not directly related to the policy being applied.

To mitigate that effect, we use an assessment highlighting how a policy would impact the indicator and any other factors that might affect the indicator.

For each indicator, we should consider the following aspects:

- **Scope and extent**: The indicator should provide information regarding the operating environment.

- **Policy relevance**: What changes by the instruments might impact the indicator, what actors have been affected by the policy, and how does it impact the indicator? How does this indicator relate to the state of digitization?

- **Graphic representation and visualization**: Each indicator should visually represent the proposed goal identified in the *challenge identification* phase and its progress. Either by creating a dashboard or some graphical capabilities. Can you group **Lines of business (LoB)**, teams, or groups into best and worst performers? Is this related to the policy or other factors? What is the uncertainty?

This section explained the different stages and what goes into each one. This will give you a solid understanding of how the phases incorporate the learnings of the previous chapters. In the next section, we will be exploring the framework phases with real-world scenarios.

Exploring the framework stages

In the previous sections, an overlay framework was used to simplify the topics addressed in the first chapter. This section will use the framework presented to establish governance by creating policies in key aspects of digital enablement to solidify how this framework can be used.

Due to the lengthy process that needs to happen during a real-world example, we will shorten the examples in the following sections to give broad coverage across different goals regarding cost, compliance, and security.

In later chapters, we will be using the tools discussed in *Chapter 3*, *Policy as Code a Business Enabler*, to codify those policies as code and use them as coercive instruments.

Real-world examples

This section will tackle three examples using the framework to define the high-level steps in each phase.

The first example is cost, which is a prevalent issue as organizations are sometimes misguided on adopting digital programs, such as Cloud Platforms, **enterprise resource planning** (**ERP**), or **customer relationship management**(**CRM**) properly, resulting in costs spiraling out of control.

The second example is especially relevant for highly regulated industries that must comply with a certain standard.

Finally, we'll look at security policy goals, which can be embedded at virtually no cost during the digital transformation, making the organization more resilient by adopting those best practices.

It's the same as building a house. If you plan for fire and build structures that are resistant to fire, the cost is much less than replacing the walls and doors once the house is built.

Cost example

Let's say that an organization decided to pursue a digital strategy. One of those workstreams was to migrate their current workloads into a cloud provider. After validating and selecting the **cloud service provider** (**CSP**), the migration on some workloads happened on credits. After a few years, when the credits expired, the costs started to snowball; as such, they decided to do something about it.

Challenge identification

We would try to understand why the costs are snowballing during this phase, speaking with stakeholders across the business.

For this example, let's assume the challenges identified were as follows:

- **Shadow IT**: Lines of businesses, and teams are using resources with their corporate credit cards.

- **Wrong sizing**: Developers use expensive virtual machines based on IaaS that are left on for a very long time for testing purposes.

- **Lack of cost visibility**: The **Chief Financial Officer** (**CFO**) cannot tie costs to products or projects.

We would meet with the key stakeholders during this phase and understand the business processes to map activities leading to the goals.

In the next phase, we would design the instruments to mitigate the identified issues.

Policy design

To tackle the challenges identified, we will use a mix of instruments, as discussed here:

- **Shadow IT**: The best instrument, in this case, is coercive. A policy that would enforce all resources requiring a valid cost center and tags associated with the product would mitigate this problem.

- **Wrong sizing**: In this case, we could use a mix of instruments to create several layers. The first layer would be based on suasion instruments, such as nudging to alert the developer of the cost incurred, especially if they are trying to deploy those resources to a testing environment.

  The second layer would be based on a coercive instrument to ensure that once a budget threshold is crossed, it will not be possible to launch these resources and automatically select smaller resources.

- **Lack of cost visibility**: For this, we could use the same instrument as for shadow IT. We can expand on the implementation part by creating specific dashboards.

We selected some instruments that would be adequate for the challenge identified in the first phase. Let's see the implementation part.

Policy implementation

Since this is all in the same organization, we will share implementations to solve some of the challenges in different business units:

- **Shadow IT**: We would get confirmation from the business stakeholders that the desired policies are aligned, supporting it. Then, jointly with the advisory group of the digital board (**Cloud Centre of Excellence (CcoE)**, **Cloud Business Office (CBO)**, and so on), we'd create a policy using tools such as **Open Policy Agent (OPA)** to enforce the usage of tags defining the product associated with the resources and the cost center.

- **Wrong sizing**: Regarding the improper sizing, we could use a suasion instrument that could be implemented as a browser add-on to check for parameters when someone spins up resources on the cloud provider portal. Or, we could have a layer between (shim) using OPA to ensure the developer gets alerted to resource size and potential costs.

  For the second layer, we could use a tool to fetch budget consumption data and limit resource deployment once a defined threshold has been hit.

- **Lack of cost visibility**: We could use the same instrument as for shadow IT, requiring the resources to have a cost center and be appropriately tagged.

These instruments would allow the creation of specific dashboards regarding costs and spending so the CFO office could have a more accurate view of the resource spending.

Evaluation

As discussed in the *Framework components* section, we need to ensure the instruments respect the 3 Cs. We could use the list in this chapter to ask some top-down questions, such as the following:

- What effect did the policies have?
- Did the shadow IT decrease?
- Did costs on development resources decrease?

We can also visually represent the indicators, as follows:

- Number of resources being created without tags
- Number of developers being alerted due to high-cost machines

This set of questions would be essential to evaluate the policy and ensure it achieves the goals proposed during the first phase of *challenge identification*. If not, we could use the feedback from those questions and the indicators to *patch the policy*, as discussed in *Chapter 1*, *Introduction to Policy Design*.

Compliance example

A multi-jurisdictional organization noticed that their dataflow patterns were causing an issue with the data localization controls during one of the regulatory audits. To comply with the regulatory requirements, the organization decided to mitigate the problem.

Challenge identification

Since this is a regulatory challenge, we need to ensure that the tech teams are aligned with the risk and compliance teams. Typically, there is a considerable gap between the regulatory and technology groups.

In this example, the challenges identified were as follows:

- **Lack of alignment**: The teams are not aligned and do not share a common understanding, resulting in friction and lost productivity.

- **Cross-border data flows**: The patterns of the data do not consider data localization as a requirement, allowing teams to select services and products that keep and move their data across jurisdictional borders.

- **GDPR**: The data kept by the development teams does not have a life cycle policy, making it liable to GDPR fines.

The stakeholders for this use case are the **Chief Information Security Officer** (**CISO**), risk, legal, and security teams alongside the development teams. This use case will require these various stakeholders to have input. There should be a common language across the discussions to address the disparity of team functions and create a shared understanding.

Policy design

For this use case, the policy design would involve creating coercive instruments and a policy engine for the technical requirements. The people and processes require a closer relationship with the different teams to foster collaboration by sharing best practices, such as PolicyOps. For the people aspect, PolicyOps would cover the collaboration, early stakeholder involvement, and usage of nudges to influence behaviors.

Following are some of the challenges identified in this example:

- **Lack of alignment**: Because several teams are involved, and traditionally, the risk and regulation teams still use traditional office documents to validate compliance, it creates friction across the development teams as they usually use paradigms such as **Everything-as-Code** (**EaC**).

    Another point is the need for cross-collaboration among these teams to adapt to EaC and help define the PaC in the organization.

- **Cross-border data flows**: We will need a policy engine to track all the services and products. Once that is established, we can block their usage when incorrect regions or options are defined.

- **GDPR**: We would use either native controls or a data lineage solution to manage the data life cycle for this regulation.

As we can see, most of the challenges are not technical (related to the product) but encompass the *people* angle. Something that we need to be mindful of, especially in digital transformations, is the **3 Ps: people**, **product**, and **process**. Our policy should contain all these tenants focusing on people, as the most significant challenge lies there.

Let's see what that would look like in practice.

Policy implementation

We need to address the people and processes in this policy implementation by creating the necessary collaboration and building the foundational technology building blocks to enable it, such as source code management, data lineage and the processes associated with it.

- **Lack of alignment**: This is a people challenge that could be mitigated with the product (technology) and supporting paradigm. Having **source code management** establish PaC and having a shared responsibility across the teams would enforce collaboration and create a shared responsibility.

  Have a process such as code owners in the SCM review the policies involved and make sure they fulfill and mitigate the risks. The risk and regulation team would incorporate their requirement into the product development life cycle and have a better-shared understanding.

- **Cross-border data flows**: A policy engine or native capabilities from the cloud providers could be used, as detailed in *Chapter 8*, *Policy Engines*, and *Chapter 11*, *Cloud Providers Policy Constructs*.

The following snippet shows a native policy for AWS that would allow development teams to run virtual machines and databases, and invoke serverless functions in a specific Region, Frankfurt (eu-central-1):

```
{
    "Version": "2012-10-17",
    "Statement": [
        {
            "Effect": "Allow",
            "Action": [
                "ec2:RunInstances",
                "rds:CreateDBInstance",
                "rds:CreateDBCluster",
                "lambda:InvokeFunction"
            ],
            "Resource": "*",
            "Condition": {
                "StringEquals": {
                    "aws:RequestedRegion": "eu-central-1"
                }
```

```
        }
      }
    ]
}
```

The preceding snippet would ensure there would not be any infringements in the data localization, as we specify the Region with `"aws:RequestedRegion":` `"eu-central-1"`.

Next, we will see how we could tackle the GDPR requirements.

For GDPR, the list of rulesets would be extensive depending on the controls implemented.

One solution could be to select appropriate coercive controls through third-party policy engines and tools containing some of these rulesets, build it on your own using PaC, use the cloud-native policy, or a combination.

As an example, Fugue uses OPA to establish some of these controls in several cloud providers. The following is a representation of some controls in AWS using a third-party tool such as Fugue:

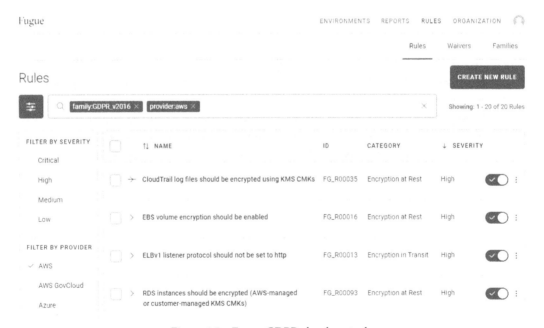

Figure 4.5 – Fugue GDPR cloud controls

As you saw in this section, we implemented the policies using a holistic approach, using a technology product such as a policy engine to provide the controls and instruments. We created a new process to guide the ways of working by requiring two groups to collaborate.

Using a policy paradigm, we can integrate the policies within the product release, gain agility and speed to market while being compliant, and improve team collaboration.

Evaluation

As in the previous section, we should use top-down and bottom-up questions to determine the efficacy of the instruments and the policy.

Here, I wanted to show how a wireframe graphical representation might be used to track the effort regarding GDPR compliance:

Figure 4.6 – Policy visual indicators GDPR controls wireframe

This simple wireframe could be used as an indicator for the coercive instruments regarding the enforcement of GDPR controls. This type of representation can be used to communicate with the stakeholders and track progress more efficiently.

OSCAL, which we will talk about in later chapters, can also view the current level of compliance programmatically.

Next, we will be looking at a security example.

Security example

A big multinational company is having issues with its cloud program regarding agility. Since it's a huge organization, there are many stakeholders, regulations, and groups, which adds complexity to add security to the services and products from the organization.

Challenge identification

This company is undergoing a digital transformation and wants to embed security within its delivery capability. They have been having issues with the alignment of the teams, especially with security and the **Security Operations Center** (**SOC**) blocking the efforts of the development and infrastructure teams.

In this example, the challenges identified were as follows:

- **Alignment**: The teams are not aligned and are not sharing a common understanding, resulting in slow deployment cycles and friction launching products.
- **Security controls**: The environment is lacking security controls. There have been multiple security defects found in production.

The stakeholders for this use case are the CISO, SOC, security, and application development teams. Next, we will see a possible policy to address the challenges identified.

Policy design

As we saw, the biggest hurdle is the teams not having alignment regarding the security posture and the lack of any security controls during the creation of the products:

- **Alignment**: For the alignment, as we discussed in this and previous chapters, having a common language is important; as such, implementing the NIST CSF will make sure all stakeholders can talk about the same thing.

  The framework uses the following functions: *identify*, *protect*, *detect*, *respond*, and *recover*. These five functions work together to form the foundation that other elements can be built upon to enforce successful cybersecurity risk management. This would create the necessary common language across the stakeholders.

  The policy would use coercive instruments, such as guidelines and training, to enforce a common framework across these teams.

- **Security controls**: The environment lacks security controls. There have been multiple security defects found in production. Building on the previous usage of the NIST CSF, there would be coercive instruments to enforce controls aligned to the framework and nudging during development to implement best practices such as DevSecOps. A PolicyOps team could help implement these policies in the CI/CD pipeline.

Next, let's see how the implementation would happen.

Policy implementation

In this phase, we would implement the policies. Since there are two main areas, let's break them down:

- **Alignment**: The actual implementation of the policy in this regard would be to do training and enforce the same terminology across the teams.

  Use the NIST CSF on assessment, high-level documents, and mapping of the technical activities.

  There would also be the usage of DevSecOps, such as integrating tools such as Prowler, Sentinel, and OPA. Combining these tools with a clear process to highlight security issues makes the process more transparent while increasing collaboration among the application/infrastructure and security teams.

  An example of building a dashboard of issues found in a cloud environment can be seen here: `https://quicksight-security-dashboard.workshop.aws/`.

- **Security controls**: We can use PaC for security controls by using either the native constructs discussed in *Chapter 12*, *Integrating Policy as Code with Enterprise Workflows*, a policy engine (see *Chapter 8*, *Policy Engines*), or a mix of both. Either way, what needs to be considered is how these security controls are implemented and tie into the NIST CSF.

  A good practice is to start with a framework such as CIS or NIST 800-53v5 and create custom controls if needed. Tools such as Sentinel, Chef InSpec, and OSCAL can help you measure the posture and how those controls are being enforced.

Evaluation

As discussed previously in the last use case, to make sure we use indicators to show the progress being made, in this case, we could use the following:

- A dashboard highlighting security controls in use, being enforced, and transgressed
- A dashboard showing security defects over time found in production

The goal is to have indicators that translate the bigger picture of the enabled policies into the progress being made.

These small examples showed at a high level the usage of a framework to split the identification of the goal, the policy design, and implementation and measure it successfully.

Summary

This chapter introduced a digital policy framework that simplified the steps and phases we discussed in the first chapter. We also made sure to create a framework that would be easy to understand and use in the field.

This chapter detailed a framework that we can refer to when tackling digital policies. We also discussed each phase, challenge identification, policy design, policy implementation, and evaluation in detail during this chapter.

The real-world example sections should give you an idea of what could be achieved through each phase to help you solidify your knowledge of the framework and its phases.

While the challenge identification was massively simplified in this chapter, it's the phase that takes the most time when designing policies, especially as different stakeholders are involved.

As we highlighted, we can identify potential for instrument synergies and a possible mix of policies during the challenge identification phase. In this chapter's examples, we tried to cover the *people* aspect from the *3 Ps*, as it's the angle that is usually forgotten. These activities fail due to placing a massive onus on technology alone. We tried to show how creating new processes to enforce collaboration brings advantages to multidisciplinary teams, bringing to fruition policy goals, usually in compliance, security, and risk.

The next chapter will cover cloud-native environments, what containers and serverless policies are available in the landscape, their differences, and what tools and frameworks are available.

5
Policy for Cloud-Native Environments

In this chapter, we will be covering **cloud-native environments**. We will discuss the term itself, the communities behind it, and how containers, microservices, and serverless paradigms play a role in this ecosystem.

Because of the minor variations of the offerings between **cloud service providers (CSPs)**, we will show architectures that depict the general concepts that apply to most cloud-native services.

We will highlight the role of microservices and serverless functions in an event-driven architecture and its benefits to an organization that would want to adopt this paradigm, especially with the advent of big data, **machine learning (ML)**, and **artificial intelligence (AI)**.

Finally, we will cover an example of a cloud-native policy that depicts an architecture for a **container as a service (CaaS)**, we will discuss the components used, and we'll consider the configuration of each service to support a policy using the framework from the previous chapter.

We will be covering the following main topics:

- Cloud-native environments
- Native policy constructs for CaaS
- Native policy constructs for FaaS
- An example of a cloud-native policy

Technical requirements

To follow this chapter, it will help to have an understanding of cloud technologies, the shared responsibility model, continuous integration and delivery, and concepts of serverless paradigms and containers.

Cloud-native environments

We often hear the term **cloud-native**, but it has become an overloaded term. For this section, we will expand on the cloud-native construct, its ecosystem, and the policy landscape for it.

When defining cloud-native environments, we refer to concepts such as 12-factor app development, the **CAP theorem**, and **cloud infrastructure usage**. Cloud-native combines tools, technologies, and paradigms at a high level. They are generally split into containers and serverless technologies from a tech stack implementation, which we will expand in this section.

Also, it's important to highlight that these cloud-native environments are the evolution of the traditional virtualizations from on-premises data centers, fueled by the needs of organizations who want to reap digital benefits. These benefits include big data analytics with access to highly efficient datastores and warehouses, innovation that utilizes AI and ML tools, and speed-to-market and organizational agility.

These drivers pushed organizations to move to cloud environments, either by using a lift-and-shift approach or by modernizing to make their applications cloud-native.

Some of these modernizations involve shifting development efforts to containers to address portability and a more mature development effort, or going serverless to reduce the management and overhead of owning infrastructure. Another big push for going serverless is focusing on business value by not being preoccupied with underlying activities such as network security and software patching. It also allows the organization to move into an event-driven architecture. We will be looking at each case in more depth in this chapter.

One thing that we need to be aware of is the complexity of cloud-native environments:

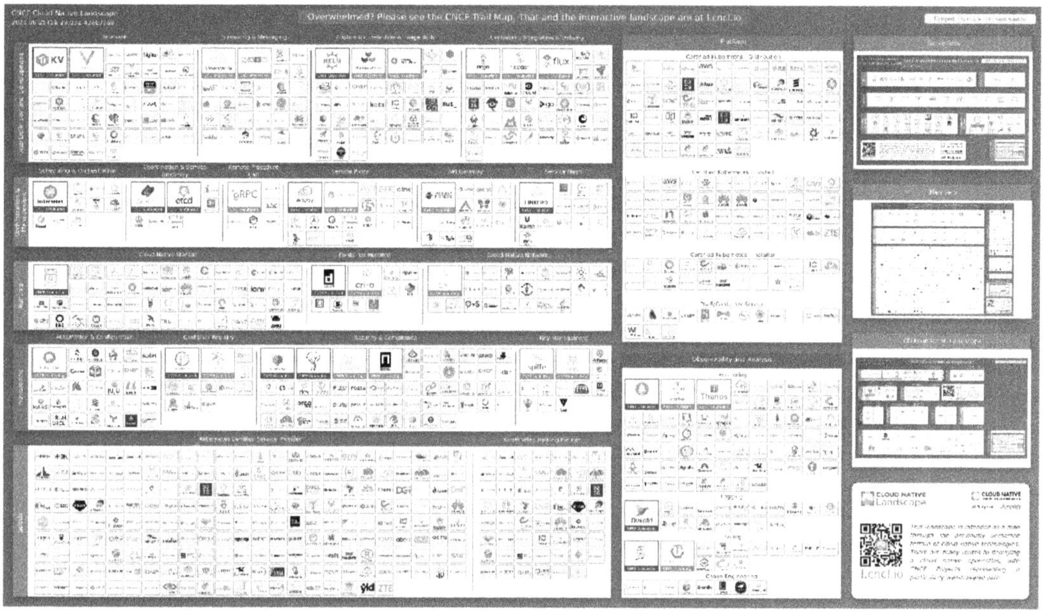

Figure 5.1 – The CNCF cloud-native landscape

These tools and services make up the **Cloud Native Computing Foundation** (**CNCF**) **cloud-native landscape**. This can look intimidating at first, but rest assured, you don't need to know every aspect of it.

One area that we are going to delve into in later chapters is the security and compliance area:

Figure 5.2 – The CNCF cloud-native security and compliance area

Some of these tools and vendors are important because they allow us to construct the necessary access controls mechanisms as coercive instruments to achieve the goals of the policy.

Be mindful that the CNCF cloud-native landscape is very container-focused. While we will highlight ways to use some of the tools to implement policies in the serverless landscape, it still needs more integration work than using the native CSP serverless policies. A good resource created recently to guide practitioners and learners of security in the cloud-native landscape can be consulted here (`https://cnsmap.netlify.app/`), which provides a mapping of CNCF and open source projects while also bringing a practical viewpoint on topics in the cloud-native security landscape.

The **Cloud Native Security Map** (`https://github.com/cncf/tag-security/blob/main/security-whitepaper/cnsmap/README.md#about-the-cloud-native-security-map`) provides a framework to use when developing cloud-native security solutions and architectures.

Containers

I think everyone will agree that containers became ubiquitous in the last years, as they became the de facto method for adopting cloud paradigms, bringing benefits such as reproducibility, dependency management, speed of operations, and ease of deployment. While there are several container engines nowadays, the revolution started with **Docker** democratizing access to the container landscape and popularizing the term and adoption.

While there was already similar technology to containers 30 years ago, in 2008, the necessary patches **Linux Containers** (**LXC**) landed on the **Linux** kernel to take full advantage of Linux **namespaces** and **cgroups**. Fast forward a few years, and **Kubernetes** popularized containers for infrastructure and cloud environments.

A container is comparable to a **virtual machine** (**VM**), which allows isolating a specific workload from other workloads, as shown in the following figure:

Containerized Applications

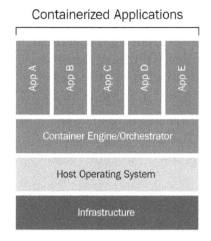
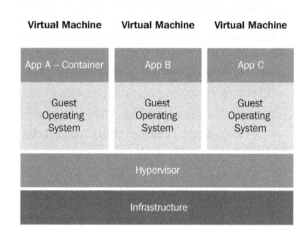

Figure 5.3 – A diagram showing container and virtual machine approaches

As you can see in the preceding figure, the left graphic shows containers with a self-contained application running on top of an engine. Applications A through E contains all of the libraries and files to run the specific service/application.

However, a VM is shown on the right, which is a heavier alternative as there is a complete **operating system** (**OS**) on top of the hypervisor. Applications are installed in such a way that they share libraries and resources within the underlying OS or other applications installed in the VM.

The main advantage of using containers is that they enable the following:

- **Portability**: By bundling specific versions of libraries and the necessary files to run the application, the container is self-contained, making it ideal to use in microservices and deploying to different environments such as private and public clouds.

- **Standardization**: As the processes to create and manage containers are tied to best practices in DevOps, their use establishes standardization by creating integration and release processes (CI/CD) while improving the operations, as it allows teams to expect the same behavior of containers independently of the environment that is deployed.

- **Efficiency**: As stated previously, containers support DevOps, which accelerates development, testing, and production release, creating more organizational value by improving agility.

Let's now expand on some of the key technology/paradigms in the containers realm:

- **Docker**: This can be seen as the package manager. It allows teams to package their application into a Docker image and publish it into a container registry, akin to a **software configuration management** (**SCM**) repository that can be referenced for specific images.

  Docker also has a lot of other key components, such as a container runtime and a private registry (**Docker Hub**). You can find more information at the following link: `https://www.docker.com/products` or `https://github.com/docker`.

  A getting started guide can also be found here: `https://docs.docker.com/get-started/`.

- **Kubernetes**: Also known as **k8s**, this is a widely used platform to run containers/microservices. Kubernetes is an orchestrator, which means that it takes care of allocating the right amount of resources such as storage, network, and compute into the underlying host, making sure services can run and scale concurrently.

  Kubernetes enables service discovery, automated rollouts, self-healing, and configuration management. Originally designed by **Google**, with similarities to their internal system, **Borg**, it is now open source and maintained by the CNCF.

  Kubernetes is highly complex and powerful, and you can read more on its concepts here: `https://kubernetes.io/docs/concepts/`.

- **Microservices**: While we have talked about some tools and paradigms, it's essential to establish the meaning of **microservices** and their relationship with containers.

  A microservice is a small and independent piece of software that is self-contained. This means that each microservice can talk directly to the outside world or other microservices. One of their most significant benefits is decoupling applications into small units, allowing teams to update the specific microservice. The following diagram helps put this into perspective in comparison to the traditional **monolith** paradigm:

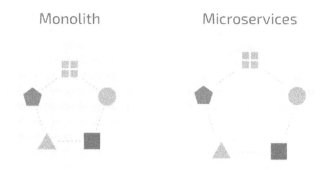

Figure 5.4 – The difference between the monolith and microservices paradigms

From the preceding diagram, we can quickly see that this paradigm brings some advantages. It is easier to scale, the components are independent, and it allows for better maintenance, as each element is simpler. Microservices are an approach to **service-oriented architectures** (**SOAs**), and they can also be designed to fulfill a serverless approach by using **Knative**. We will talk more about the serverless paradigm in the next section.

The use of microservices is a trending topic due to the popularity of tools such as Docker and Kubernetes. In the next section, we will talk about serverless approaches, another trending topic part of the cloud-native landscape.

Serverless computing

Serverless computing is a cloud-computing execution model in which the cloud provider is responsible for allocating the compute, network, and storage resources needed to serve the specified workload. In this model, the application owner does not need to specify and manage how many resources are required at a given time. Serverless computing is also categorized as a *pay-as-you-go* approach, where payment is generally made based on the usage of the resources, such as storage consumed or CPU time spent.

In this paradigm, application teams provide code that will run and manage the CSP.

The main advantages of serverless computing are as follows:

- **Agility**: Enabling teams to develop business applications without being concerned with the infrastructure allows them to build and deploy at a much faster rate – fostering innovation as experimentation becomes frictionless.

- **Cost**: Serverless computing is usually priced on a per-event basis and is cost-efficient on burst workloads, as you do not need to maintain the infrastructure, which reduces **Capital Expenditure** (**CAPEX**) on things such as hardware equipment (servers, firewalls, switches), buildings, software licenses, and so on, as well as the **operational expenditure** (**OPEX**), which relates to the teams running the day-to-day activities to support the business, such as the IT team, the network team, and so on.

- **Scalability**: Serverless computing auto-scales based on usage without any management from administrators. This scalability is automatic, without the need to plan and provision resources.

There are many serverless hosting models, the most common being the following:

- **Amazon**: **Lambda**, **Fargate**, **AWS Batch**
- **Google**: **Cloud Functions**, **Knative**, **Cloud Run**
- **Microsoft Azure**: **Azure Functions**, **Azure Container Instances**
- **IBM**: **Redhat** (**Knative**)
- **Others**: **Knative**, **OpenFaas**, **Apache OpenWhisk**, **Fission**, **Kubeless**

All these hosting models abstract the underlying resources so that you can focus on writing code. Some fall into the CaaS model and others into **function as a service** (**FaaS**).

The following section will discuss the main differences between CaaS and FaaS.

CaaS versus FaaS

As seen in the previous section, containers and serverless computing simplify an organization's operations. The focus of the applications teams can be on developing business value instead of needing to manage and provide the necessary resources to support workloads.

Two of those services related to the deployment model of serverless computing and containers are CaaS and FaaS. It's essential to understand the main differences between these, as policies for each model have different instruments, depending on the user-managed layer.

The following diagram will help to illustrate the differences in responsibility between the different service models:

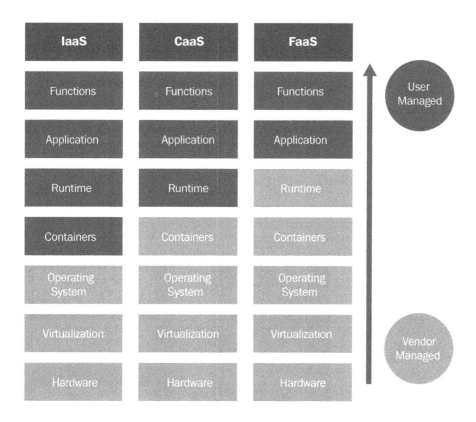

Figure 5.5 – An IaaS versus CaaS versus FaaS responsibility model

As you can see, the runtime's responsibility is still something the application owners have in the CaaS model, such as EKS. When we develop policies, we need to consider the model we are targeting to make sure we can use instruments on the user-managed stack.

Be mindful that a service such as Google App engine would fall under **platform as a service (PaaS)**. In this service model, you are responsible for securing its applications, thereby having a different responsibility from a CaaS and FaaS.

Most CSPs provide solutions such as managed Kubernetes – for example, **Google Kubernetes Engine (GKE)**, Amazon **Elastic Kubernetes Service (EKS)**, and **Azure Container Instances (ACI)** – which would fall into CaaS.

The following section will discuss event-driven architectures and the role containers, serverless computing, and cloud computing have in the major cloud-native architectural paradigm.

Event-driven architecture

As we have seen in the previous sections, serverless computing and microservices propose decoupling services and make them as modular as the simplicity of a unit. This type of simplicity makes it easier to create small actions to respond to situations or **events**.

The event-driven paradigm is built on events that happen in an environment, such as requesting a password change, a suspicious log entry, or a product being placed in the shopping cart. These events will execute an action in response, such as sending an email, alerting the **security operations center** (**SOC**), or updating the existing stock after the user buys something, respectively.

The following is a figure describing this type of architecture:

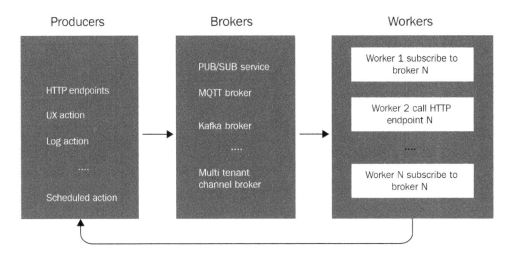

Figure 5.6 – Event-driven architecture

These architectures enable loose coupling, fault tolerance, real-time APIs, and resilience.

At a macro level, these architectures are composed of three components:

- **Producers**: These can be created by a simple request (for example, HTTP, TCP, or UDP) or any action on a website, for example, from a scheduled activity that runs at a specific time or from a log source.

  The event's producers are the units responsible for creating the events and sending them to the **brokers**.

- **Brokers**: These are responsible for temporarily receiving events and storing them before sending them to the appropriate **worker**. Most message brokers, such as **Apache Kafka**, Google Pub/Sub, and RabbitMQ MQTT, can be used as brokers.

- **Workers**: These form a service that processes and executes the events received. A simple example could be sending a notification or an email.

This type of architecture is very suitable for CaaS and FaaS, as you can construct, route, and parse events through several services. It can lead to simple or complex designs, as the following figure shows:

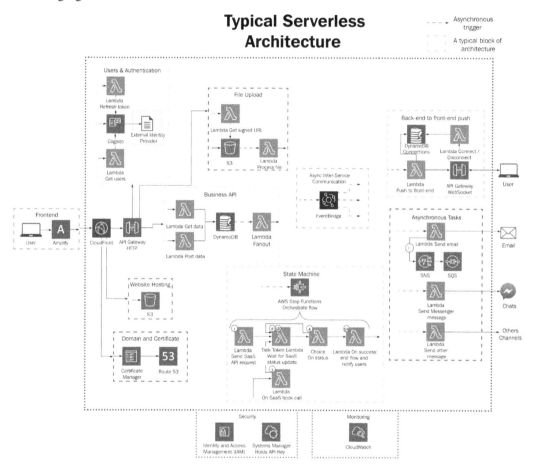

Figure 5.7 – Serverless architecture

If you want to know more about event-driven architecture, you can read more about Knative, OpenFaaS, OpenWhisk, and Kubeless.

The purpose of this section was to make you aware of the capabilities of cloud-native solutions, inform you about ongoing trends, and how these paradigms work.

More importantly, the responsibility depends on the service mode. This is an important notion to understand, as the type of instruments for the policy will differ.

The following sections will be split into native policy constructs for CaaS and FaaS, approaching the policy constructs for each of those environments.

Native policy constructs for FaaS

As we saw in the previous section, both FaaS and CaaS enable teams to increase agility and focus on business value. This section will show you how to use coercive instruments to enforce specific authorization policies for FaaS environments.

First, let's define a FaaS architecture visually, as this will help highlight points for enforcement:

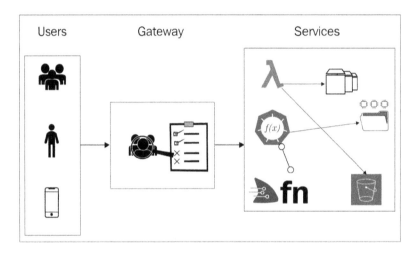

Figure 5.8 – A simple FaaS serverless architecture

As you can see, we have two major points in which we can influence and apply coercive instruments such as access controls, the gateway, and the services. Be mindful that a gateway might not be present in some cases, which will require us to apply policies to the resources and services.

Let's break them down and discuss the options at each stage.

Components

Applying policies at each component can be achieved by using **Policy as Code**, a **policy engine**, or the cloud-native policy constructs, which can be done in **JSON**, **Python**, **Terraform**, and so on.

In this section, we will highlight a couple of examples.

Gateways

Both FaaS and CaaS architectural patterns can leverage a gateway to manage and secure the APIs. The gateway, traditionally, is responsible for accepting and routing requests, authorizing certain users or services, monitoring, and for the life cycle management of APIs.

Next, we will see two patterns to enforce authorization and access policies. The first will use the gateway as the policy engine to provide authorization and access control. The second will achieve authorization and access control by using **Open Policy Agent (OPA)** in a proxy pattern.

The API gateway level

In this pattern, a gateway such as **AWS API Gateway**, **Azure Application Gateway**, **Google API Gateway**, **NGINX**, or a third-party solution is used to authenticate, authorize, and manage access controls for our APIs.

In this pattern, we can leverage API resource policies to enforce authorization.

The following is an example of this in AWS API Gateway:

```
01: {
02:     "Version": "2012-10-17",
03:     "Statement": [
04:         {
05:             "Effect": "Allow",
06:             "Action": [
07:                 "execute-api:Invoke"
08:             ],
09:             "Resource": [
10:                 "arn:aws:execute-api:eu-west-3:*:*"
11:             ]
12:         }
13:     ]
14: }
```

As there is an implicit deny in this snippet, we need to add an `allow` statement. Then it would only allow resources in the eu-west-3 (France) region to invoke the API gateway.

You can test resource policies for AWS at `https://policysim.aws.amazon.com/home/index.jsp`.

We will talk more in-depth about these CSPs' policy resources in *Chapter 12, Integrating Policy as Code with Enterprise Workflows.*

You can read more on access controls for the different CSPs at the following links:

- **AWS**: `https://docs.aws.amazon.com/apigateway/latest/developerguide/apigateway-control-access-to-api.html`.

- **Azure**: `https://docs.microsoft.com/en-us/azure/api-management/api-management-access-restriction-policies`.

- **Google** (at this stage, **Google Cloud Platform** (**GCP**) has an API gateway, but it is very limited in functionality, so you would be better served by using **Apigee**): `https://docs.apigee.com/api-platform/reference/policies/access-control-policy`.

- **OPA**: We will approach OPA in *Chapter 9, A Primer on Open Policy Agent.* Be mindful that due to the extensible nature of OPA, it is possible to use it with the majority of FaaS products, as it can be deployed as an HTTP admission hook. There is more information on OPA at the following link: `https://www.openpolicyagent.org/docs/latest/http-api-authorization/`.

As you can see, you can use policies in the API gateway directly. But as there is more adoption of a multi-cloud environment, the variance between different API gateways in CSPs creates friction in the user experience, as there will be different maturity types regarding their API gateways.

OPA integration

One way to mitigate the variance in capabilities between CSP policies is to use a common proxy pattern, where the gateway talks with a policy engine such as OPA and retrieves the decision of the authorization, as shown in the following figure:

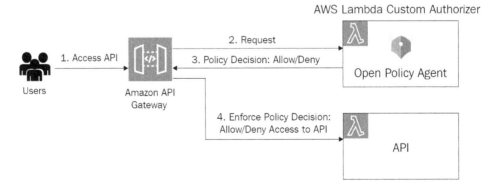

Figure 5.9 – A serverless proxy pattern using OPA for gateway authorization

In this pattern, OPA offloads the authorization capabilities out of the gateway to provide those capabilities.

We will talk more in-depth about OPA in *Chapter 9, A Primer on Open Policy Agent*, but for now, it's important to realize that OPA can be used as a shim to provide policy for FaaS, albeit more tailored for CaaS and the Kubernetes ecosystem.

Next, we will look at policies that we could implement at the resource level.

Resources

As we saw in *Figure 5.8*, there are two major enforcement points – they're either in the gateway, using a proxy pattern, or they're at the resource level.

By *resources*, we mean resources directly tied to FaaS constructs. For example, while FaaS traditionally does not require a network, it can be attached to a network, by default the functions can access anything available on the public internet.

Functions, compute, and storage

Regarding the policies in serverless functions, it depends on the environment we use, AWS has the **Serverless Application Model (SAM)**, a templatized way to build serverless functions.

Policies in the AWS SAM can be attached as part of a Policy as Code approach. Let's look at following the snippet:

```
"Statement": [
  {
    "Effect": "Allow",
    "Action": [
      "s3:PutObject",
      "s3:PutObjectAcl",
    ],
    "Resource": [
      {
        "Fn::Sub": [
          "arn:${AWS::Partition}:s3:::${bucketName}",
          {
            "bucketName": {
              "Ref": "BucketName"
            }
```

```
            }
          ]
        },
        {
          "Fn::Sub": [
            "arn:${AWS::Partition}:s3:::${bucketName}/*",
            {
              "bucketName": {
                "Ref": "BucketName"
              }
            }
          ]
        }
      ]
    }
  ]
```

This snippet allows the function to store data in **Amazon S3**, a **blob storage** offering from AWS. Here, we specify the resource and use variables to enable the function to store data in the S3 bucket.

As you can see, the function must be explicitly given access to the resources it will access. Since we talked about the decomposition brought by FaaS, it is a good idea when developing the functions to specialize as much as possible, meaning that one function should only be responsible for one task, and the permissions should follow best practices such as the **principle of least privilege**.

In the previous example, if the function stores data, there is no need for it to have permissions that would allow it to list all the objects or to read objects from the bucket.

As you can see, we can apply policies to limit the function's scope, following the *least privileged* paradigm we discussed in previous chapters.

Network

Serverless deployments do not require an explicit network, and by default, the functions can access external endpoints and the public internet. Currently, there is the possibility to attach the functions to a network. Having the functions as part of a network is helpful, as it allows segmentation at the network level. In AWS, this is achieved by **Amazon Virtual Private Cloud** (**Amazon VPC**), which is a similar construct as a network domain. Thus, placing the function in an Amazon VPC instance and giving the functions free access to all resources and services in the VPC.

This pattern of using a function inside a VPC is something the major CSPs support, as you can see in the following:

- **GCP**: `https://cloud.google.com/vpc/docs/serverless-vpc-access`

- **AWS**: `https://docs.aws.amazon.com/lambda/latest/dg/configuration-vpc.html`

- **Azure**: `https://docs.microsoft.com/en-us/azure/azure-functions/functions-networking-options#virtual-network-integration`

There is flexibility in applying authorization and access control for serverless computing in public cloud provider environments, as we can use the gateway or a third-party solution to serve as an authorization proxy.

Next, we will look at the policy constructs for CaaS.

Native policy constructs for CaaS

We discussed the FaaS and its authorization and enforcement policies in the previous section. This section will do the same for CaaS, which has a more extensive ecosystem and is currently more widely adopted than FaaS, especially with the popularity of Kubernetes.

CaaS has a bit more complexity – architecturally speaking – than FaaS. Take a look at the following architecture:

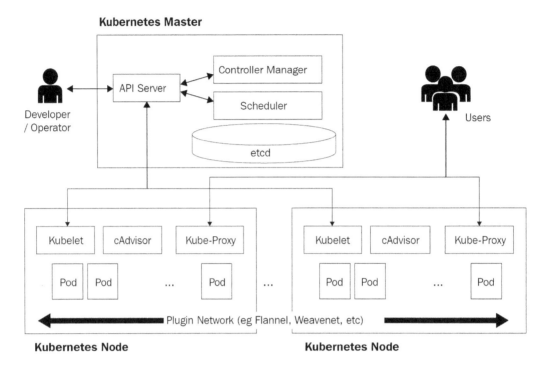

Figure 5.10 – An example of the Kubernetes architecture

One way to separate this into simpler terms is to split it into the *control plane* at the top and the *data plane* at the bottom.

Since CaaS is a wrapper on top of Kubernetes, without the complexity of managing it, two very successful offers are **Google Cloud Run** or **Google Kubernetes Engine** (**GKE**) from GCP. At the same time, AWS offers **Amazon Elastic Container Service (ECS)** and **Elastic Kubernetes Service(EKS)**, and finally Azure offers **Azure Container Instances (ACI)** and **Azure Container Instances (AKS)**.

In this section, we will use examples from Kubernetes. Still, the concepts can be applied to the CaaS ecosystem from the CSPs.

First, let's look at the components.

Components

This section will discuss the components that can act as enforcement gates and serve as policy points either natively, via a third-party plugin, or in a proxy pattern.

The API server

As most CaaS solutions are based in Kubernetes – or with a slight variation such as Openshift – the API server is a good point to enforce authorization policies, especially on the control plane.

The recommended way to establish authentication and authorization is via **identity and access management (IAM)** and **role-based access control (RBAC)** using service accounts. In an enterprise setting, this can be extended to **LDAP**, **SAML**, **Kerberos**, **X.509** schemes, and so on.

The authentication can also be extended to a proxy or an authentication webhook.

Using ingresses

In CaaS, an ingress pattern can route the traffic from internal or external sources. Depicted as follows, an ingress is used to route traffic from the public cloud to services:

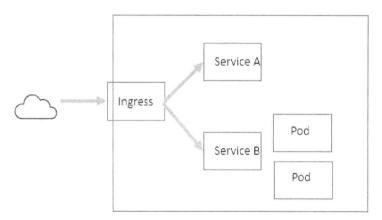

Figure 5.11 – Ingress architecture

As shown in the previous image, the ingress can be extended and integrated with the CSP's load balancers. An example in AWS is as follows: `https://aws.amazon.com/blogs/opensource/kubernetes-ingress-aws-alb-ingress-controller/`. Another example in GCP is as follows:

`https://cloud.google.com/kubernetes-engine/docs/concepts/ingress.`

In this component, Kubernetes supports the usage of network policy to restrict traffic. One simple example might look like this:

```
apiVersion: networking.k8s.io/v1
kind: NetworkPolicy
metadata:
  name: pac-network-policy
  namespace: default
spec:
  podSelector:
    matchLabels:
      type: data
  policyTypes:
  - Ingress
  ingress:
  - from:
    - ipBlock:
        cidr: 172.17.0.0/16
    - namespaceSelector:
        matchLabels:
          project: pacproject
    ports:
    - protocol: TCP
      port: 3306
```

This snippet would enforce the following:

- A network policy to isolate *data Pods* in the default namespace for ingress traffic

This would allow connection to all Pods in the default namespace with the `type=data` label on TCP port `3306` from Pods with the `project=pacproject` label namespace the IP range in `172.17.0.0/16`.

In the CSPs – for example, in GKE – you can enable a network policy, as detailed here: `https://cloud.google.com/kubernetes-engine/docs/how-to/network-policy`

Now, let's look at some third-party integration.

Third-party integrations

As discussed in this chapter, by using a proxy pattern or a third-party solution, we can also augment authorization and authentication policies to the base system.

The popularity and integration of OPA with Kubernetes make it one of the most widely used policy authorization systems. There are also other systems, such as NGINX, or more tailored services for APIs, such as **Kong** or **Istio**.

There is a good book on **service mesh** that covers Istio, **Linkerd**, **Consul**, and others: *Mastering Service Mesh, by Anjali Khatri, Vikram Khatri, Packt Publishing*.

Let's now look at the resource policies for CaaS.

Resource policies

When building policies for CaaS, it is important to enforce controls for who can access the systems and resources. Establishing limits, quotas, processes, and so on is a great practice, and this will reduce surprises and attacks, such as **denial of wallet** (**DoW**) attacks.

Let's look at some of the policies that can be configured in a CaaS system.

Resource quotas

A resource quota is a tool that can be used to enforce the fair usage of resources – for example, Pods, services, and so on – across the cluster. It provides constraints on the total resource consumption per namespace. For example, it can limit the number of computing resources addressed in a specific namespace.

As an example, consider the following scenario. We have a cluster with different namespaces: one for testing, and one for production. We could limit the testing namespace to a small percentage of the overall available resources while not constraining the production namespace. We could also configure the resource quotas for more complex scenarios, such as allocating resources per team or specific workloads.

The types of resources that can have constraints applied can be compute (such as CPU), memory, storage (such as persistent volume claims), object counts (such as services), deployments, jobs, replication controllers, and more. This is very useful when we are trying to create policies that address resource allocation.

Next, we will look at *limit ranges*, which apply policies to individual containers.

Limit ranges

On Kubernetes, containers will run without a limit on the compute resources. This means they will have access to all RAM and CPU defined at the namespace level.

Limit ranges apply policies to the individual container on how much resources can be used, let's look at an example for CPU:

```
apiVersion: v1
kind: LimitRange
metadata:
  name: limit-range-pac-example
  namespace: pac-example
spec:
  limits:
  - default:
      cpu: 300m
      memory: 100m
    defaultRequest:
      cpu: 100m
      memory: 50m
    type: Container
```

In the preceding code example, we used the `pac-example` namespace and set the defaults the container can use:

- `default`: This is the number of resources the container *will be limited to using*, if not specified.

- `defaultRequest`: This is the number of resources the container *will request to use*, if not specified.

You can learn more in the official Kubernetes documentation, located here:

`https://github.com/kubernetes/community/blob/master/ contributors/design-proposals/resource-management/admission_ control_limit_range.md`

Most of the CaaS systems in the majority of the CSPs will have these constructs, or you can use these policies in the YAML files.

There are also other policies for specific resources that depend on the CaaS system you are using, if we look at the documentation for ECS, we can see that there are some non-default values: Amazon ECS tasks hosted on Fargate use the default resource limit values set by the operating system with the exception of the nofile resource limit parameter which Fargate overrides.

 You can check it at AWS ECS task definition documentation:

```
https://docs.aws.amazon.com/AmazonECS/latest/developerguide/
task_definition_parameters.html#container_definition_limits
```

Next, let's look at some native policies in a Kubernetes admission controller.

Pod security policies

A **PodSecurityPolicy (PsP)** is an **admission controller**, which means that it helps the operator of the cluster control the Pod's specification.

A PsP would create some resources in the cluster and then define the Pod's requirements using RBAC rules. This is important, as we can use PsPs to enforce policies such as *not allowing privileged users on nodes* in these clusters.

Unfortunately PsPs have been deprecated, however, a native substitution is being worked on. In the meantime, the effort can be tracked here: `https://github.com/kubernetes/enhancements/issues/2579`.

In the meantime, OPA can fill this requirement, as we will see in *Chapter 9, A Primer on Open Policy Agent*. For now, let's say that the OPA gatekeeper library and constraint templates can be used for these purposes. This is the default approach for **Google Cloud Anthos**.

Containers

Defining trusted container images in our environment is essential as the number of imported libraries due to the images import creates supply chain issues. Attestation is the process of checking the container image, running through specific checks, and approving it for use.

Google Cloud uses the concept of binary authorization, which only allows an image that has been previously checked and signed to be enforced.

From a cloud-native perspective, **Notary** is the project incubated by the CNCF, which provides attestation to the container images and can be used with most CSPs, for example, **AWS ECR cosign**.

As you can see, there are many ways to apply coercive instruments to enforce a specific policy. The CaaS environment is currently a bit more mature than FaaS, but both of them enjoy a healthy community and different options for policy instruments.

Examples of cloud-native policies

This section will expand on some real-world policies related to CaaS and FaaS consumption. Some of these can be more technical than others, and this list is not exhaustive, but it is intended as an example of policies that can be implemented.

- **Stakeholders**:

  - Common language framework: Use a framework to create a unified language across teams and stakeholders, such as NIST CSF.

  - Service-level objectives policy: Ensure the services and applications are published following a cloud best practice by leveraging error budgets (`https://sre.google/workbook/error-budget-policy/`).

- **Security**:

  - Data encryption: Encryption is ubiquitous, as most security frameworks (CIS, NIST, CSA) will mandate data encryption in transit and at rest. You can enforce these practices with native cloud tools such as OPA or the CSP's native tooling. We will discuss this in more detail in *Chapter 12*, *Integrating Policy as Code with Enterprise Workflows*.

  - Data sovereignty: This chapter presents some solutions that can enforce data sovereignty through a third-party authorization engine (see *Chapter 8*, *Policy Engines*) or the CSP constructs.

  - Service identity: Create a policy based on best practices, either using a third-party engine or cloud-native constructs. We will discuss this in more detail in *Chapter 9*, *A Primer on Open Policy Agent*.

- **App development**:

  - Security provenance: Some CSPs have services such as binary authorization. Building your own could be achievable, but there are ready-to-use tools to validate and sign your containers and the provenance and quality of the code used in the functions by using some kind of attestation software. One example would be using **Docker Notary** or **SPIFFE**.

- Git workflow: Establish a workflow with several stakeholders that review collaboratively. An example would be the network security team being the code owner for the firewall-as-code, but the code getting reviewed and merged by the application team.

- Security development life cycle: Establish a life cycle that considers best practices and enforces policies scanning and testing at every stage of the development pipeline.

- **Infrastructure**:

  - **Infrastructure as Code** (**IaC**): This establishes policies that scan resources for broad permissions, key rotation issues, and IAM password policies. One cloud-native tool is **Checkov** (`https://www.checkov.io/`), which allows the scan of IaC resources – for example, Azure Resource Manager (**ARM**), Terraform, Docker, and so on – for security issues.

- **Compliance**:

  - **NIST**, **FedRAMP**, **HIPAA**: Using an **Everything as Code** (**EaC**) approach, we can leverage **Open Security Controls Assessment Language** (**OSCAL**) to build the information-sharing capabilities between tools to maintain the necessary compliance requirements in the organization.

Summary

This chapter focused on both CaaS and FaaS environments and how to develop a policy for these environments. We discussed the CNCF, the most prominent organization in the cloud-native landscape. We also discussed how OPA has grown in recent years, demonstrating widespread adoption, open governance, and a solid commitment to the community.

We explored the main concepts of the CaaS and FaaS architectures, highlighting the primary components used as enforcement points. As noted, the CSPs' CaaS offerings, such as GKE, ECS, AKS, and so on, due to being based on open source Kubernetes, will support the same policies with minor nuances.

We also added some cloud-native policies with some toolsets, and provided references to chapters where we approach policy creation in more depth.

The next chapter will discuss applying policies to hybrid environments, covering both on-premises and cloud environments. It will also discuss how we can maintain cohesive policy visibility across environments.

Further reading

- A collection of AWS policies can be consulted here: `https://github.com/aws/serverless-application-model/blob/develop/samtranslator/policy_templates_data/policy_templates.json`.

- The official AWS documentation for the SAM policy is located here: `https://docs.aws.amazon.com/serverless-application-model/latest/developerguide/serverless-policy-templates.html#serverless-policy-template-table`.

6
Policy Design for Hybrid Environments

In this chapter, we will be covering hybrid environments. Typically, these environments span across different cloud providers, making them far more complex than using cloud-native tools, processes, and policies, especially when it comes to centralizing and integrating policies across such a large footprint.

We will touch on some of the challenges of hybrid environments, illustrating the typical architecture, definition, and pain points.

Following this, we will touch on systems that require a policy, such as **authentication** and an **access policy**. Additionally, we will discuss the constructs of those architectures. By now, it should be no surprise that even in hybrid environments, automation is one of the critical tenets; we will expand on how it enables you to scale segmentation and enforcement across environments.

Finally, we will highlight some of the concepts that have been discussed, such as having automation to provision multiple environments across cloud providers across environments and adding policy checks on top of **Infrastructure as Code** (**IaC**), using zero trust to have a single place of authentication, and making the best use of the cloud provider's native functionality.

In this chapter, we will be covering the following main topics:

- The challenges of hybrid environments
- Policy as Code for hybrid environments
- Automation, segregation, and enforcement – an approach to policy overlay
- An example of a policy spanning hybrid environments

Technical requirements

Prior knowledge of traditional computing and technologies to interact with cloud providers such as curl, JSON, basic command line are required for this chapter.

The challenges of hybrid environments

In *Chapter 5*, *Policy for Cloud-Native Environments*, we discussed cloud-native environments and how policy tools for **Container as Service** (**CaaS**) and **Function as a Service** (**FaaS**) might help create enforcement patterns.

This chapter will look at the hybrid environments and their definitions, compositions, and challenges.

While I believe that the future is on public cloud platforms using service models such as FaaS, the current reality is multi-cloud with private and on-premises environments. This pattern is still prevalent in large organization segments where there is a need for a hybrid environment due to legal, regulatory, and localization requirements. This is evident as the EU launched efforts such as **GAIA-X** in 2020 and a draft of the candidate **European Union Cybersecurity Certification Scheme for Cloud Services** (**EUCS**) scheme in 2021.

In this section, we will define a hybrid environment and discuss its architecture, along with the benefits and challenges that come with a mixed environment.

Hybrid environments

Let's start with a definition: a **hybrid environment** is a type of environment that can contain a mix of public cloud, private cloud, and on-premises models.

The following diagram should help you to understand the nuances between the different models:

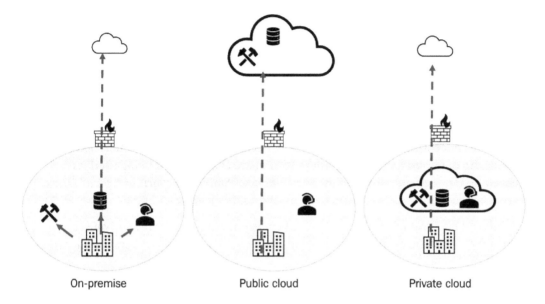

Figure 6.1 – The differences between the consumption models

As you can see, there are differences between the usage of the resources. The consumption models can be summarized as follows:

- **On-premises**: Here, the organization has a perimeter that can be segregated using network devices such as a firewall, and all the resources located inside the perimeter, work tools (such as Customer relationship manager, Enterprise resource planning, Active Directory, and more), and resources such as databases, computers, and the help desk are all managed inside the organization. The dotted line represents the connectivity between the internet and the outside world.

- **Public cloud**: In the public cloud model, connectivity is used to reach resources on a cloud provider such as **AWS**, **Google**, or **Azure**, which will provide **Infrastructure as Service (IaaS)** to FaaS. In this model, the organization can manage resources on the public cloud provider or use **Platform as a Service (PaaS)**, **software as a Service (SaaS)**, CaaS, Faas, or **Contact Center as a Service (CcaaS)** to relinquish the responsibility of managing the services on the cloud providers.

- **Private cloud**: In this scenario, the organization creates a private cloud inside the organization using tools such as **VMware vSphere**, **OpenStack**, and **OpenShift**, which allows it to control the resources and hardware and build services. Additionally, operational management becomes the responsibility of the organization.

A hybrid environment can be a multitude of the preceding configurations. It can span an environment that uses storage resources from a cloud provider, AI/ML APIs from another provider, and even a private cloud for specific workloads.

The trend in the industry has been multi-cloud, which is a hybrid model. This has been the majority of the operating model in regulated industries such as banking and insurance to reduce the concentration risk. Regulators are becoming increasingly concerned as only a handful of **Cloud Service Providers** (**CSPs**) are available and being used, as referenced by UK regulators in the July 2021 *Financial Stability Report*: https://www.bankofengland.co.uk/financial-stability-report/2021/july-2021

In the following diagram, we can see a hybrid environment composed of private cloud functionality within the on-premises environment, which extends to several public clouds:

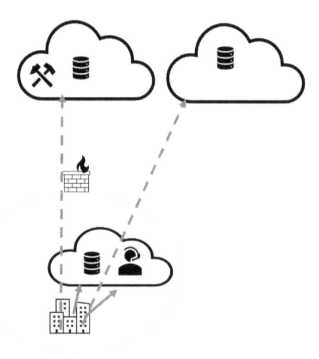

Hybrid Enviroment

Figure 6.2 – A hybrid environment

The hybrid environment has the best of both worlds. Typically, it is chosen to provide the following requirements:

- Reducing costs: By reducing the footprint of the organization such as CapEx and IT spending.

- Flexibility: By using the best of breed from different cloud providers and being able to better adapt to changing market demands.

- Advanced analytics: This is one area in which CSPs shine, as their analytics capabilities are way ahead of what a traditional organization might have on-premises in terms of advanced analytics services.

- Availability: By using CSPs to improve the availability of a service or to implement **Disaster Recovery (DR)**.

- Risk concentration: Using different cloud providers to reduce risk concentration and prevent network outages, identity provider outages, or general service outages, which happen frequently and can impact the business depending on the CSP. Outages for the year 2021 can be consulted at `https://totaluptime.com/notable-network-and-cloud-outages-of-2021/`.

These points can be seen as valid arguments in which to adopt a hybrid strategy. On the other hand, it can be very challenging to create a single plane of policy across the organization, and in the next section, we will discuss the challenges this introduces.

The challenges within hybrid environments

Instead of focusing on pure technological components for this section, let's look at the challenges from a people, processes, and technology lens.

People

As discussed in previous chapters, the people element is crucial. Quoting *Peter Drucker's culture eats strategy for breakfast*, any digital program should prioritize people and processes before technology.

Friction arises by having teams with differing operating models. Just go and talk to your cloud-native infrastructure team regarding the challenges they face. If there aren't any war stories about the on-premises team, something must be off.

However, to summarize this point, there are different teams, such as on-premises teams, private cloud teams, and public cloud teams. There will be friction among these teams due to the inherent nature of each group and their priorities, skillsets, and alignments to the business.

Additionally, success in your digital transformation journey requires a policy layer on top of these environments. There needs to be a policy targeting people in the people, process, technology (**PPT**) to ease off the different operating models. You can refer to *Chapter 1, Introduction to Policy Design*, *Chapter 4, Framework for Digital Policies*, and *Chapter 7, Building a Culture of PolicyOps*, to develop policies targeting the organization.

Operating models

Although they have been referenced, we will not delve into the enterprise architecture operating models. Instead, we will abstract and talk about two significant elements related to the people angle.

From an enterprise architecture perspective, the operating model has elements that include governance, behaviors, structure, and accountability, and how people, processes, and technology are integrated to develop business capabilities.

So, taking into consideration that the people angle must be supported, we will talk about the major challenges within the people element:

- **Expertise**: This element is key during transformative efforts, as newer paradigms must complement the existing skillsets. One example of this is compliance. In a new paradigm such as the public cloud, you want automated, reproducible, and near real-time checks. This is achieved through Compliance as Code, but you also want the existing compliance teams with deep business processes to be part of the effort; otherwise, the organization will not be able to transform itself by leveraging the expertise of new and existing teams.

- **Incentives**: Broadly speaking, the incentives within an organization, especially in a hybrid model, are not adjusted. Organizations start to focus on new technologies without realizing the synergies of combining new technology with in-house expertise. This was discussed in *Chapter 1, Introduction to Policy Design*, along with the need for incentives to be distributed equitably to the teams that are involved.

- **Behavior**: Going back to *Chapter 4, Framework for Digital Policies*, in these digital paradigms, we need to make sure that we design policies and behaviors that align with the key elements of DevOps to bring groups together and foster a collaborative ethos. The challenge of these hybrid environments is the various ways of working for different teams, including the workflow, lack of standards, and different operating models.

These are some of the most common challenges for organizations in a hybrid environment related to people.

Next, we will talk about processes. Be mindful that they are similar due to the organizational structures between people and processes.

Processes

As learned in the *People* section, most challenges stem from a lack of expertise, incentives, behavior, and more. They are all elements of the operating model that a specific team is working on, be it the private cloud, public cloud, or the on-premises team.

This section will highlight that many of these challenges are due to teams having their linkage to the business processes, which will be very different depending on their environment and the operating model.

For example, supporting a business call center depending on the environment will require a different integration effort; how it is designed, implemented, and supported, whether it is inside the premises, whether it uses a public cloud provider, or even CCaaS.

The lack of alignment to the business process

The challenge is in a hybrid environment that comes from different teams. If you work for a big organization with more than 10,000 employees, go to other groups, such as the team responsible for the cloud services and the team responsible for providing identity services such as Active Directory, and discuss the business processes integration of giving access to a user for a specific service. If not all organizations, at least the majority will have different processes for each team.

From an efficiency perspective, we can all understand that having the business process integration follow a template to provide **identity services** to the user across different teams inside the same organization would be the way to go. Still, it becomes hard in practice due to the operating models and different priorities between separate groups.

The lack of linkage between teams

This issue has been the subject of books on team performance and collaboration from Agile Squad models and DevOps to security-focused DevSecOps, to more specific implementations such as **Site Reliability Engineering** (**SRE**) and PolicyOps. *Chapter 7, Building a Culture of PolicyOps*, highlights the need for policies to adjust to new digital paradigms and be part of the software development and IT operations, especially as most business processes lean on these two to create value.

As we know, organizations have been struggling to implement and operate efficiently with these new collaborative paradigms. Big corporations such as Google studied the synergies produced by their teams and what made them effective; a study was commissioned in *Project Aristotle*.

But for the rest of the world, effective team collaboration has been elusive and very hard to implement. This becomes more pronounced in hybrid environments, as the different teams will have different toolsets, workflows, and other **Key Performance Metrics** (**KPIs**), making it hard to align them to a cohesive process.

An ambiguous source of truth

Data is the new oil. To support different processes across the business and generate insights, it is necessary to have a centralized source of truth across the organization. We all know the CRM that reads from one database, the ERP from another, and the required effort to consolidate records across both.

Organizations already struggle to maintain a centralized source of truth for their consumption, so imagine adding more environments such as the ones presented in the hybrid model. Each of those environments will add their data, which needs to be integrated into the **Single Source of Truth** (**SSOT**) to generate insights and effectively use advanced analytics on the data.

Technology

Now, let's look at the last tenet, the technology paradigm. Technology is hard to use, especially in hybrid environments. While a standard tech stack might resolve some issues, it also introduces new ones, so ensuring the right balance in terms of technology is key.

As discussed throughout this chapter, technology is fundamental but never the single tenet. As we design, implement, and validate policies, we should be mindful of the people and the processes. So, hybrid presents some exciting challenges that we will identify in this section.

Next, we will look at both angles of using a tech stack in hybrid environments.

A diverse tech stack

A diverse stack is the most common pattern as cloud adoption and transformation happen when the company is already operating. Except for companies *born in the cloud*, the most common practice is to have multiple tools used by different teams and departments.

While this might bring some benefits such as initial speed due to familiarity, experience, and vendor support, in the long run, it causes challenges due to the lack of standardization. One technology that tries to mitigate the lack of standardization is containers, where, even if teams have different workflows, the output is consumable across the organization.

Another important pattern is to also achieve an SSOT across the organization, which is easier said than done.

So, to summarize, using a diverse tech stack brings challenges regarding transformative efforts, as some operating models are misaligned. On the other hand, it can also have some resilience benefits. This is because, if something happens to the technology, groups can quickly migrate into another piece of technology without losing too much efficiency.

A common tech stack

Having a common stack in large organizations is rare. Usually, it is more prevalent in start-ups or small organizations.

Having a common tech stack brings standardization as a benefit and naturally increases the organization's agility; that's why start-ups are more efficient at developing MVPs.

The only downside is the risk of the technology being out of trend or something happening to the technology provider. For example, let's say that Google decided to shut down some vision APIs that a start-up was using. This would be a huge blow to the strategy of the small organization. This leads us to the next section about the exit strategies that organizations should have in place.

Exit planning – a hybrid panacea?

One of the biggest arguments for using hybrid environments is having an exit strategy, and it is a topic of interest in highly regulated industries.

There are two types of **exit plans**:

- **Planned**: We decide to exit due to a CSP deciding to increase its service costs or notify the customer that the account will be terminated.
- **Stressed**: This is the unlikely scenario where a CSP goes bust or the government steps in and mandates that it cease its operations with a specified company.

Both these scenarios can happen very quickly, and the concern is about maintaining critical business functions. This overlaps with the hybrid story, as nowadays, there are more CSP offerings such as **Outpost**, **Anthos**, **Arc**, and more. If we think about the preceding risks, how these hybrid technologies can help isn't clear.

This section presented the architectural building blocks of hybrid architectures and some of their challenges. To summarize, a hybrid model brings its own challenges, especially in aligning different teams with their operating models such as security, risk, and more in a coherent way.

In the next section, we will approach the idea of Policy as Code in hybrid environments.

Policy as Code in hybrid environments

In the previous chapter, we talked about cloud-native environments and how policy tools for CaaS and Faas might help create enforcement patterns.

This section will look at the hybrid environments and discuss the tools and patterns you might use in such environments to support the creation of Policy as Code.

If an organization considered an on-premises environment exclusively, it would be more simplistic from a delineation perspective. Creating enforcement points would be trivial at the edge of our perimeter, and segmentation based on network, identity, and physical enforcement points would be achievable. With hybrid environments, these need to extend to have something akin to an overlay. A zero trust architecture can help in terms of authorization and access. However, as discussed in previous chapters, there are some requirements to implement such systems and reap the benefits.

Identity management

Having different environments creates a lot of friction regarding user and identity management, especially since users require access to applications and services on-premises and various cloud providers.

One solution is to implement a hybrid identity management system to provide syncing between users on-premises and in the cloud environments to implement SSO using the corporate credentials and the usual security best practices such as MFA, smartcards, and so on.

The following diagram shows the concept of having an identity that spans between the on-premises model and the cloud providers:

Figure 6.3 – A high-level overview of an identity and access overlay

While this diagram is simplistic, the real-world implications of having federated identity management are quite extensive. All these systems have identity and access management in their silo. While **Identity as a Service (IDaaS)** solves one aspect of the challenge by providing SSO across the systems, it still lacks access policies and an identity directory.

While solutions from Microsoft, such as Active Directory, or third-party vendors, such as Okta, provide access management across SaaS, it is still a challenge. Organizations still use IaaS and PaaS across different cloud providers that require a new strategy.

This is where distributed identity management comes into play. It creates the overlay layer that allows your organization to have identity access and control across the hybrid environment.

SSO is not going anywhere and is part of the required multi-cloud operations. Still, managing identities and policies across multiple environments such as public, private, and on-premises platforms require a decentralized approach.

There are some start-ups within this space, but it is growing as the field of hybrid multi-cloud becomes more mature.

Identity orchestration, **automation**, and **central policies** are connected to the change in how we perceive the security of the environments and platforms. That's why discussing **zero trust** in this hybrid chapter is important, as it can help with authorization and access in mixed environments.

Zero trust

As discussed earlier, having hybrid environments makes it hard for us to create enforcement points because the environments are hugely distributed, which is why perimeter-less environments are prevalent. In hybrid environments, when the organization consumes services from multiple public cloud providers, has remote workers, and ingests data from different sources, this perimeter extends to various locations, users, and applications, rendering the usual patterns somewhat obsolete.

While everything is possible with the right number of tactical solutions and increasing technical debt, zero trust architecture is becoming the reigning champion for these environments where the trust needs to be determined.

So, instead of trying to build a perimeter to encompass these edges, zero trust proposes an architecture based on three principles:

- **The application and user authentication**: Traditionally, one or the other has been used to ascertain provenance and trust. For example, the application is deemed safe in on-premises environments, while the access control happens at the user level. With zero trust, both of those qualities are assessed.

- **Device authentication**: This is related to how a device is authenticated and authorized. It can be achieved with technology such as **network access control (NAC)** or **endpoint security**.

- **Trust score**: This is the final part of the framework in which a score is computed from the application, user, device, and context. Additionally, a policy might be applied regarding the score.

Recall the access controls from *Chapter 2, Operationalizing a Policy for Highly Regulated Industries*. You will notice the similarities with **Attribute-Based Access Control (ABAC)**, as zero trust architecture also uses a policy engine to make decisions. This is the best-suited place to enforce the Policy as Code paradigm to have the policies defined in an SSOT.

Zero trust components

Since numerous books and papers are dedicated to the zero trust architecture, we will only cover its basic concepts:

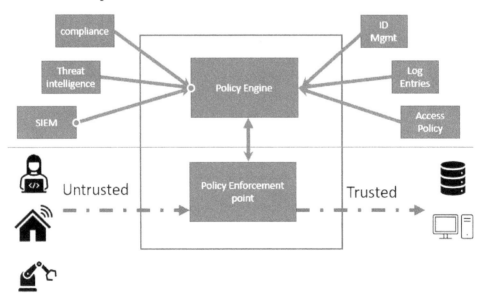

Figure 6.4 – The zero trust architecture

So, as you can identify in *Figure 6.4*, there are several elements, people, applications, devices on the left-hand side that are treated as untrusted. Since they want to connect to the specified resources on the right, they need to be approved by the **Policy Enforcement Point (PEP)**.

The PEP using available data will determine a trust score that will allow access to the resources on the right-hand side.

To understand how that decision is made, let's look at the following major elements:

- **Policy engine**: This is the component that is responsible for making the decision. It takes data from several sources such as the SIEM, threat intelligence, compliance rules, and log entries to allow or deny a specific resource. Be mindful that the authorization happens in the PEP, but the policy engine is responsible for crunching all data.

- **PEP**: This component will allow and maintain the session for the authorized resources. Like a proxy, it will receive the score from the policy engine and be responsible for authorizing and managing the connection.

- **Trust assessment**: This is the score given to the PEP to make a decision. It uses data from several sources to reach a score compared to a policy, and access and authorization are given.

- **Data sources**: All of the external and internal sources used to compute the trust value can be data from the SIEM, the endpoint, log sources, or some running agent.

As you can see, zero trust is a helpful architecture, but it requires coordination and assessment from all the components in the architecture, from the user and device to the context data. For more information, you can refer to *NIST 800-207*.

Automation, segregation, and enforcement

There are many challenges of architecting for zero trust, especially as it requires integrating many existing products and platforms. Automation is the most significant enabler of a zero-trust architecture. It makes it possible to operate it at scale, as changing policies across distributed environments would simply not scale.

As illustrated in *Figure 6.4*, if the policy enforcement point cannot be dynamically operated in an automated fashion, the concept of zero trust is not achievable because this paradigm relies on automation as a first-class element.

However, automation does not stop here, especially in hybrid environments. Some technologies that we have discussed previously, such as containers, **Everything as Code (EaC)**, and more, are required to create a posture in which segmentation and enforcement are byproducts of the enforcement policy overlay.

Next, we will talk about the different controls and technologies available to make the process smoother in hybrid environments.

Detective controls

Detective controls are key for teams and organizations to respond to threats and malicious activities. Detective controls provide the capabilities for the SOC to identify and alert you about malicious behavior. There are a set of tools that we will touch on briefly; be mindful that a pattern such as a log sink needs to be configured in all hybrid environments. This allows us to consolidate all of the events, properly analyze and use the detective controls, and have a central place to deploy alerting policies.

Security controls can be divided into two types: **technical** or **administrative**. We will focus on the technical. The best practices for this revolve around establishing your central point to aggregate all the logs. Once that has been established, we can address the following issues regarding logs:

- **Capturing**: If we use multiple public cloud providers in our environment, we need to activate the logs, such as **AWS Cloud Trail**. Additionally, we need to configure the service-specific logs, such as **GCS**, **Athena**, or **VPC Flow Logs**. The logs from deploying our environments such as IaC security, compliance, and policy checks should be captured.

- **Analyzing**: This is where we will examine the logs. The most common pattern is to use cloud-native capabilities from each provider and send the most important ones to the central location. Tools such as **Google Chronicle**, **Elasticsearch**, and **BigQuery**, can help with this.

- **Storing**: Depending on the regulation, you will need to keep logs for a determined amount of time. A popular pattern is to use the storage from the cloud provider where the service is running, coupled with their retention policy, and create a central metadata repository to have an SSOT of all the log locations and attributes.

- **Retention**: Similar to the preceding point, as the cloud providers have different storage tiers, with reduced pricing for infrequently accessed data, their policy on retention is quite flexible, allowing you to move the logs within different tiers.

- **Notification**: Some solutions facilitate the notification process, but your notifications must come from a centralized place after being sifted through the usual checks to avoid operations fatigue.

As you can see, most detective controls revolve around logging and the capabilities we have to analyze and understand the event to respond to it effectively. In a hybrid environment, this requires a lot of integration between different teams. Next, let's look at preventative controls.

Preventative controls

Preventative controls are set in place to strengthen the system against malicious activity. They work based on sound governance using organizational policies, good practices such as DevSecOps, strong authentication, and more importantly, a robust feedback loop to other controls.

We will talk about the ability to set up organizational policies in each provider, use security by design when developing services in each CSP, and make sure the **Identity Access Management** (**IAM**) follows the best practices including the **Principle of Least Privilege** (**PoLP**), **Segregation of Duty** (**SoD**), and more.

Governance

Having strong governance by using organizational policies depending on the cloud provider is the first step in creating a robust policy mechanism. We discussed these cloud provider policy constructs in-depth in *Chapter 12, Integrating Policy as Code with Enterprise Workflows*, and in the next chapter, we will learn how to enable PolicyOps.

Another aspect to bear in mind is the required integration with the different CSPs to ensure there is only a central SSOT; we will discuss this in the next chapter.

Having a governance process in place helps us enforce policies at the top level, for each one of the environments. For example, GCP provides a constraint library that can be used with **Terraform** as part of the DevSecOps process or with **Forseti**, a security tool to audit, monitor policies, and enforce rules.

More information about the GCP policy library can be found at `https://github.com/GoogleCloudPlatform/policy-library`. It uses the same language as Open Policy Agent: the **Rego** language. Additionally, it allows teams responsible for creating policies to have a single language to refer to, similar to what Terraform does with HCL for its IaC.

DevSecOps

As security becomes more ubiquitous in today's world, it is essential to bring out the security best practices during the product development life cycle.

DevSecOps is based on applying the principles of DevOps to security threads. For example, take a look at the following:

- Internal security: This is achieved by providing a risk assessment, either using a framework such as NIST 800–160, inventory and asset management, or more broadly, providing vulnerability assessments, security monitoring, analytics, and dashboards to empower the organization to improve their security posture.

- Business security: This is the security work that deals with the IAM aspect by providing access to particular users and **Lines of Business** (**LoBs**), making sure compliance efforts align with the regulatory needs, and encryption and other security mechanisms are applied correctly.

- Operational security: This is the day-to-day security work usually done by the SOC, including upgrading vulnerable software, applying patches, generating alerts, and getting in touch with teams regarding security issues.

These activities are essential, highlighting that security is a pillar in any organization. DevSecOps takes it further by enabling cross-collaboration among different teams to deliver a product that security-minded teams have checked. Besides, it's also making sure processes, tools, and people share the expertise of the security teams.

There is also a concept called the **shift left**. Security activities begin when the code has been produced and during the life cycle. The term "shift left" also means that the feedback loops from every stage are used to inform the previous stage, as shown in the following diagram:

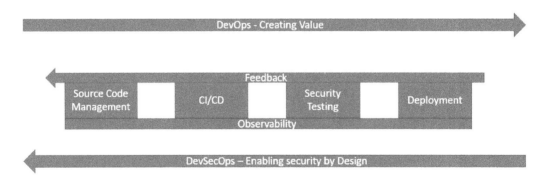

Figure 6.5 – DevSecOps Shift Left

The principles highlighted in previous chapters, such as automation, continuous monitoring, EaC, and more, are fundamental as they enable the necessary agility in an organization to ship products that have security by design practices, which will ensure the products strike the right balance between security and development speed.

Since hybrid environments have multiple ecosystems, a pipeline that deploys infrastructure is critical, and automation should be a first-class element. For example, using Terraform or similar tools allows the teams to use a single language (HCL) to deploy across the environments and have everything defined as code.

From a policy perspective, we can create policies to automate the security and compliance checks in our pipeline, using the continuous integration and delivery tools to create feedback loops, using dashboards to monitor and ensure our pipeline deploys to our different cloud environments, taking the necessary security steps for each environment, and notifying and alerting when appropriate.

IAM

This section discusses how to leverage zero trust architecture using data sources from different environments to enrich the policy engine. Another aspect is that while we should use SSO, there is still the requirement to have a layer of distributed identity management across our environments.

The main goal is to have all our applications behave like cloud apps. One way in which we can achieve this is by extending the standards-based authentication from the cloud to on-premises and making sure that zero trust identity is used as the **perimeter model**.

As discussed earlier, there are different types of controls we might use. The main challenge is the integration among the different environments. Additionally, we talked about some possibilities to create an overlay.

In the next section, let's look at some real-world policies that we might use.

An example of a policy spanning hybrid environments

Similar to the previous chapter, let's expand on some real-world policies related to hybrid environments. We will address some key components that we might use to build policies across environments:

- Organizational policies:

    - One of the aspects of hybrid environments is the necessity to implement policies at the environment, for example, AWS SCPs. The challenge is in using a single source of truth to manage all of the environments.

    - By using OPA or other third parties, there might be an overlap, especially if the organization is mature enough to be using containers.

- IAC policy checks:

    - As the organization uses multiple environments, the need for a mature deployment infrastructure pipeline is vital. More important is the requirement to check if the policy is being maintained or whether there are security issues within the deployed infrastructure.

    - Using HashiCorp HCL might be an option, but the choice needs to be weighed against other tools such as Chef, Puppet, or Salt. We cover *in Chapter 10*, *Policy as Code Tool Evaluation,* how to compare these tools. Some tools will support policy checks, such as Chef Inspec and Terraform Sentinel, or you can also use a more comprehensive tool such as Checkov.

- Configuration management:

    - One of the aspects of automating, correcting, and enforcing is also having a good configuration manager that is integrated with the different environments. There is no doubt that Ansible plays an important role in today's world.

- Federated identity:

    - As discussed earlier, different environments have different identity sources of truth localized in their environment. Using SSO requires a distributed identity engine that can integrate the enterprise with the various cloud providers. Currently, I'm only aware of start-ups in this domain (strata).

- Zero trust:

  - A key architecture should be the starting point for an organization using hybrid environments. We discussed this earlier, and would recommend any organization with multiple distributed environments to onboard the zero trust journey, as the integration by design will be much easier to deploy, configure, and maintain.

- People policies:

  - As with any program, creating people and process policies is essential. One policy that can be implemented for the people aspect is cross-assignment, where a person is allocated to a group for one quarter or several weeks. I've seen this having success with security people working with applications and infrastructure people for a limited time to bring their expertise into the group. I've also seen technical folks from applications doing the same with a non-technical audience to understand the requirements and design accordingly.

  - Another person-based policy can be the approval of **Pull Requests** (**PRs**) in source code management. This is done by at least one junior member alongside a senior member to transfer knowledge and create a more inclusive environment.

  - Finally, creating policies for development either for upskilling, reskilling or retraining can be a force multiplier for digital enablement. One example is organizations creating their badges, certifications, and training programs. Alternatively, you could try using the vendors' certification to learn in a particular area such as the cloud, data analytics, cybersecurity, and more.

These are some technology tenets that should be looked at and researched for organizations using a hybrid approach.

The paradigm with hybrid is far more complex to manage and operate efficiently, especially from a policy perspective as there is fragmentation. Currently, no product solves the siloed identity, policy, and management issues required to properly abstract all the environment and create a single plane of glass.

Summary

This chapter defined and highlighted some of the challenges of hybrid environments. We touched on several points, including the architecture, challenges, and how some components, such as zero-trust, can help achieve a standard layer among these environments.

Additionally, we touched on the different types of controls as they are also part of the authorization and access policies.

In the first part of this book, we looked at policies more broadly because as we move toward coercive instruments for authorization and access, especially in hybrid environments, we need to understand that there are also possibilities in which to create systems that use nudges to shape behaviors regarding security, especially using behavioral economics to encourage safer practices.

In the next chapter, we will look at building a culture of PolicyOps. Due to the complexity of multi-cloud environments, many gaps exist and require integration not just from the technology side but also with the several involved teams and processes.

PolicyOps solves this problem by creating a team that is responsible for designing and maintaining policies for digital adoption, security, and trust in the organization.

7
Building a Culture of PolicyOps

As a wrap-up to this book's second part regarding the framework for digital policies, this last chapter will focus on supporting policies from a people and process perspective.

PolicyOps is a framework to influence change in an organization's adoption of digitization. On one hand, it is responsible for establishing guardrails which are preventative rules to prevent people from doing activities that could go against the policy rules; on the other it is responsible for changing behaviors to influence transformation in an organization.

This chapter will also serve as a lightweight manifesto for PolicyOps. It discusses ways to address people and processes for advancement and digital transformation.

We will discuss how to design, embed, and manage policies, looking at the culture and processes changes that would support such a function, going a bit more into the best practices of the policy design three Cs and life cycle.

Lastly, we will take advantage of some methods to highlight how using digital tools can be helpful for the engagement of the organization and the selection of effective instruments.

In short, this chapter will explore PolicyOps, its definition, what it tries to influence, and the benefits of having a PolicyOps framework. By the end of the chapter, you will realize the positive influence of PolicyOps and how it can be used as an augmentation to **DevOps** and other agile methods.

In this chapter, we will be covering the following:

- PolicyOps – designing, embedding, and managing policies
- Policy DLC – coherence, congruence, and consistency
- Agile policy design

Technical requirements

A prior understanding of cloud paradigms such as DevOps, DevSecOps, Everything as Code, and agile methodologies is required for this chapter.

PolicyOps – designing, embedding, and managing policies

PolicyOps is a framework that brings public policy methods into organizations' digital adoption. In the previous years, there has been a change in the way organizations release software, through new paradigms such as agile and DevOps.

PolicyOps as an augmentation to DevOps

PolicyOps introduces a change in how organizations establish their digital enablement by introducing policies and instruments to achieve digital adoption and integrating policies in a modern software development life cycle.

PolicyOps uses concepts from DevSecOps and can be integrated with it, such as using security best practices as part of coercive instruments to enforce policies. Still, it exceeds it, as it also uses other instruments, such as suasive instruments to drive adoption through behavioral changes.

PolicyOps, in simple terms, does the following:

- Introduces public policy design into digital transformation
- Uses instruments and campaigns to fulfill a digital goal
- Uses instruments, such as coercive, financial, and suasive instruments, to nudge behaviors and establish guardrails

While some of you might rightly find that DevSecOps already covers some of these points, PolicyOps works across **DevSecOps** to extend to more than just coercive instruments.

The main benefit of having a PolicyOps team that designs campaigns for digital adoption, is that such a team can leverage instruments such as suasion, that go beyond the traditional coercive instruments.

An analogy that can be used is the elements of a highway. Let's look at the following figure:

Figure 7.1 – An image of a highway

We can all agree that to build a road to travel fast, it needs to have several mechanisms for the driver to feel safe and allow travel at higher speeds. If we look at the above image, we can see security mechanisms, such as the white paint on the floor that serves to alert the driver that they are crossing a boundary, the noise band to alert the driver that there are driving off-limits, and finally the guardrail to reduce the hazard to the driver in case of an accident. All these mechanisms work to make the driving safe at a higher velocity than on an unmarked road.

If we transpose these security mechanisms to DevSecOps, which is also concerned with creating guardrails such as white lines, a sound band, and so on, it highlights an interesting point related to the organization's velocity. If the guardrail is narrower without room for error, a simple mistake will get it against it. It is much more productive to have different mechanisms to alert and nudge users before they get to the guardrails, and that's what we should strive for when designing policies.

As such, PolicyOps teams work in tandem with the security teams (DevSecOps) in a similar agile fashion to create the road, the rest stops, the signs, and the guardrails.

If we look at the road analogy, it would be the feedback loop mechanisms that integrate all the road elements such as the signs, the rest stops, and so on (the organization's digital adoption) with the security features such as the paint, guardrails, and so on (DevSecOps).

The following diagram visually represents the influence of PolicyOps and the spheres of influence:

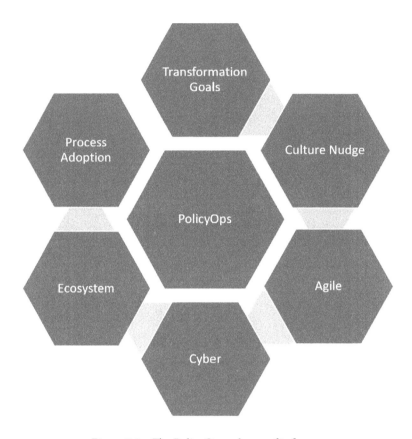

Figure 7.2 – The PolicyOps spheres of influence

As you can see, PolicyOps extends the concept to several spheres of influence, not only the coercive instruments in information security but the culture nudge and integration with the ecosystem.

The benefits of PolicyOps

So, having a team that is proficient with policies and can create campaigns brings several advantages. In the following section, we will list some of the main benefits of adopting PolicyOps.

An expansive footprint

Digital transformation is hard; most organizations struggle because it requires an orthogonal approach in the organization. It requires the alignment and nudging of a work culture toward a new mindset without alienating existing teams and building on top of the current teams' deep business know-how.

Because new digital environments are used, it requires solid foundations in agile and DevOps methodologies, security (DevSecOps), and, more importantly, the right balance of agility.

Integrated feedback loops

One of the key tenets of policy design is viewpoints and making sure that stakeholders are listened to when designing and implementing effective policies. As such, PolicyOps looks at the security aspect and makes sure that more than coercive instruments are used. Before you hit the guardrail, you should see the white line or hear the rumble of the steering wheel. PolicyOps builds feedback loops into these coercive instruments within the overarching goals associated with increased digital uptake by an organization.

Controls tie-in

One of the aspects of DevSecOps is the shift left and the short feedback loops created between different phases. PolicyOps, in a sense, works similarly, as it uses design thinking and other methodologies to have feedback loops integrating not only controls but also how teams and users interact with the system.

PolicyOps ties in the coercive factors with the suasion instruments to achieve a specific goal, becoming more expansive than just focusing on the coercive instruments and security controls.

As you now have a bit more information on the benefits of PolicyOps, let's look at the three Cs and how to manage the policies in an organization.

Policy DLC – coherence, congruence, and consistency

As seen in the first chapters, policies are a mix of goals and instruments. As time passes, policies go through several iterations that can introduce drifting from the original intent, either by introducing a new layer as they are updated, changing instruments as they are converted to other goals, or completely being replaced due to new goals.

In this section, we will talk about the life cycle and the key concern to maintain fit between the policy design elements, such as ensuring we get congruence of the goal and instrument, consistency at an instrumental level, and making sure that goals are coherent.

The three Cs

It is crucial to refer to the ability of the PolicyOps team to manage different policies with coherent goals, which means that as long as the goals refer to the same policy objectives and can be pursued concurrently, there is coherency.

The most pressing issue that affects the need for a PolicyOps team is the instruments and how they are labeled consistently. This is only possible (using our road analogy from *Figure 7.1*) if we build the road and the supporting instruments to highlight where we are, and create supporting guardrails and controls that tie into the higher goal.

Lastly, congruency can be defined by the balance of goals (what) and instruments (how) if they are both aligned to a specific purpose; take a look at some examples in an organizational context:

- Standards and rules applied in the same fashion across an organization or **Lines of Business (LoB)**
- Consistency on what to expect and how it works
- Transparency and clear intentions
- Action consistent with stated cultural values

One interesting approach is the **Nadler-Tushman congruence model**, which can be adapted to policy design and reflects how the impact of changes made in an organization can ripple throughout teams and groups.

To simplify, take a look at the next figure to get a sense of how the three Cs work together and how a PolicyOps team should strive to achieve that balance between goals and instruments with congruency:

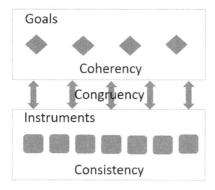

Figure 7.3 – A policy design fit

One aspect that I would like to highlight is being mindful when choosing consistency over everything, as it can lead to a focus on maintenance and admin tasks ignoring a user's knowledge. While it might be useful as a framework, we need to be sensitive to the use case.

And that's why having a slight bias for coherence that increases clarity can enable better, more flexible, and more resilient policies; take a look at the following diagram:

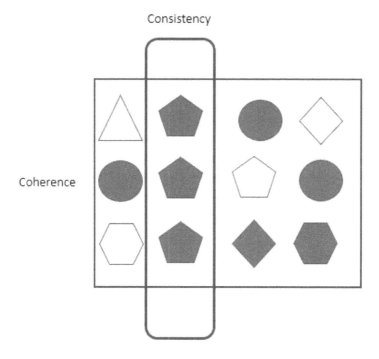

Figure 7.4 – Coherence over consistency

When we have a slight bias for coherence, the focus is slightly shifted not solely on building consistent instruments but also on groups that we are trying to help. This enables a natural flow as those groups will feel familiar with the goal and will interact much better with the instruments.

As such, flexibility can increase by taking a coherent approach, although it requires covering the organization and group's needs, which can be achieved by incentivizing teams in the same way or using a security control across teams (consistency).

Facilitating incentives across teams or building security controls aligned to the existing group experience will change how the users consume and interact with the policy.

To wrap up, building on the concepts of the three Cs, as stated in *Chapter 2, Operationalizing Policy for Highly Regulated Industries*, is key. Still, we also need to be mindful of the trade-offs.

This section highlighted that, while having consistency by using the same type of instruments can be perceived as a cleaner and more standard way, it can represent a bad experience for different groups that respond better to other types of instruments. Having a slight bias for coherence with the right balance of flexibility is important, as it helps achieve a more human-centric policy.

This section follows *Chapter 2, Operationalizing Policy for Highly Regulated Industries*, where the different design systems were all based on stakeholders' feedback and the simplification of several frameworks, such as design thinking and persuasive system design, which we discussed in *Chapter 4, Framework for Digital Policies*.

The policy life cycle

As we saw in the last section, designing policies requires alignment to the basic principle of three Cs, but how do we manage the policies, and update, reform, and improve them?

This section will touch on the life cycle management of policies and how to integrate them with the **Software Development Life Cycle** (**SDLC**) to reap business benefits.

Automation as enabler

From a PolicyOps perspective, it is essential to build on the foundations of the *Agile Manifesto*, especially those that focus on interactions, collaboration, and responding to change.

There is quite good information on this at the following URL: `https://agilemanifesto.org/`. Despite having a software development flavor, the concepts have been used in many industries to build more collaborative teams, which is the basis for the DevOps framework.

While many of the coercive instruments already exist in a machine-readable format, such as Infrastructure as Code and Policy as Code there is a lack of suasion instruments that could be codified in the IT industry and research toward transposing suasion instruments to machine-readable formats. While some immediate benefits would be possible using a **Domain-Specific Language** (**DSL**), as far as I'm aware, there is nothing in the field that would allow the design and management of suasion instruments.

Regarding coercive instruments, the field is ripe, especially fueled by everything-as-code paradigms that focus on Policy as Code, detection as code, compliance as code, controls as code, and so on.

The next chapter will be the beginning of the third part, which focuses on tools for policy as code, mostly from a coercive standpoint.

A suggestion for suasion instruments would be to use the already existing toolset where it makes sense, such as the following:

- **Source Code Management** (**SCM**): To store and enable collaboration of PolicyOps in defining goals, instruments, and other related activities regarding workflows.
- **Domain-specific Language** (**DSL**): To re-use any unified language framework that could be used to describe the instruments. I would also put Wardley mapping in this category, despite not being machine-readable (yet), to enable groups external to PolicyOps to understand and collaborate in establishing digital goals.

Designing and maintaining policies

Organizations, groups, and policies are not static; as such, extending the policies to support the evolving needs of a business can be achieved by a change introduced by conversion, replacement, layering, or drift.

One important aspect is that there can be existing policies that are hard to change in most circumstances, limiting the freedom of policy designers.

In these cases, layering, conversion, and drift are introduced as **patches** to reshape existing policies.

The main point is that it might not be a bad thing in these cases, as it can have positive outcomes. For example, using layering can enhance the effectiveness of different instruments.

Using a DSL coupled with an SCM system in this context would greatly help track and show the changes taken in the policy and the reason why. We did something similar to this in *Chapter 9*, *A Primer on Open Policy Agent*, for access control with the Rego language of Open Policy Agent.

Automation is necessary and should be used as much as possible, especially in native digital platforms, but let's look at the benefits of bringing an agile paradigm to some phases of our digital framework.

Agile policy design

As we saw in the initial chapters, agility is key. This also goes for policy design, especially when using the collaborative nature from design thinking embedded within PolicyOps.

This section will approach techniques that allow us to bring a **Minimum Viable Product** (**MVP**) into the policy design process and get initial feedback from the stakeholders.

Remember the framework in *Chapter 4*, *Framework for Digital Policies*. We will introduce some methods that can make each phase more agile.

Speed as a key tenet

As with any design approach, having a quick iterative model such as an MVP, prototype, and mockup helps solicit feedback from users and stakeholders.

Desire paths are also a great tool in design to help us understand a user's real interaction; the following diagram exemplifies desires paths, something that we are accustomed to:

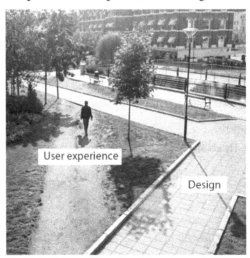

Figure 7.5 – Desire paths

These desire paths are important to factor in early prototypes, as they allow us to look at where instruments should be used instead of trying to shape a new behavior. This can save a lot of time and frustration in policy implementation if we think about it in the challenge identification and policy design phases.

Let's move on to the next section to see some examples and applications of agile policy design.

Policy design in practice

As we all know, we currently live in an environment filled with data. The signal-to-noise ratio has never been so low, so having analytics at our disposal helps a PolicyOps team understand and influence behaviors and make coercive instruments more efficient.

So, let's ask some questions that an organization should consider regarding its policies:

- When was the last time anyone talked about testing a combination of security controls to try to influence the invisibility of guardrails?

- When was the last time guardrails were updated, and was it in the past 6 months?

- When was the last time guardrails were updated to meet business time to value?

- What is the digital enablement policy, and how frequently are instruments revised?

The answer to most of these questions in most organizations isn't positive, and in order to change it, a simple analysis method would be sufficient.

One way to do the analysis is to take advantage of agile methods during the *challenge identification* and *design phase* discussed in *Chapter 4, Framework for Digital Policies. We* can include monitoring of the organization media sources such as social media, internal wikis, and business process documentation to understand the users' preferences, values, and behaviors.

Nowadays, with **Natural Language Processing** (**NLP**), attributing a sentiment is quite easily done, which can be combined with a quantitative measure regarding an actual or proposed policy change.

NLP coupled with rapid prototyping can be used to get an initial reaction from users in an environment affected by the policy. That way we can quickly assess the response and tweak the policy. More importantly, it also allows us to review the network effect and see which groups and teams are adopting or rejecting policies.

Using A/B testing and perpetual beta paradigms, PolicyOps teams can extend their collaborative effort within DevOps, DevSecOps, and FinOps teams. The workflow allows them to monitor the affected environment in real time, respond to a policy, and make small adjustments, bringing more agility to our framework policy implementation and evaluation phase.

These techniques allow PolicyOps teams to modify and adjust policies quickly. A/B testing is such a powerful tool, which you can read a bit more about at the following link: `https://hbr.org/2017/06/a-refresher-on-ab-testing`.

As the field of data analytics grows, PolicyOps can employ novel and emerging techniques to take advantage of the huge amount of generated data in digital environments and the analytics that enable a much quicker iterative process.

The following are some of the most common techniques that can be used:

- Perpetual beta
- Rapid feedback
- A/B testing
- Direct feedback

As you saw in this section, PolicyOps should take advantage of existing methods such as A/B testing and leverage emerging analytics capabilities to make small adjustments and see the reaction. The explosive growth in big data, machine learning, and artificial intelligence makes it suitable for PolicyOps teams to be at the forefront of policy design, using either coercive or suasion instruments, for the benefit of digital adoption.

Summary

As we saw in this chapter, PolicyOps takes traditional capabilities beyond conventional authorization and access control to influence an organization's behaviors toward digital adoption.

By bringing automation, analytics, and the best design thinking practices, PolicyOps is a fundamental stepping stone for an organization to build digital roads that can safely be navigated at full speed. Using the framework described in *Chapter 4*, *Framework for Digital Policies*, organizations can split a design into different phases and bring agile methods to each phase.

In this chapter, we highlighted the role of PolicyOps within an organization; we focused on the methods and constructs of policy design and how PolicyOps can integrate orthogonally across an organization to define, establish, and evaluate policies.

The next chapter will focus on tooling, where we will be talking about policy engines, their uses, and their architectures, and illustrating some small snippets. The policy engine's role is more aligned to coercive instruments, which allows us to build guardrails or different layers of defense. Some of the frameworks discussed will be full-blown policy engines, such as Sentinel, jsPolicy, and others not as big but tailored for Kubernetes workloads. We will also talk about compliance and what tools can be used to share information among tools to build a near-real-time, continuous, compliant environment.

Section 3: Tooling

This section is focused on the tooling aspect. We cover a number of policy engines, including Sentinel, jsPolicy, and the most popular policy engine, *Open Policy Engine (OPA)*. We discuss ways to be data-driven regarding the choice of policy engines for organizations and how to integrate with existing services and frameworks such as ITIL and COBIT. We have a chapter that focuses on cloud policy native tooling from the major cloud providers. Finally, we wrap things up by using the framework defined in the previous section to highlight real-world scenarios and architectures.

This section comprises the following chapters:

- *Chapter 8, Policy Engines*
- *Chapter 9, A Primer on Open Policy Agent*
- *Chapter 10, Policy as Code Tool Evaluation*
- *Chapter 11, Cloud Providers Policy Constructs*
- *Chapter 12, Integrating Policy as Code with Enterprise Workflows*
- *Chapter 13, Real-World Scenarios and Architectures*

8
Policy Engines

Now that we have established concepts such as **Everything as Code** (**EaC**), talked about the different instruments, and discussed the implementation of PolicyOps, this chapter will begin highlighting the more technical part of coercive instruments to help understand how to establish authorization and access to resources.

We will define policy engines, their role, and their benefits. We will see some examples of the most common policy engines in the ecosystem, such as **Kyverno**, **Sentinel**, and **K-Rail**.

Each section will be focused on a small introduction to the policy engine, with an example policy being shown. We will also show the architecture when it makes sense, followed by the main benefits and a summary.

By the end of this chapter, you will understand the main policy engines, how to start using them, what use cases they cover, and their main strengths.

In this chapter, we'll cover the following main topics:

- Policy engines
- Pod Security Policies
- Kyverno
- Sentinel

- Open Security Controls Assessment Language
- K-Rail
- jsPolicy

Technical requirements

Prior understanding of YAML, Kubernetes scripting, and some **Infrastructure as Code (IaC)** is required to get the most out of this chapter.

Policy engines

As discussed in previous chapters, one way to create policies can be with suasion and coercive instruments. When we try to decentralize the decisions of authorization and access, it's important to have a separate engine that allows us to make decisions on policy enforcement across the APIs, IaC, message bus, and so on in a decoupled way.

As we will see in *Chapter 9, A Primer on Open Policy Agent*, **Open Policy Agent** (**OPA**) is one very versatile policy engine, it allows us to make decisions on the frontend, backend, and even **Continuous Integration/Continuous Delivery (CI/CD)** pipelines.

As such, discussing the different policy engines and their benefits, architecture, and usage will undoubtedly help us choose and select the right coercive instrument for our organization.

The coercive instruments part of the policies should be coupled with the environment best practices, for which you can refer to the following links:

- **Amazon Web Services**: `https://aws.amazon.com/security/`
- **Azure**: `https://docs.microsoft.com/en-us/azure/security/azure-security`
- **Google Cloud Platform**: `https://cloud.google.com/security/`
- **Alibaba Cloud**: `https://www.alibabacloud.com/trust-center`
- **Oracle Cloud Infrastructure**: `https://www.oracle.com/security/`

So, in the next section, we will discuss what a policy engine is and discuss a bit of its architecture.

What is a policy engine?

A policy engine, similar to what we discussed in *Chapter 2, Operationalizing Policy for Highly Regulated Industries*, in the *Attribute-Based Access Control* section, can be defined as a hardware or software component that allows querying policies to make decisions on authorization and access to a specific resource.

A policy engine contains rules that define access or revoke access or authorization, and those rules can be updated. It can also use data from different sources, such as logs, browser versions, and IP addresses, to make a better decision.

The following is a diagram of a policy engine:

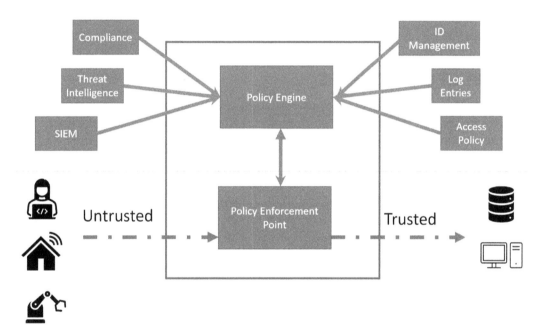

Figure 8.1 – Policy engine diagram

In other chapters about policy engines, we also recommend looking at *NIST Special Publication 800-207*. Despite being tailored to a zero-trust architecture, the concept remains the same for the policy engine.

This architecture and concept of having a policy engine brings a fundamental change, the ability to decouple policy decisions from users, applications, and the environment, bringing benefits such as the following:

- **Centralized policy**: The enforcement can be done from a single plane, which can be distributed across environments, especially important in organizations with operations across different countries, cloud providers, or **Software as a Service (SaaS)** applications.

- **Automation**: By treating the rules following the principle of EaC, you can test different policies and introduce A/B testing, resulting in a reduction in manual provision and configuration error.

So, let's get started by looking at the most common policy engines.

Pod Security Policies

Pod Security Policies (**PSP**) is one way to enforce policies in microservices. It can enforce the control for the Pod specification, for example, the use of host namespaces, the use of specific networking rules, and the user and group IDs of the containers. The entire list can be consulted here: `https://kubernetes.io/docs/reference/generated/kubernetes-api/v1.22/#podsecuritypolicy-v1beta1-policy`.

It works with an **admission controller**, a shim that intercepts API requests and either accepts or rejects the requests.

Currently, it is being deprecated starting from version `1.21` but will still be supported until it gets phased out. We will briefly touch on the existing policies and will discuss the upcoming changes.

The PSP works based on a **Role-Based Access Control** (**RBAC**) access model, as discussed in *Chapter 2, Operationalizing Policy for Highly Regulated Industries*, and it can be used to authorize policies.

An example can be seen in the following snippet:

```
kind: Role
apiVersion: rbac.authorization.k8s.io/v1
metadata:
  namespace: testblockexecns
  name: blockexec
rules:
  resources:["pods/exec"]
```

```
- apiGroups: ["*"]
  resources: ["pods"]
  verbs: ["get"]
```

The important bit is defining the `rules` stanza and adding `pods/exec` to the resources. In another snippet which does the `RoleBinding`, we define the following:

```
kind: RoleBinding
apiVersion: rbac.authorization.k8s.io/v1
metadata:
  namespace: testblockexecns
  name: blockexecpod
subjects:
- kind: Group
  apiGroup: rbac.authorization.k8s.io
  name: blockexecgroup
roleRef:
kind:Role
name:blockexec
apiGroup:""
```

The `RoleBinding` YAML will apply the rules to the group called `blockexecgroup`.

A replacement for PSP is called **Pod Security Admission (PSA)**, which we will talk about in the next section.

Pod Security Admission

PSA is the successor to PSP, and offers a built-in admission controller to ensure Pod security standards. This feature, which is currently in alpha at the time of writing (version 1.22), uses the existing security standards based on three different profile policies to cover security use cases from highly permissive to highly restricted.

The profiles are as follows:

- **Privileged**: This policy is wide open and unrestricted. This policy is for system and infrastructure workloads managed by trusted users.

- **Baseline**: This policy is geared toward ease of adoption while maintaining a good balance to prevent known privilege escalations. This policy is for application operators and developers of non-critical applications.

- **Restricted**: This policy is the strictest, and it applies Pod hardening best practices in exchange for compatibility. The use cases are for security-critical applications, environments, and users with low trust.

It also contains several modes, **enforce**, **audit**, and **warn**, to create automated guardrails depending on the level of security necessary. The policies can be enforced at the namespace level through labels, adding necessary flexibility for widespread adoption.

The simplicity of profiles and policy modes has all the building blocks for enabling policies in new and upgraded clusters with the dry run and audit-only modes. This feature makes it easier to be adopted by non-security people.

You can view the controls defined for each security standard at `https://kubernetes.io/docs/concepts/security/pod-security-standards/`.

For those of you that are thinking of upgrading to PSA, you can take a look at the official documentation for more information on migrating the existing PSP to PSA: `https://kubernetes.io/docs/tasks/configure-pod-container/migrate-from-psp/`.

PSA is a good effort to replace something that was at times cumbersome to use by non-security operators, and as such it will bring relevant features in the upcoming releases. As we discussed in the previous section, with the deprecation of PSP, there is also interest in using third-party policy engines, such as the ones we are going to be talking about next.

As PSA is not a policy engine, it has the drawbacks of not being as flexible as true policy engines, such as the ones we are going to discuss next.

Kyverno

Kyverno is a project with growing popularity within the microservice community. It competes with OPA in terms of popularity.

Kyverno, meaning *to govern*, is a **Kubernetes-native policy engine**, meaning that the policies are managed as another resource in the Kubernetes ecosystem, taking advantage of the same tools as Kubernetes, the declarative model, label selectors, metadata, events, kubectl, and so on.

This allows Kyverno to validate, mutate, or generate new configurations on the fly. The generation ability is one of Kyverno's main strengths. Now let's look at policies and how they can be used.

Kyverno policies

A Kyverno policy is composed of a policy stanza that will have one or several rules. Every rule will needs to be associated with at least a resource, and one option. The options in Kyverno are **Mutate**, **Verify**, **Validate**, and, as you can see in the following image:

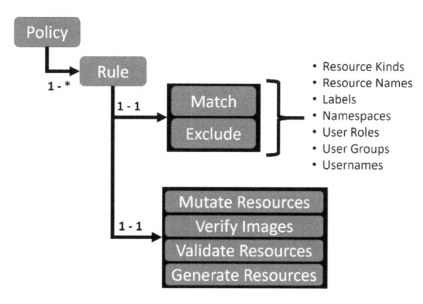

Figure 8.2 – Kyverno policy structure (Policies and Rules | Kyverno)

Let's look at, in terms of code, what it would mean to write a simple policy to block `exec` into pods:

```
apiVersion: kyverno.io/v1
kind: ClusterPolicy
metadata:
  name: blockexecpod
spec:
  validationFailureAction: enforce
  background: false
  rules:
  - name: denyexeclabel
    match:
      resources:
        kinds:
        - PodExecOptions
```

```
    context:
    - name: podexeclabel
      apiCall:
        urlPath: "/api/v1/namespaces/{{request.namespace}}/
pods/{{request.name}}"
        jmesPath: "metadata.labels.exec"
    preconditions:
    - key: "{{ request.operation }}"
      operator: Equals
      value: CONNECT
    validate:
      message: Exec 2 Pods with the label `exec=false` denied.
      deny:
        conditions:
          - key: "{{ podexeclabel }}"
            operator: Equals
            value: "false"
```

The key bits are as follows:

- `validationFailureAction`: This means that it would block the request as it is enforced. We could change the audit to have the failure logged but not blocked, for example, to learn about offending Pods.

- `match`: Where we specify the specifics of the matching resources; in this case, we match against `PodExecOptions`.

- Variables: Kyverno supports JMESPath, which is a query language for JSON to retrieve the label metadata.

- `preconditions`: Allowing the execution control based on variables, in this case, based on the label we set on our Pods.

- Validate resources: The final piece uses a validate policy coupled with conditions that try to validate what was defined previously, and in the case that the pod label is set to false (`'exec=false'`), it will deny the request.

While this simple policy touches on many Kyverno policy definitions, it shows the flexibility you can have to write more powerful policies for Kubernetes environments.

Just a reminder that every policy can only have one declaration of either `validate`, `mutate`, `generate`, or `verifyImages` child declarations.

You can check how to write policies and their extensive capabilities here: `https://kyverno.io/docs/writing-policies/`.

Architecture

The way Kyverno works is based on a dynamic admission control, similar to a shim that intercepts the API and makes a decision. The following figure illustrates this point:

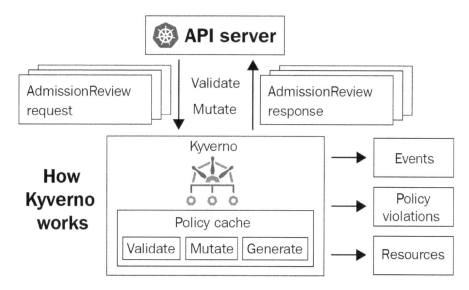

Figure 8.3 – Kyverno architecture

As you can see in the preceding figure, the API server talks with Kyverno through the `AdmissionReview` request, and after evaluating the request in the policy engine, it will make a decision and respond to the **API server**.

Kyverno main benefits

Kyverno's main advantage is that it does not require learning a new language as the policies are managed as Kubernetes resources. The biggest differentiator is that Kyverno was purposely built for Kubernetes, which differs from OPA. The latter is more extensible but not native to Kubernetes. Some capabilities, such as open API validation and mutation (while OPA now supports mutation, it is still in alpha) are very well supported in Kyverno.

Kyverno is a very accomplished policy engine that can be used very extensively with Kubernetes. While not as popular as OPA, it still remains one of the most popular policy engines in the ecosystem. Next, let's look at a commercial offering from HashiCorp.

Sentinel

Sentinel defines itself as a compliance-as-code framework from *HashiCorp*. Sentinel, being from HashiCorp, has an ecosystem that is very integrated with **Terraform**, the major IaC provider. Sentinel allows machine-readable code to be used to write policies, especially at the infrastructure level.

For more information on Terraform, you can consult this link: `https://www.terraform.io/intro/index.html`.

Sentinel allows establishing best practices such as making tags mandatory in the infrastructure to be able to associate resources with cost centers, restricting usage of expensive virtual machines for development environments, or ensuring resources are disposed of after a certain time.

As we have seen in previous chapters, we can create the necessary guardrails by expressing rules that would enforce specific standards, such as a naming convention, standardization across environments, or making sure costs are contained and managed.

The last aspect is regarding visibility, making sure we have a consistent environment regarding images and types. Sentinel, the policy engine, allows us to design coercive instruments for our policies and validate and publish them.

We do need to remind you that Terraform policies through Sentinel are a paid feature from the Team & Governance upgrade package.

Like other policy engines, Sentinel also has different enforcement levels to define behavior when the policies fail to evaluate. The following are Sentinel enforcement modes:

- **Mandatory**: In this mode, Sentinel requires the policy to pass; if not, the run is halted and may not be applied until it is resolved. The keyword in Sentinel is `hard-mandatory`.

- **Audit**: Similar to the mandatory level but allows operators with specified permission to override the policy failures. The Sentinel keyword is `soft-mandatory`.

- **Warning**: This mode will not interrupt the run and will flag the policy failures as information to the operator. The keyword is `advisory`.

Let's now look a bit more in depth at the policies Sentinel can provide.

Sentinel policies

As discussed, the types of policies provided by Sentinel are more tailored for infrastructure, while Kyverno is more for the Kubernetes ecosystem. Sentinel can be a preferred policy engine, especially if the organization already uses Terraform and is trying to bring policies to the **Cloud Service Provider (CSP)** resources.

Be mindful that Sentinel has three generations of policies that are dependent on the version of Terraform that you are using. You can read more about it here: `https://github.com/hashicorp/terraform-guides/blob/master/governance/third-generation/README.md#important-characterizations-of-the-new-policies`.

The following example is a third-generation policy that enforces types of policies. Remember one of the first examples regarding coercive instruments only to allow a subset of virtual machines? It can be recreated in a Sentinel policy to achieve cost control, as seen in the following snippet:

```
import "tfstate-functions" as state
allowed_types = ["t2.small", "t2.medium", "t2.large"]
allEC2Instances = state.find_resources("aws_instance")
violatingEC2Instances = state.filter_attribute_not_in_
list(allEC2Instances,
                        "instance_type", allowed_types, true)
main = rule {
  length(violatingEC2Instances["messages"]) is 0
}
```

The Sentinel folder structure includes a folder with the policies using the Sentinel language. All of the policies will be evaluated to a predefined enforcement level set in the `Sentinel.hcl` file, which the following snippet illustrates:

```
policy "preventEC2unaprovedinstances" {
  source = "./mypolicyinsentinel.sentinel"
  enforcement_level = "advisory"
}
```

`Sentinel.hcl` can define the enforcement level per policy; in this case, it is `advisory`, meaning only a warning will be shown if the policy fails.

Now, let's look at the architecture of HashiCorp Sentinel.

Architecture

Sentinel is a paid feature of HashiCorp that inserts a shim between the plan and apply steps of the Terraform workflow, as shown in the following figure:

Figure 8.4 – Sentinel workflow

The architecture is very simple, with the policy code being used as part of the Terraform workflow. When resources are instantiated, it gives the operator and organizations the requirements to apply the policies in their IaC repositories.

Be mindful that Sentinel can also be integrated with other HashiCorp products, making it ideal for heavy users of Terraform with Enterprise plans.

Benefits

One of the biggest benefits of Sentinel is the integration with the HashiCorp ecosystem, such as Terraform, Vault, Nomad, and Consul. Since it is deeply embedded, it is easy to enable policy enforcement or the alert but not enforce mode to provide the necessary guardrails.

It is compatible with the Terraform modules, making it multi-cloud compatible. The major cloud providers offer strong support. Since it uses the Sentinel language, it can enable programmatic activities and is able to express complex policy use cases.

One of the best resources out there regarding Sentinel is the Medium page of *Roger Berlind*, which provides a lot of information on Sentinel (`https://medium.com/@rberlind`), or the *HashiCorp* official documentation (`https://www.terraform.io/cloud-docs/sentinel`).

Now let's look at a different framework, one that is used to create an information exchange medium between tools.

Open Security Controls Assessment Language

Open Security Controls Assessment Language (**OSCAL**) is an effort led by *NIST* and the industry to reshape how machine-readable code can represent control catalogs such as *NIST 800-X*, baselines as in *FedRAMP* (low, high), security plans, and security results.

One of the biggest issues currently is keeping track of environments and making sure they are compliant. This is very hard to do with traditional methods, such as Excel spreadsheets and Word documents. Hence, automation is key to enabling security solutions that track compliance and risk.

As organizations adopt multiple environments, their environments become more complex, which makes vulnerabilities more prevalent.

As seen in *Chapter 2*, *Operationalizing Policy for Highly Regulated Industries*, ensuring we fulfill regulatory frameworks across **Lines of Business** (**LoBs**) and geographies is hard, especially maintaining a risk profile that changes in real time as organizations evolve.

OSCAL positions itself as the de facto foundation to allow different groups and professionals to exchange data in a common format using YAML, JSON, or XML in an automated fashion. So, OSCAL is not a tool but a standardized way to share data between tools.

Architecture

OSCAL architecture is built in a layered fashion that contains seven models distributed in three layers. The layers can be seen in the following figure:

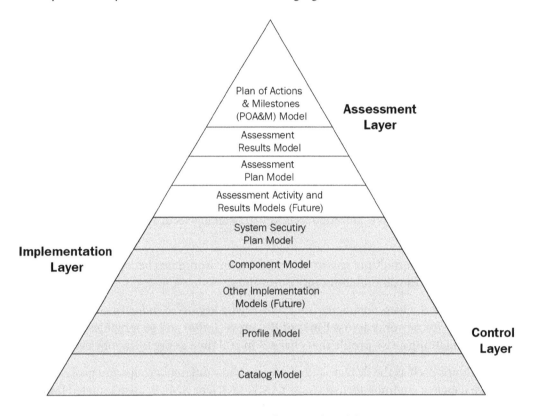

Figure 8.5 – OSCAL layers and models

OSCAL architecture is based on layers, where the lower layer provides information such as references, structures, and data to be used by the higher layers:

- **Control**: The control layer, which contains the catalog and profile model, is used to organize the controls used by the organization risk framework. It also includes the profile model, a set of controls from several catalogs to establish a baseline, similar to a FedRAMP high or low baseline.

- **Implementation**: The implementation layer contains the component model and the security plan model. The component model is the description of the controls supported by a policy, procedure, or compliance artifact. This allows the grouping of related components into capabilities and documenting how the interaction between components can satisfy specific controls.

The second model, the **System Security Plan** (**SSP**), allows the security implementation to be represented by an OSCAL baseline. The main benefit is that the SSP is expressed in machine-readable code, hence it can be used by automation tools.

- **Assessment**: The last layer is responsible for describing the assessment, plan, and results. It contains three models: the plan model, the results model, and the plan of action model. The plan represents the information regarding the plan of an assessment, the results represent the information related to the findings, such as violation, and the plan of action highlights the risks, deviations, and remediation plan.

Within each layer, there is a set of models. These models represent the information structure for a specific purpose:

- **Catalog**: Represents a collection of security controls, such as *800-53*, *Cobit 5*, or *ISO 27002*, which can be used as a risk management program.

- **Profile**: Used to establish a baseline of controls to be implemented; for example, the organization might want to implement controls from a single catalog or multiple catalogs, start with the moderate *800-53*, and then remove some controls and add some from another catalog.

- **Component**: The components can be used to represent controls for a specific policy, process, procedure, or validation. It can bring advantages for validations or standardization efforts.

- **Security plan**: The SSP describes controls implementation, containing the points of contact, system specificity, inventory, attachments, and other detailed items related to the controls.

- **Assessment plan**: The assessment plan contains the necessary information to carry out the assessment.

- **Assessment results**: The assessment results show the information from the assessment, what was done, how it was done, and who was responsible for doing it, highlighting what was found in terms of risks.

- **Assessment plan of action**: Serves to identify and track the risks highlighted by the previous models and keep track of remediation activities.

The following figure will help you understand how the different layers and models use the information:

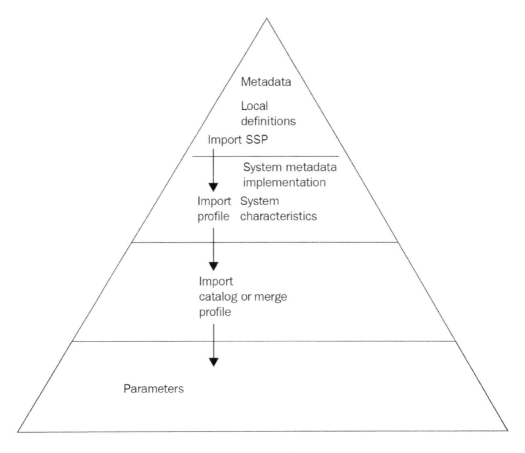

Figure 8.6 – OSCAL stack

The preceding figure shows the models and several parameters inside each model. As you can see, the source of information is always the layer below ending up in the profiles and catalogs which are the basis for achieving compliance.

OSCAL document properties

Every OSCAL model has the following properties:

- **Root element**: Serves to indicate the model of the data – whether it is a catalog, an assessment plan, assessment results, and so on.

- **Root UUID**: The UUID changes every time the document is adjusted to maintain a single source of truth.

- **Metadata**: Can be used to fill in information about the document.

- **Body**: This is the main section, which is specific to the model in question.

- **Back matter**: Used to link and attach resources.

You can see a catalog example in the following snippet:

```
controls
  - id: sc-28
        class: SP800-53
        title: Protection of Information at Rest
        params:
          - id: sc-28_prm_1
            select:
              how-many: one-or-more
              choice:
                - confidentiality
                - integrity
        props:
          - name: label
```

As you can see in the snippet, OSCAL can use a *NIST 800-53* control, in this case, *SC-28*, and codify it, making sure we get entries such as the description and how it relates to the CIA triad.

As part of any risk management program, having a catalog of controls is necessary. As you can see in the snippet, it contains the control description and many other references that tie the controls together and their role. Feel free to check out the entire listing here: `https://github.com/usnistgov/oscal-content/tree/master/nist.gov/SP800-53/rev5`.

OSCAL is being adopted in the risk and compliance industry. It allows for the creation of automated workflows in these environments, which have been using legacy mechanisms for a while now, creating friction with the digital teams. It is definitely a project to keep your eye out for.

Now let's look at a workload policy engine for Kubernetes, called K-Rail.

K-Rail

K-Rail is a tool with a focus on Kubernetes to establish security guardrails. Due to the many privilege escalation routes in Kubernetes, it is important to secure workloads. The methods to protect workloads can be with a full-blown policy engine, a shim, or an admission webhook.

K-Rail takes a lightweight approach that uses a mutating admission webhook to simplify workload policy enforcement.

K-Rail architecture

The K-Rail architecture is very simple. It uses a mutating webhook, and when the operator or system applies a resource against the cluster, the API server will check the webhook endpoint which K-Rail uses as an admission review, similarly to the following figure:

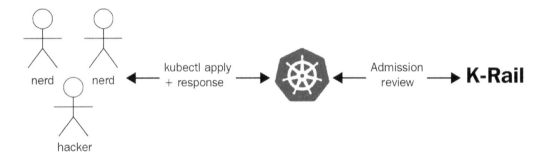

Figure 8.7 – Rail architecture

As such, K-Rail is one of the simplest policy engines you can use to protect your workloads, and with the huge amount of already written policies, it can be used straight away. Let's look at some of those policies.

K-Rail policies

One of the biggest strengths of K-Rail is the amount of pre-written policies that it comes with, from blocking `exec` to network access and a trusted image repository.

Similar to other policy engines, it also supports different methods of operation:

- **Report mode**: This flags violations to the policies but does not block enforcement mode.
- **Enforcement mode**: This acts and blocks based on the defined policy.

The way that K-Rail works is based on a YAML configuration file that contains the different policies and how to enable them, as you can see in the following snippet:

```
- name: "pod_no_shareprocessnamespace"
  enabled: True
  report_only: False
- name: "pod_image_pull_policy"
  enabled: True
  report_only: False
```

The configuration file based on YAML is easy to use, and the three parameters are very simple:

- **Name**: The name of the policy we are using.
- **Status**: `True` or `False`, to designate whether or not we are enabling the policy.
- **Operation mode**: Whether the policy will run in report or enforcement mode.

Custom policies can also be written based on the HashiCorp go-plugin, which requires knowing how to use Golang.

You can find out more about K-Rail at the following URL: `https://github.com/cruise-automation/k-rail`.

Now, let's look at a new policy engine that uses JavaScript.

jsPolicy

jsPolicy is a new contender in this field from *Loft Labs* that tries to make policies easier to create and maintain. It is an interesting policy engine that, despite being quite new, is an alternative to OPA and Kyverno.

jsPolicy tries to remove the complexity of learning a new language to create policies. It uses JavaScript and TypeScript, which have a very mature ecosystem, to allow the creation of policies to be as easy as possible.

Another strong point is the ability for jsPolicy to run on a very simple architecture, supporting some of the advanced capabilities that other policy engines still struggle with, such as mutating policies and controller policies, with more mature tooling as it runs on JavaScript.

Let's look at how jsPolicy works.

jsPolicy architecture

In this section, we will talk about the architecture of jsPolicy, which has some small nuances as a policy engine:

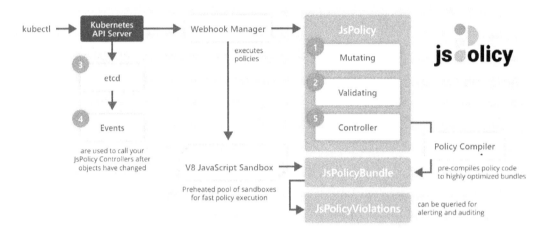

Figure 8.8 – jsPolicy architecture

jsPolicy runs everything on a container. We will expand on the three different components:

- **Webhook manager**: This is the part responsible for interacting with the admission webhooks from the Kubernetes API server.

- **V8 JavaScript sandbox pool**: This is a departure from other policy engines as it uses the V8 JavaScript sandbox pool, which is the same JavaScript engine used by the Chromium project.

- **Policy compiler**: This is a controller that precompiles the policies to optimized bundles so they can be queried by the V8 sandbox.

Now that the architecture has been defined, let's look at a policy example.

jsPolicy policies

jsPolicy uses JavaScript inside YAML. An example that blocks the creation of resources in the default namespace can be seen in the following snippet:

```
apiVersion: policy.jspolicy.com/v1beta1
kind: JsPolicy
metadata:
```

```
    name: "deny-default-namespace.mycompany.tld"
  spec:
    operations: ["CREATE"]
    resources: ["*"]
    scope: Namespaced
    javascript: |
      if (request.namespace === "default") {
        deny("Creation of resources within the default namespace
  is not allowed!");
      }
```

This YAML snippet is very similar to what we have seen throughout this chapter in other policy engines, except that it uses embedded JavaScript in the YAML. While this can put off some people, the good news is it can support separate JavaScript, even using npm packages.

So, writing policy logic can be done in three ways:

- **Embedded**: Provides an easy way to integrate JavaScript at the cost of readability and limited testing

- **Separate JavaScript**: Provides more support in IDEs and generates unit, functional, and end-to-end tests, with the ability to offer npm packages containing policies

- **TypeScript**: Provides type safety and all of the previous benefits of having the JavaScript separate

This new concept can be an interesting proposition as it enables an organization to create policies much quicker as there is no need to learn a new language.

You can read more on policies here: `https://www.jspolicy.com/docs/writing-policies/configuration`.

Summary

As you have seen in this chapter, there are quite a few policy engines out there in the community. We selected some, but this was not a comprehensive list.

We decided to introduce Kyverno, as it is one of the competitors to OPA.

We also touched on PSP and PSA. While not being policy engines in the definition of the word, they can still be useful for basic use cases when a full-blown policy engine is not necessary.

OSCAL, despite not being a policy engine but a standard of exchanging information, ties into this topic of policies as it can be used as the medium to represent how controls are being enforced, paving the way for automation in the risk and compliance functions in the organization throughout.

We also touched on Sentinel, which, depending on the organization and relationship with the HashiCorp ecosystem, can be an interesting approach despite not being free; a paid plan is required.

Finally, we also approached quite a novel policy engine, jsPolicy. From an architectural perspective, it is quite interesting how it uses the V8 JavaScript engine and JavaScript as the language, which is prevalent nowadays. So, this is something to keep on your radar.

In the next chapter, we will look at OPA, the leading policy engine in the container ecosystem. We will talk about the engine, its language Rego, the main benefits, and how to integrate it with our use cases.

9
A Primer on Open Policy Agent

After the primer on policy engines in the previous chapter, we will now focus on **Open Policy Agent** (**OPA**), the most popular policy engine out there.

This chapter will briefly introduce OPA, its architecture, how it can be used, and the main benefits and challenges, while also going a bit deeper into its policy language, Rego, which is used to build coercive instruments for access control.

Since Rego is the key to expressing policies, we will show some snippets and discuss them. OPA contains a playground that we will leverage, and you can also follow along to solidify your understanding of the concepts explained.

We will also talk about how integration with IT environments and platforms nowadays is becoming more complex due to the numerous products and services, and the shift to microservices requiring an overlay that can deal with all the pieces. We will discuss the ecosystem and how we can integrate OPA with microservices, CI/CD, service meshes, API gateways, and so on.

In this chapter, we'll cover the following main topics:

- Open Policy Agent
- Rego
- Open Policy Agent extension and integration

Technical requirements

A prior understanding of cloud environments, policy engines, YAML, and basic coding skills will be required to follow along with this chapter.

Open Policy Agent

As we have seen in the previous chapter, there are a lot of policy engines out there. OPA is one of the most popular policy engines out there and will be the focus of this chapter.

This section will discuss OPA, its architecture, and components, with a brief tutorial on installing it and testing some policies. Next, we will show some use cases of deploying OPA and the use cases it can help with.

Introduction

OPA is an open source project created as an abstraction layer for policy decisions across different environments, applications, and microservices. OPA's main strength is building on its expressive language, Rego, which we will discuss in another section.

As we discussed in previous chapters, a policy can be a set of best practices, procedures, guardrails, and standards to help achieve a goal. These policy engines, such as OPA, focus more on authorization, which corresponds to coercive instruments.

OPA and other **policy engines** (**PEs**) allow users, systems, and applications to query the **policy decision point** (**PDP**) for a specific decision, typically *ALLOW* or *DENY*. These decisions are based on the library contained in the PE and external sources, aligned to how a zero-trust architecture uses data for context. For a quick recap, check *Chapter 8, Policy Engines*, and *Chapter 2, Operationalizing Policy for Highly Regulated Industries*, the section named *Access controls for policy enforcing*.

For example, in a zero-trust architecture, the browser version, the time, and the location may be used to make a decision. These are all external sources that help create a picture of the context. Is the user accessing a resource from a commonly used browser and location?

So, in summary, OPA allows us to abstract those policy decisions from the applications, users, and services. OPA's flexibility in deployment means that it can be co-located with the organization's services and used as a standalone daemon, sidecar, or library, making it suitable for a wide variety of environments.

Architecture

One of the properties of OPA is the decoupling of policy-making decisions.

The following figure represents this decoupling:

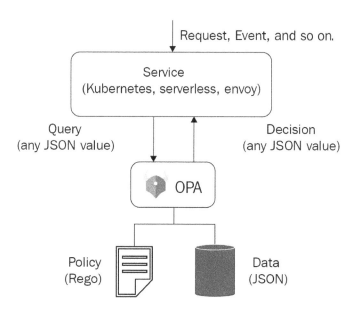

Figure 9.1 – OPA policy decoupling

The preceding image represents the architecture of OPA. It allows access to services to abstract the authorization and access.

For example, a service would receive a request and then ask OPA if the request should be authorized. OPA would internally consult its data and policy and return a decision to the service. Be mindful that the responsibility of the authorization and enforcement still lies with the service; OPA is only responsible for making the decision based on the policy and data.

Let's look at how OPA works for **Kubernetes** as it uses something called **Gatekeeper**.

Gatekeeper architecture

As we discussed in previous chapters, Kubernetes has the concept of **admission controllers**, which enforce policies on objects during *CREATE*, *UPDATE*, and *DELETE* operations. This allows us to use OPA as a decision point or a set of engine rules for the Kubernetes admission controller via the Gatekeeper plugin (more information here: `https://kubernetes.io/docs/reference/access-authn-authz/admission-controllers/`) to enforce policies such as the following:

- **Provenance**: Requiring images to come from approved image registries

- **Limits**: Requiring pods to have limits enforced

- **Inventorization**: Requiring labeling of all resources created

OPA Gatekeeper provides first-class integration with Kubernetes, and at a high level it works as shown in the following figure:

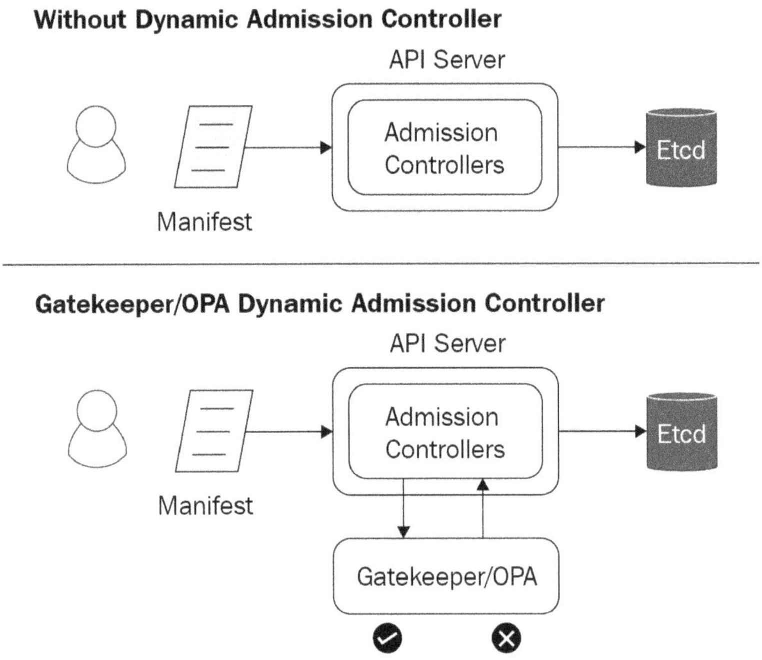

Figure 9.2 – OPA Gatekeeper

As you can see in *Figure 9.2*, Gatekeeper allows the decoupling of the decision from the API server to Gatekeeper. Gatekeeper then becomes a custom admission webhook that enforces the policies executed by OPA.

The current version of Gatekeeper is 3.0, which means that the admission controller is integrated with the OPA constraints framework (which can be consulted here: `https://github.com/open-policy-agent/frameworks/tree/master/constraint#Introduction`), allowing **Create**, **Read**, and **Delete** (**CRD**) policies to be shared. Since version 3.0 is built with **Kubebuilder**, it provides an integrated validation admission control and the creation of policy templates.

Another alternative to Kubernetes policies is using OPA and **kube-mgmt**, but Gatekeeper is recommended.

Let's now look at some resources that can be used to help you get started with OPA and learn a bit more about OPA.

Benefits

As we discussed in the previous chapter regarding PEs, OPA has some interesting benefits:

- **Broad**: OPA can be used to implement policies against structured data (YAML, XML, JSON, and so on). The most common use cases are in the Kubernetes world, in the admission controller. Because OPA can be integrated with **Golang**, **WASM**, or a **REST API**, it makes it very flexible as a single platform for policy enforcement across cloud environment infrastructure, microservices and serverless workloads authorization, and application authorization.

- **Open source**: OPA is open source using the Apache 2 License, which gives freedom to an organization to adopt, and in some cases even build, services based on OPA, such as *Netflix*, *T-Mobile*, *Yelp*, and many others have done.

- **Community**: OPA is one of the most supported PEs with a strong community (over 6,000 GitHub stars). Also, the integration ecosystem lists 55 corporations and individuals that can integrate OPA with programming languages, data filtering, and **Everything as Code** (**EaC**), to build system integrations leading to a proper policy mesh.

- **Rego language**: The OPA language is a **Domain-Specific Language** (**DSL**) that gives policy designers immense flexibility to design policies around structured data (YAML, JSON, and so on). A purpose-built language allows for extra expression and the composing of hierarchical policies, as seen in the Rego section. Rego contains more than 140 built-in functions to help write policies, such as functions to manipulate strings, time, **JSON Web Tokens** (**JWTs**), networking, and so on.

- **Control plane**: The OPA management API allows for comprehensive report creation, dashboarding, and pulling policy data from central locations. There is an offering for Styra, the **Declarative Authorization Service** (**DAS**), which provides a control plane using the management APIs. The control plane is called DAS, built from the original creators of OPA, and is a control plane for OPA in distributed environments, as you can see in the following figure:

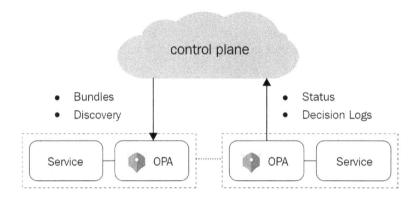

Figure 9.3 – Control plane example for distributed OPA instances

DAS makes it easier to manage huge distributed environments at scale. They have an enterprise paid version as well as a free version. You can check it out here: `https://www.styra.com/`.

OPA is one of the most comprehensive PEs, and that's why it has its own chapter. Next, we will learn how we can start writing some policies.

Getting started

This section will highlight several methods we can use to kickstart OPA.

First, we will show how you can install OPA via the command line and run it in server mode, which will accept JSON requests with a tool such as **curl**.

We will also talk about the **Rego Playground**, a browser-based GUI alternative to test and experiment with policies.

Standalone installation

To get started, you can download the OPA binary into your computer:

```
rsff@xps:~$ curl -L -o opa https://openpolicyagent.org/
downloads/v0.35.0/opa_linux_amd64_static
```

% Total		% Received	% Xferd	Average Speed		Time	Time
Time	Current						
				Dload	Upload	Total	Spent
Left	Speed						
100	88	100	88	0	0	138	0	--:--:--	--:--:--
--:--:--	138						
100	659	100	659	0	0	500	0	0:00:01	0:00:01
--:--:--	19382						
100	22.8M	100	22.8M	0	0	4833k	0	0:00:04	0:00:04
--:--:--	7800k						

Once the download finishes, you should have the binary in your current folder. The file will be missing execute permissions so you will need to add them with chmod:

```
rsff@xps:~$ ./opa
-bash: ./opa: Permission denied
rsff@xps:~$ chmod 755 ./opa
```

You can also use chmod +x ./opa to give the right executable permissions. Once that is done, you are ready to run OPA as a server that will listen for connections on port 8181, as you can see in the following:

```
rsff@xps:~$ ./opa run --server
{"addrs":[":8181"],"diagnostic-addrs":[],"level":"info","msg":"
Initializing server.","time":"2021-12-29T22:20:26Z"}
```

Once you have OPA installed, you can run it in server mode, standalone or in an evaluation mode, such as the Python interpreter.

Other operating systems

The instructions in this section were for Linux; if you are using another operating system, such as Windows or OSX, you can follow the same instructions, changing the curl command in the first snippet for the version required. The list of supported operating systems and latest releases can be found here: https://github.com/open-policy-agent/opa/releases.

Playground

If you are a fan of GUIs, there is the ability to use OPA in the Rego Playground, where you can paste policies and quickly evaluate them without any installation process at https://play.openpolicyagent.org/.

In the following figure, you can see the Rego Playground GUI with its several panes (four in total), showing a role-based access control example. We will explain each pane.

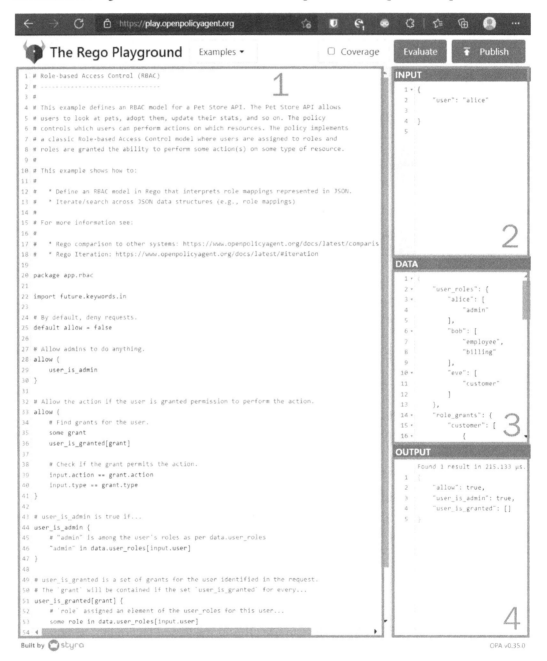

Figure 9.4 – OPA Rego Playground

As you can see, there are four main areas. The first is where the policy will be written; the Rego Playground also has some examples you can leverage.

The second pane is where you input the data to be evaluated. In this example, we can check the permissions of the different users by sending the following JSON snippet:

```
{

    "user": "alice"


}
```

And you will see the response in the fourth pane:

```
{

    "allow": true,

    "user_is_admin": true,

    "user_is_granted": []
}
```

The preceding snippet shows us that Alice is allowed and has admin permissions.

Looking at the third pane, which contains the data or the assigned permissions, we see that Alice is the admin by default on this example.

But let's change Alice to customer and execute again:

```
{

    "user_roles": {

        "alice": [

            "customer"

        ],

        "bob": [

            "employee",

            "billing"

        ],
```

If we change Alice's role to customer and evaluate, we will get the following response:

```
{

    "allow": false,

    "user_is_granted": [
```

```
        {
            "action": "adopt",
            "type": "cat"
        },
        {
            "action": "adopt",
            "type": "dog"
        },
 [..]
```

After changing the description of Alice in the data, she becomes a customer and inherits the associated permissions.

You can test many more examples regarding **role-based access control (RBAC)**, **attribute-based access control (ABAC)**, Kubernetes, and Envoy policies in the Rego Playground.

Be mindful that the **Publish** button also allows sharing the current policy, making it a handy resource to share policies and increase collaboration.

Styra Academy

Another good resource to learn about OPA is **Styra Academy** from the creators of OPA. It introduces OPA and its language, Rego, with videos, quizzes, and hands-on labs to solidify knowledge.

The most exciting module is where they explain packages, as it is very useful to build several policies and use them as packages in other policies. You can find Styra Academy at the following link: `https://academy.styra.com/`.

Let's now look at the use cases in which OPA excels and is most commonly used.

Use cases

OPA is quite flexible and can be used for many use cases. The most common are the following:

- **Application authorization**: With Rego, OPA allows you to write and enforce rules. With the rich ecosystem and tools, we can embed policies into applications.

- **Serverless policy enforcement**: OPA excels in cloud-native environments, and is used in projects containing Kubernetes and Envoy. Up until version 0.32, integrating with serverless was a shortcoming due to the temporary nature of serverless functions. A plugin made by *GoDaddy*, located here, `https://github.com/godaddy/opa-lambda-extension-plugin`, makes those issues disappear by allowing OPA to run as a Lambda extension for AWS serverless functions.

- **Kubernetes admission controller**: This is one use case where OPA shines. Thanks to Gatekeeper, it allows deep integration with the existing admission controller, extending the basic capabilities provided by Kubernetes. This enables the creation of robust policies to create provenance policies for your container images, enforce cost-center allocation, eliminate shadow IT, and much more.

- **Service mesh authorization**: OPA helps controls service meshes, as you can add a layer of authorization into the service mesh, increasing compliance, improving security, and limiting lateral movement in case of a breach.

- **Infrastructure as Code (IaC) validation**: OPA can be integrated with Terraform to enforce policies on resources provisioned by Terraform, especially in highly regulated industries, as we discussed in *Chapter 2, Operationalizing Policy for Highly Regulated Industries*, for example, in HIPAA and PCI environments. Another use case can be validating resources to a specification, for example, no public access to object storage. A resource that shows this in detail is `https://github.com/mjlshen/terraform-aws-opa`. For a more automated way of doing things, you can use **Terratest**, which automates the OPA validation on the Terraform source code: `https://blog.gruntwork.io/automatically-enforce-policies-on-your-terraform-modules-using-opa-and-terratest-d6a3f34330a1`.

These are some of the use cases that you can leverage OPA to help you achieve policies in your environments. As you noticed, OPA gets its strength from its flexibility and Rego, so let's spend a bit of time on it.

Rego

Rego, pronounced *ray-go*, is a DSL that can be used to express policies so that OPA can evaluate them.

In this section, we will be talking about the language at a high level, giving links to the official documentation as much as possible, and providing some examples of policies for the most common environments.

Introduction

Rego is a language based on **Datalog** and is used as a query language due to its expressiveness and ability to extract information from complex queries. Rego extends it to support structured data such as YAML, JSON, and XML.

For those familiar with the .NET ecosystem, think LINQ but for data that describes authorization.

Rego allows defining policies that are easy to read and write; for example, look at the following policy snippet (you can follow along using the Rego Playground: `https://play.openpolicyagent.org/`):

```
package example
default allow = false
allow = true {
    input.method == "GET"
    input.path = ["readData", user]
    input.user == user
}
```

Let's say you try to query the service as Bob to read data from Alice, as shown in the following path field:

```
{
    "user": "bob",
    "method": "GET",
    "path": ["readData", "alice"]
}
```

It will fail:

```
{
    "allow": false
}
```

The policy only allows the user to get data from his own account; for example, his bank account.

As you can see, a policy can be written in five lines of Rego, allowing OPA to evaluate it and indicate to the service if the user is allowed or not. This is one of the main benefits of Rego, succinctly defining policies. Rego is also declarative because the imperative equivalent would be more complex, and the philosophy of Rego is for authors to focus on what it should return rather than how it should be executed.

Basics

Let's look at a simple example of Rego. Since most of the cloud-native world works with a structured data format, such as JSON or YAML, Rego uses **references** (https://www.openpolicyagent.org/docs/latest/policy-language/#references) to be able to access nested data.

In the following snippet, we will define three cloud environments and access them with Rego.

First, we initialize OPA in evaluation mode:

```
rsff@xps:~$ ./opa run
OPA 0.35.0 (commit a54537a, built at 2021-12-01T02:11:47Z)
Run 'help' to see a list of commands and check for updates.
>
```

Once that is done, we can define environments as containing three values:

```
> environments = [{"name": "Amazon"}, {"name": "Google"},
{"name": "Azure"}]
Rule 'environments' defined in package repl. Type 'show' to see
rules.
```

We did an assignment operation that transferred the content to the environment variable. To list the contents of the variable, we can type its name as follows:

```
> environments
[
  {
    "name": "Amazon"
  },
  {
    "name": "Google"
  },
  {
```

```
    "name": "Azure"
    }
]
```

As you can see, the values are returned as part of a nested structure.

We can also define an `allow` statement to evaluate to `true` when it contains `Amazon` with the following snippet:

```
> allow = true {
    environments[_].name == "Amazon"
}
```

Let's call `allow` and see what it returns:

```
> allow
true
```

It means that Rego iterated over the values of `environments` and there was a match with `Amazon`.

If the array did not have the object, Rego would return `undefined` by default.

Let's create another array:

```
environments2= [{"name": "Ozon"}, {"name": "Google"}, {"name": "Azure"}]
```

Then, use the same process for `allow` and evaluate it:

```
> allow
undefined
```

As you can see, the value now returned is `undefined` as OPA cannot find an object with the name `Amazon`.

Now, we are going to iterate over the objects, which can be done with the following syntax:

```
# iterate over values
val = obj[_]
```

So, we assign the value of the iteration to `query _names`:

```
> query_names[name] { name := environments[_].name}
```

```
Rule 'query_names' defined in package repl. Type 'show' to see
rules.
```

Once that is done, we can check the value of query_names:

```
> query_names
[
  "Amazon",
  "Azure",
  "Google"
]
>
```

Thus, we get the environments.

So, in this small example, we used assignment, operations, and iteration.

The most valuable functions will probably be the built-in ones, which can be checked here: https://www.openpolicyagent.org/docs/latest/policy-reference/#built-in-functions.

Let's now look at some policy examples for different types of services.

Examples in the Rego Playground

In this section, we will lean on the examples in the Rego Playground and some custom modifications to understand how to build them.

RBAC

The Rego Playground contains an RBAC policy that shows how to interpret the mapping represented in the nested data structure.

We will change it slightly for the sake of simplicity; the policy will be the following:

```
package app.rbac
import future.keywords.in

default allow = false
allow {
    user_admin
}
```

```
allow {
    some grant
    user_is_granted[grant]

    input.action == grant.action
    input.type == grant.type
}
user_admin {
    "admin" in data.user_roles[input.user]
}
user_is_granted[grant] {
    some role in data.user_roles[input.user]
    some grant in data.role_grants[role]
}
```

So at a high level, we have the imports at the beginning of the policy, with the default deny.

The import syntax is actually a very important concept as it allows us to create packages and then use them later. In this example, we are importing the in keyword, which allows us to iterate over a collection to see if an element is present and then return either false or true.

future.keywords.in is used because Rego maintains its backward compatibility by making transitional (beta) keywords available through an import, future.keywords. Later, when the function has been made part of the Rego standard, we will not need to import the keyword.

After explicitly allowing based on the grant, we use a function called user_is_ granted. We also have another function to check if the user is an admin.

This allows us to build a simple banking system with three actors: Alice will be the admin, Bob the employee who can read accounts, and Eve the customer who can read her account and make deposits.

The following would be the data definition:

```
{
    "user_roles": {
        "alice": [
            "admin"
```

```
    ],
        "bob": [
            "employee"
    ],
        "eve": [
            "customer"
        ]
    },
```

So, first, we would create the roles:

```
    "role_grants": {
        "customer": [
            {
                "action": "read",
                "type": "account"
            },
            {
                "action": "deposit",
                "type": "account"
            }
        ],
        "employee": [
            {
                "action": "read",
                "type": "account"
            }
        ]
    }
}
```

In the previous snippet, we granted the necessary permission. Now, we can use OPA to evaluate.

Let's try one scenario, which is trying to have Bob deposit in the account.

Let's pass the following input:

```
{
    "user": "bob",
    "action": "deposit",
    "type": "account"
}
```

This will generate a deny response, as you can see in the following:

```
{
    "allow": false,
    "user_is_granted": [
        {
            "action": "read",
            "type": "account"
        }
    ]
}
```

Let's say we change the name of the user to Eve:

```
{
    "user": "eve",
    "action": "deposit",
    "type": "account"
}
```

We will be able to see that she is allowed to make a deposit:

```
{
    "allow": true,
    "user_is_granted": [
        {
            "action": "deposit",
            "type": "account"
        },
        {
            "action": "read",
```

```
        "type": "account"
    }
  ]
}
```

While there are some shortcomings, a more robust system could be implemented in the policy for the user to only access their own account.

The purpose of this section is to show you the flexibility of OPA, how to iterate, and the basic syntax of the policies. You can see an example based on this one, which went a step further to implement RBAC for a blog API, here: `https://github.com/ashutoshSce/opa-rbac/blob/master/rbac.rego`.

Terraform

Since OPA can only work on structured data formats, we need to be mindful that the Terraform source code language, HCL, is not in a structured data format. As such, after the planning phase, we can output the result into JSON using the `terraform show -json` native Terraform capability so that OPA can consume and evaluate. There are also other tools to convert HCL to JSON, for example, `hcl2json`: `https://github.com/tmccombs/hcl2json`.

So, the workflow would look like this.

1. Create the Terraform plan
2. Convert terraform plan to JSON
3. Run OPA checks on the JSON

On the official page of OPA, there is a Terraform example. You can check it out, but be mindful that it uses weights to classify whether the deployment is safe or not, making it a bit more complex: `https://www.openpolicyagent.org/docs/latest/terraform/`.

Also, there will be use cases where you can just check the JSON for fields. For example, see the next snippet:

```
            "type": "google_storage_bucket",
            "values": {
                "cors": [],
                "default_event_based_hold": null,
                "encryption": [],
                "force_destroy": false,
```

```
              "labels": null,
              "lifecycle_rule": [],
              "location": "EUROPE-WEST2",
              "logging": [],
              "name": "testplantojson69420",
              "requester_pays": null,
              "retention_policy": [],
              "storage_class": "STANDARD",
              "versioning": [],
              "website": []
            }
          }
        ]
      }
    },
```

In the preceding example from a Terraform plan, if we look at the encryption data structure, it is empty. As such, making a policy to iterate through the data structure to check the field encryption and only allow instances that have encryption enabled can be an easy and fast way to create a policy that increases encryption use.

Kubernetes

Building on the example from the Rego Playground called **Label Existence**, say we define the following policy:

```
package kubernetes.validating.existence

deny[msg] {
      not input.request.object.metadata.labels.costcenter
      msg := "Every resource must have a costcenter label"
}
deny[msg] {
      value := input.request.object.metadata.labels.costcenter
      not startswith(value, "costcenter-")
      msg := sprintf("Costcenter code must start with
`costcenter-`; found `%v`", [value])
}
```

This policy requires that all the resources on Kubernetes have a label identifying the cost center. Say we pass in the following input:

```
{
    "kind": "AdmissionReview",
    "request": {
        "kind": {
            "kind": "Pod",
            "version": "v1"
        },
        "object": {
            "metadata": {
                "name": "myapp",
                "labels": {
                    "costcenter": "-42069"
                }
            },
            "spec": {
                "containers": [
                    {
                        "image": "nginx",
                        "name": "nginx-frontend"
                    }
                ]
            }
        }
    }
}
```

It will fail and give an error message like the one defined in the policy, as shown in the following:

```
{
    "deny": [
        "Costcenter code must start with `costcenter-`; found
`-42069`"
    ]
}
```

Say we correctly supply the cost center in the right format:

```
"object": {
            "metadata": {
                "name": "myapp",
                "labels": {
                    "costcenter": "costcenter-42069"
                }
            },
```

We will get an empty response:

```
{
    "deny": []
}
```

OPA and Rego are very powerful and flexible when it comes to writing policies and evaluating them. If you are writing policies for microservices and service meshes, be mindful that performance is key. As such, there are comprehensive best practices on how to write policies that are evaluated with minimal overhead here: `https://www.openpolicyagent.org/docs/latest/policy-performance/`.

The main takeaways for high-performance use cases are as follows:

- Write policy code that follows big O notation best practices to minimize loops and searches.
- Use objects when you have an identifier for the elements instead of an array, making lookups faster.
- Write policies with indexed statements so that indexing can be done.
- Use the profiler to help identify policy portions that require improvement.
- There is also **Conftest**, a framework on top of OPA to help test policies and shift left to developing policy assertions. More information can be seen here: `https://www.conftest.dev/`.

In the next section, we will be looking at how to extend and integrate OPA.

Open Policy Agent extension and integration

OPA's biggest strengths are extending it via functions or custom plugins and integrating it with any service. This final section will briefly discuss our options to integrate and extend it for our custom needs. Let's look at API integration.

API integration

As with any service, product, or platform, integration is important. It allows organizations to reduce operational overhead and team fatigue by having to *translate* different services, resulting in reduced operating costs.

OPA is well suited to integration thanks to its agnostic APIs, which your products and services can use.

There usually are two cases to integrate OPA with external sources:

- **Management**: To create a control plane to manage and operate policies across environments, get operational metrics from across the agents deployed, especially in multi-cloud with microservices environments, and retrieve logs and status for operational teams.

- **Policy enforcement point (PEP)**: Providing access to services, tools, and platforms to use OPA as a PEP requires integration. This allows for the decoupling of policies from applications and services and creates a consolidated strategy and a single pane of glass for policy authorization and enforcement.

I'll describe and link the APIs required to integrate and evaluate with OPA:

- **Policy and data distribution**: The **Bundle API** helps with OPA downloading bundles of policy and data from remote locations. This can help with an EaC posture as you have a central repository and OPA can fetch periodically from that location. This API is important as it allows us to push massive policies in one go to achieve near real-time enforcement. There are also capabilities to sign the bundle to validate the integrity of the policies. You can read more here: `https://www.openpolicyagent.org/docs/latest/management-bundles/`.

- **Monitoring and observability**: The **Status API** coupled with the **Health API** allows us to check the operational health of the services. The Status API provides us with the capabilities to know when bundles are downloaded and activated and when a plugin state changes. You can read more here: `https://www.openpolicyagent.org/docs/latest/management-status/`.

The Health API checks that the server is operational, which is handy when load balancing several OPA services and we want to know when the service is active. You can read more here: `https://www.openpolicyagent.org/docs/latest/rest-api/#health-api`.

- **Logging**: As we want to consolidate all the decisions made by OPA agents, the **Decision Log API** allows us to report the evaluation decision to remote locations via HTTP. It comprises the events that led to the policy querying, the input, the bundle metadata, and other information that allows us to audit. This is one of the most important APIs, especially for **PolicyOps** and the monitoring of coercive events in a single pane of glass. More can be read here: `https://www.openpolicyagent.org/docs/latest/management-decision-logs/`.

Besides the management APIs described, we can also evaluate policies in different ways:

- **REST API**: The decision is returned as JSON via HTTP. This is the most common method, as it's easy to use and makes upgrading OPA easy. Due to the nature of HTTP, it also needs security best practices, such as the following:

  - Limit API access to trusted local clients executing policy queries.

  - Configure TLS.

  - Do not pass credentials as arguments.

  - Run OPA as a non-root user, ideally inside a specific account.

- **Golang library**: Only works for **Go** software, and upgrades to OPA will require redeploying the software. Looking at evaluation performance, it is faster than REST APIs. It requires the management APIs to be enabled or implemented.

- **WebAssembly (WASM)**: While this functionality is still being implemented, it will be the option with the most negligible overhead, as the policies are compiled to a low-level instruction set. It will also be possible to embed this with any language with a WASM runtime (this includes most of the popular languages).

  You can check the Bytecode Alliance at `https://bytecodealliance.org/`, which shows the organizations backing this effort. In my opinion, this is the option with the most promise once the functionality gets fully implemented along with the language's SDK.

OPA has a lot of integration capabilities, not only from an operational and management perspective but also from an evaluation perspective, supporting the REST API and going into the future with **WASM**.

Let's now look at extending OPA through functions and plugins.

Extending OPA

As with any platform, there needs to be a way to bring custom functionality. OPA does this by providing the creation of custom built-in functions for the Rego language, which you can find more information about here: `https://www.openpolicyagent.org/docs/latest/extensions/#adding-built-in-functions-to-the-opa-runtime`.

Finally, there is also the possibility of extending the OPA runtime with plugins, which can be desirable for custom behavior. The details can be found here: `https://www.openpolicyagent.org/docs/latest/extensions/#custom-plugins-for-opa-runtime`.

Summary

In this chapter, we focused on OPA to show you the basics, the architecture, the language, and how to get started.

As we have seen, OPA is one of the most popular PEs due to its flexibility and community support. It is more mature than other projects as it has graduated from **Cloud Native Cloud Foundation** (**CNCF**).

Its flexibility lies in decoupling the policy decision from the applications, services, or tools, thus making it suitable for complex environments, and not only cloud-native ones. While it can integrate natively through Gatekeeper with Kubernetes and service meshes, its ability to extend through REST API also makes it suitable for legacy and heterogeneous environments with different services and tools.

While there is an overhead of learning a new language for writing policies, the flexibility and the constructs of the Rego language allow you to express complex policies. I would say that OPA is the de facto engine to implement and enforce coercive instruments for digital enablement.

Now that we have covered PEs, we will be looking at how to classify and make a case for organizational PEs' needs in the next chapter. We will use a framework to rank different maturity levels across people, processes, and technology to make data-driven decisions when starting the Policy as Code journey.

10
Policy as Code Tool Evaluation

So far, we have covered **policy engines**, their uses, architectures, and their main benefits. In this chapter, we will talk about evaluating **Policy as Code (PaC)** ecosystems. We will cover cloud-native capabilities and vendors and highlight the main advantages and challenges of each.

More importantly, this chapter will examine the different tools, products, and vendors, all of them with different features and capabilities that need to be weighted and compared to our goals to have an objective approach when selecting them, thus we discuss how to evaluate them in an data-driven approach.

Additionally, we will touch on the organizational policies of **Cloud Service Providers (CSPs)** and their interaction with **Identity and Access Management (IAM)**, albeit at a high level, to show how to create effective policies combining both tools.

The key part of this chapter is the tool evaluation framework, where we discuss a method to rank and vizualize the different tools' approaches, policy engines, and policy management.

With these topics, we can gain a high-level overview of the landscape and, more importantly, be able to refer back to this chapter every time we want to evaluate and compare different policy tools. Additionally, the framework can be used for maturity assessment, for example, to figure out different levels of maturity and work on areas that require improvement.

In this chapter, we'll cover the following topics:

- Cloud-native ecosystems
- Vendor ecosystems
- CSP-native capabilities
- The evaluation framework

Technical requirements

To follow along with this chapter, a prior understanding of cloud environments, policy engines, YAML, and basic coding is required.

Cloud-native open source ecosystems

As discussed more thoroughly in *Chapter 5, Policy for Cloud-Native Environments*, cloud-native environments have several policy engines and languages to establish PaC. This section will discuss open source tools and frameworks that can help you to build policy engines and authorization policies. This list is not exhaustive, but it highlights the tools that you can evaluate.

Cloud Custodian

Cloud Custodian is an open source security, governance, and management tool. Similar to **Open Policy Agent** (**OPA**), it uses a **Domain-Specific Language** (**DSL**), YAML, to define rules for cloud environments. It can be seen as a policy engine for the security, cost, optimization, and governance of cloud environments. One of its main characteristics is that it provides support across the major cloud providers of AWS, Azure, and **Google Cloud Platform** (**GCP**).

The integration with major cloud providers and their native tooling is a welcome addition for providing a policy engine with deep integration.

For more information, please refer to `https://cloudcustodian.io/`.

SPIFFE

SPIFFE is an open source set of standards for workload identity. It is essential in modern environments that use cloud computing, serverless, microservices, and orchestrators such as **Kubernetes**, as traditional network policies do not scale for these use cases.

As such, SPIFFE provides a framework specification that uses X.509 certificates or JWTs in the form of a **SPIFFE Verifiable Identity Document (SVID)** to prove service workload verifiability and to make a decision.

The following diagram shows the architecture of SPIRE, which is an implementation of the SPIFFE framework:

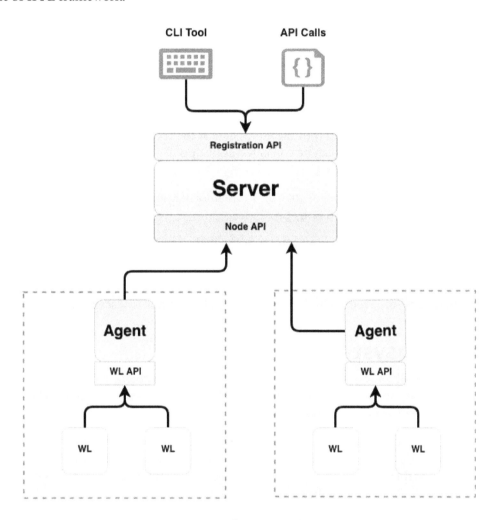

Figure 10.1 – The SPIRE architecture

As you can see in the preceding diagram, there is one server and several agents. The server is responsible for maintaining the list of workload identities, signing identities, and creating the trust domain of the environment.

The agents run on every node containing the **Workload** (**WL**), which communicates with the server via the API, provides SVIDs from the server, facilitates communication with the workload API, and ensures the workloads get their SVIDs.

For more information, you can visit `https://spiffe.io/`.

Parliament

Parliament is a linter tool for IAM. It can detect malformed IAM JSON, whether there are any missing elements in the IAM policy, whether the resources are allowed to have the conditions and actions specified, or simply for lousy policy patterns.

Parliament is an open source tool specific to **AWS**.

For **Google Cloud**, an official API is in the alpha state at the time of writing, which provides similar functionality. It can be consulted at `https://cloud.google.com/iam/docs/linting-policies`.

You can navigate to the GitHub repository for more information on Parliament at `https://github.com/duo-labs/parliament`.

We covered some examples of tools and frameworks that allow us to build policies for cloud resources, methods to authorize and validate workloads, and enable us to validate the CSP IAM constructs.

Next, we will look at some tools and frameworks from the vendor landscape.

Vendor ecosystems

In this section, we will introduce some tools from the PaC ecosystem. Here, the main difference is that we will focus on paid tools, in some cases listing vendors that provide a free version and an enterprise version at a cost.

As you might know, **Terraform**, an **Infrastructure as Code** (**IaC**) tool, is part of **HashiCorp**, which also provides an enterprise paid version called Terraform Enterprise. It makes sense to list them, primarily in organizations that need assurances, such as **Service-Level Agreements** (**SLAs**), and dedicated support.

HashiCorp

As discussed in *Chapter 8, Policy Engines*, HashiCorp Sentinel provides a PaC framework for enterprise users. One of the great benefits of this is integrating with the HashiCorp ecosystem, especially Terraform, the de facto tool for IaC, and providing comprehensive policies to the Terraform code.

You can find more information at `https://www.hashicorp.com/sentinel`.

Styra

Styra provides **OPA** enterprise support and the **Declarative Authorization Service** (**DAS**) tool, which leverages the existing management APIs of OPA to build a control plane, which is beneficial for distributed OPA deployments.

Styra DAS comes in two versions: a free version for small deployments, which supports up to 100 rules, and the enterprise version, which provides policy packs alongside some of the most common policies and benchmarks. These include NIST, PCI, MITRE, CIS, and more.

You can find more information at `https://blog.styra.com/blog/what-is-styra-declarative-authorization-service`.

RegScale

RegScale takes compliance to the next level by providing **Compliance-as-Code** (**CaC**) constructs. It allows organizations to manage their compliance obligations. Additionally, it allows you to schedule audits, document compliance issues, attach evidence, and track corrective actions in a collaborative environment. It also allows you to integrate the compliance workflow with vendors and other tools as it is API-centric.

They have a free **Community Edition** (**CE**) distributed in a container, and ISO appliance, and the **Enterprise Edition** (**EE**), with support ideal for large, regulated companies such as governments, financial institutions, and energy and utilities organizations.

For more information, please refer to `https://regscale.com/`.

OKTA

OKTA provides an identity agent to manage authorization and authentication. It is one of the most common deployment tools due to its integration across legacy environments, APIs, and cloud-native connectors. It brings **Single Sign-On** (**SSO**) and OAuth 2.0 support across different cloud providers.

You can find more information about OKTA at `https://developer.okta.com/docs/reference/`.

Now that we have described some vendor examples, next, let's discuss some CSP-native policies.

CSP-native capabilities

In this section, we will discuss the different types of services linked to coercive instruments and how we can use the native capabilities of CSPs to build policies.

We will discuss the major cloud providers' services such as AWS **Service Control Policies (SCPs)**, **IAM**, **Microsoft Azure Policy**, and Google Cloud **Organization Policy Service (OPS)**. We will discuss how these services can be used.

These services will help us design a centralized control plane to establish guardrails and authorization for cloud environments. This allows teams to increase their agility, as the guardrails do not allow them to deviate from compliance rules.

AWS

AWS SCPs are a method to restrict actions in cloud accounts so that users and roles are limited in what they can do, for example, blocking users from using a specific database in a region. In *Chapter 11*, *Cloud Providers Policy Constructs*, we will talk about CSP policies and how to build them in more detail.

This section will briefly cover the types of native policies and provide a quick example.

SCPs

One of the most potent instruments in AWS for coercive instruments is SCP. We will discuss them in depth in *Chapter 11*, *Cloud Providers Policy Constructs*.

For now, be mindful that SCPs help to establish the necessary guardrails in different AWS accounts. In combination with IAM, it creates the de facto privileges, as the following diagram shows:

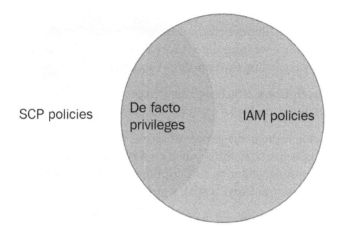

Figure 10.2 – The intersection of SCP and IAM permissions

An important point to remember is that the preceding diagram doesn't only apply to AWS; other cloud providers also share the same concept, as you will see in the following sections.

IAM

AWS IAM allows us to control access to resources such as virtual machines (EC2), serverless functions (Lambda), Kubernetes nodes, and more. It gives us the ability to express who has access to what.

In AWS, you can use the GUI to build IAM policies or create them programmatically.

We will discuss IAM and CSP-native policies, in more depth, in *Chapter 11, Cloud Providers Policy Constructs*.

However, if you want to learn more, take a look at the following blog, which explains how to write a policy to read and write to AWS S3 object storage: https://aws.amazon. com/blogs/security/writing-iam-policies-how-to-grant-access- to-an-amazon-s3-bucket/.

Let's look at how Azure manages and implements policies.

Microsoft Azure

Microsoft Azure has a very different concept from AWS and Google Cloud, as its service is called Azure Policy. Before we jump into Azure Policy, I would like to discuss how Azure differs, especially regarding the concept of accounts.

First, Azure uses **subscriptions**, which we can interpret as accounts. These subscriptions can be designed to facilitate workload separation, similar to AWS accounts.

The second consideration is the management of access, policies, and compliance across those subscriptions. Azure has something called an **Azure management group** that allows you to abstract and encapsulate different subscriptions into one management group. It is similar to AWS' **Organizational Units** (**OUs**), which allow you to group accounts.

These topics will be discussed, in more depth, in *Chapter 11*, *Cloud Providers Policy Constructs*.

Azure Policy

Like AWS SCP, Azure Policy helps to create guardrails by allowing you to define standards programmatically. It works differently from other cloud providers as it consolidates the functionality around Azure Policy, such as viewing results in a specific dashboard, bringing resources to compliance through automatic remediation, and filtering resources—all from a dedicated dashboard. Similar to other CSPs, it uses JSON.

Azure role-based access control

Azure Role-Based Access Control (**RBAC**) helps you to manage who has access to what resources in a similar way to what AWS IAM does.

If we want to control the actions of a user or a group, Azure RBAC is the right tool to use. If an individual is allowed to perform an action, and the result is a non-compliant resource, Azure Policy will block it. Hence, the combination of Azure Policy and Azure RBAC gives operators in Azure full scope control, similarly to what we see in Figure 10.2.

Now, let's look at Google Cloud.

GCP

Google Cloud has concepts similar to AWS, such as its OSP and IAM services. The concepts within Google Cloud are clearer and easier to grasp as the usage of folders makes it intuitive to apply policies, as seen in the following figure:

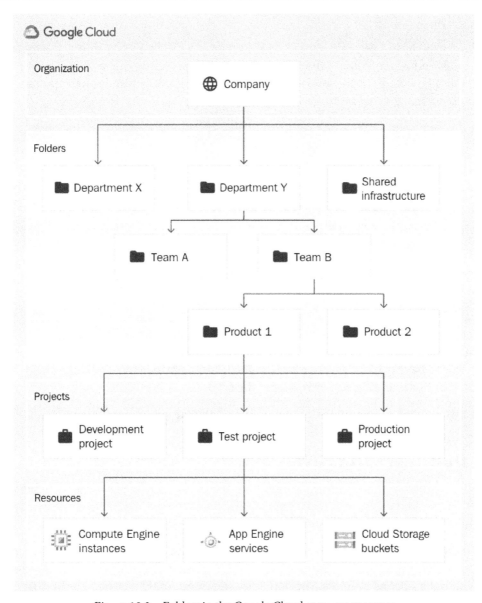

Figure 10.3 – Folders in the Google Cloud resource manager

As you can see in *Figure 10.3*, the ability to segregate at the folder level, the project level, and the resource level gives us a lot of flexibility when applying organizational policies, as they are inherited. This means that a policy applied at a parent resource will trickle down to the child resources.

OPS

OPS allows us to have a centralized view over the organization's cloud resources, similar to AWS SCPs and Azure Policy. OPS focuses on *what*, establishing the restrictions on the resources and how they can be configured; IAM, which we will talk about next, focuses on *who* can access them.

And it's the combination of these two capabilities, as highlighted in *Figure 10.2*, that gives the de facto privileges.

IAM

Like the other cloud providers discussed here, Google Cloud structures its IAM model around three parts. The principal can be a user, group, or service account with permission to access a resource.

The role is a collection of permissions. For example, the **Database_dev_reader** role can have the necessary permissions to only access databases within the development environment and only perform read operations.

Roles simplify the management processes by having standard roles that fit groups and users, such as DB_READER, ADMINISTRATOR, APP_DEV, and so on. Finally, the policy needs to have two parts to be effective: the *who* (the principal, service account), and the *what, that is, t*he associated permissions (the role).

Now that we covered the major CSPs at a high level, let's dive into our evaluation framework.

The evaluation framework

As we have learned in this chapter and the rest of the book, there are many ways to build policy engines and use PaC to achieve PolicyOps. This section will discuss the major parts you should focus on in the evaluation framework.

This framework will look at the tools from a **People, Process, and Technology** (**PPT**) lens to develop a ranking depending on your organizational needs. This is not a prescriptive framework but a starting point for your organization or group when evaluating a digital policy toolset.

The main pillars

As we discussed throughout the book, technology should only be part of the overall framework when dealing with policy, enforcement, and management. As such, we will use the three-legged stool, also known as PPT. This section will discuss the main pillars and analyze the components. We will discuss the evaluation process and finish it with the visualization part, which will help us rank different toolsets.

People

In this pillar, we gauge people's abilities, such as their digital maturity, support for reskilling or retraining, and operational excellence. A real-world example can be expressed by the friction between engineering and risk teams. It is very common for each team not to understand the other team's requirements and operating models, thus leading to an inefficient collaboration.

We will ask questions about how to introduce a policy toolset that can interact with the workforce and how a specific toolset enables people through training, documentation, or specific design courses to reskill.

We will be looking at the following aspects:

- **Digital maturity**: In this aspect, we can measure the ability of the toolset to relate to the organization's growth strategy and provide more digital maturity to the organization.

- **Operational excellence**: Here, we measure the ability of the toolset to bring operational excellence to the groups and the organization.

- **People three Rs (retrain, reskill, and retain)**: In this aspect, we measure the ability of the toolset to provide capabilities to train and reskill people, such as through well-written documentation, courses, and tutorials.

Now, let's talk about the process that keeps everything in place and ensures we tie our toolset to our organizational goals.

Process

In this pillar, we are trying to measure the policy toolset and integrate it with the organizational processes; for example, how well the toolset integrates with our digital workflow software (ServiceNow). The sub-pillars to take into consideration in the process pillar are listed as follows:

- **Self-service**: This refers to the ability of the tool to enable self-service. Does it contain management APIs to be able to create services around it?

- **Business integration**: This refers to the ability to integrate with the existing vendor base, process, or tool.

- **Analytics**: Does the tool have analytics capabilities, such as dashboards, reporting, and more?

Now, let's talk about the next pillar.

Technology

This pillar is concerned with the technology angle. How will the tool integrate with the current tech stack? Will it create more tech debt? Does it have integration points with **Continuous Integration and Continuous Delivery (CI/CD)**?

- **Tech debt**: This refers to the ability of the tool to be modular to avoid coupled components. For example, does it contain good documentation? Does it come with a test suite?

- **SDLC maturity**: Does the tool or project follow a mature SDLC? Are best practices such as OWASP followed by the project, vendor, or platform?

- **CI/CD integration**: This refers to the tool's ability to integrate with the most common systems such as GitHub, Jenkins, Spinnaker, CircleCI, and more. It does this by providing examples and documentation on it.

Now that we've talked about the three pillars and sub-pillars, let's move to understand how to evaluate each of these aspects.

Evaluation

This section will discuss the ability to give a quantitative measure to each of the sub-pillars to express a number. We will be using an adaptation of **Capability Maturity Model Integration (CMMI)**. Then, we will show how we can construct a radar graph to communicate the results of our evaluation using a simple table.

CMMI

For the overall score and how to measure the abilities of the toolset in terms of the organization, we can use an adapted version of CMMI:

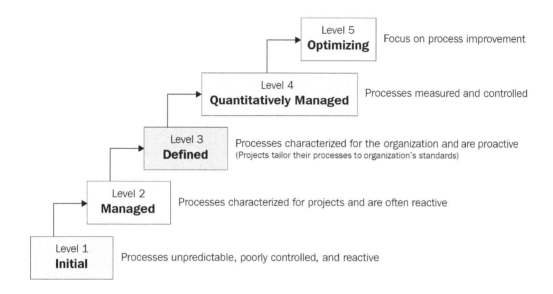

Figure 10.4 – Maturity levels

As you can see in the preceding diagram, CMMI has several levels, from 1 to 5, representing several degrees of maturity. We can use those levels in our assessment and visualization to establish the desired state and the toolset state.

We can analyze each sub-pillar based on the preceding levels to build a table. The table will contain the pillars, the sub-pillars, the target score, and the tool score in each sub-pillar.

As part of the sub-pillars, we should create questionaries or capabilities and rank them accordingly. However, that is beyond the scope of this chapter, as the most crucial bit is gaining an understanding of how to rate the tools:

	Policy-as-Code Evaluator	Target Score	Tool1	Tool2
	Overall	3.56	3.60	3.11
People	Digital Maturity	3.00	3.42	3.00
People	Operational Excellence	3.00	3.00	1.00
People	People three Rs	4.00	5.00	2.00
Process	Self Service	3.00	3.00	3.00
Process	Business Integration	5.00	5.00	3.00
Process	Analytics	3.00	2.00	5.00
Technology	Tech Debt	3.00	3.00	2.00
Technology	SDLC Maturity	4.00	4.00	4.00
Technology	CI/CD Integration	4.00	4.00	5.00

Figure 10.5 – The framework evaluation table

Now, let's look at how we can visualize our findings to make it easier to communicate them.

Visualization

Once we populate our table, we need a graphical way in which to represent the desired state and the different toolset capabilities to help us achieve that desired state.

In that regard, we can use a radar graph, which is a chart primarily used to understand deviations or commonalities among variables. Hence, this is why radar charts are the most appropriate chart type for our evaluation, as we can have the target state and different tools showing how close or away they are from our sub-pillars.

You can look at the following diagram as an example:

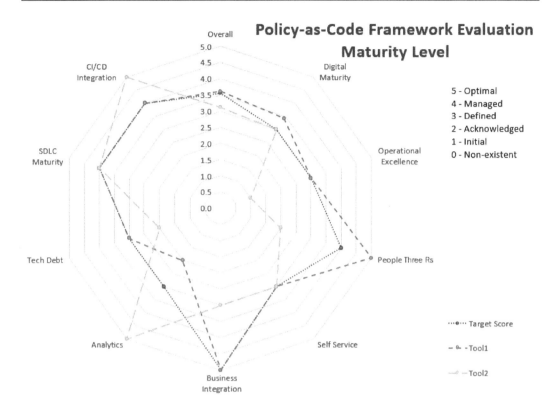

Figure 10.6 – An example of a radar graph visualization

There are other types of charts, but the radar graph is the one that I've found to show stakeholders different kinds of tools, platforms, and capabilities, being able to compare them with the desired baseline.

Summary

This chapter presented different toolsets from cloud-native ecosystems, open source platforms, and vendors. The purpose was to highlight some of the existing toolsets in those environments. I also highlighted that some vendors have a dual approach where they offer an open source version that is free of charge; this is either limited in functionality or without support. A good example is HashiCorp, which is used with Terraform.

In this chapter, we lightly touched on the native policies of CSPs, although we will cover them in more depth in *Chapter 11, Cloud Providers Policy Constructs*, to highlight some of the capabilities and differences that could be captured in our evaluation framework.

Finally, we closed the chapter by demonstrating how to create a basic framework built on PPT to capture both the desired state and the toolset state. This is important when making a PolicyOps function or bringing a PaC toolset into an organization. As the saying goes, an image is worth more than a thousand words. I've shown how you can use a particular chart type to represent what you want to achieve and how different toolsets can help you achieve the target state.

In the next chapter, we will discuss cloud-native policies. In particular, we will talk about some of the policies that the European Union has implemented to drive digital adoption, as well as focusing on the major cloud providers to highlight the tools and services they offer to design and implement policies.

11
Cloud Providers Policy Constructs

Moving on from the tool evaluation we did in the previous chapter, we will now discuss the native **Cloud Service Provider** (**CSP**) policy offerings. This chapter is divided into two sections.

In the first part, we will discuss the primary digital policy from the **European Union** (**EU**), known as *A Europe fit for the digital age*, by highlighting its goal and supporting projects.

In the second part, we will discuss **Amazon Web Services**, **Microsoft Azure**, and **Google Cloud**, which are the major CSPs. We will highlight the services and product offerings that support policy creation, enforcement, and management.

First, we will discuss cybersecurity policies and regulatory policies regarding *A Europe fit for the digital age* since these are directly associated with CSPs and the concerns surrounding their dataflows. We will also discuss cybersecurity policies, especially the revision of the **Network and Information Security** (**NIS**) **Directive** and one regulatory proposal as an example of the EU's commitment to increasing the resilience of critical sectors (financial) in the **Digital Operational Resilience Act** (**DORA**) as it specifically addresses the risk from CSPs and the existing concentration risk.

After that, we will focus on the major CSP service offerings and how we can leverage them to build **PolicyOps** functions.

In this chapter, we're going to cover the following topics:

- Types of CSP policies
- AWS native policy offerings
- Azure native policy offerings
- Google Cloud native policy offerings

Technical requirements

To complete this chapter, you will need to have a basic understanding of cloud-native services, APIs, YAML, and basic coding skills.

Types of CSP policies

In this section, we will discuss policies that directly impact the EU's digital economy beyond traditional coercive instruments. We will discuss digital and cloud adoption policies, some regulations indirectly tied to cloud providers, and the organizational policies that are associated with coercive instruments.

Adoption

As we have seen in the last few chapters, most digital policies are built on coercive instruments. For example, **policy engine** mechanisms, in new frameworks such as **Zero Trust**, all leverage coercion. Let's analyze some of the more recent policies that increase digital or cloud adoption. These policies are aligned with what we discussed in *Chapter 1, Introduction to Policy Design*, and use suasion, financial, and coercion instruments. These policies represent an organizational policy design that uses other instruments and is more complex to enact and establish.

In this section, we will highlight some policies that deal with the adoption of digital and cybersecurity at the EU level focused on *A Europe fit for the digital age*.

EU

The EU has been very active in enabling and fostering policies for digital adoption. Over the last few years, they have been launching an alliance for industry, the edge, and the cloud via the European Digital SME Alliance. These workgroups look for opportunities for business using digital means, encourage the development of trustworthy technology, and abide by proposals for green transitions to fight climate change.

A *common European data space* has also been established, which helps with regulatory proposals. This means that public bodies in agriculture, the government, energy, the environment, and so on can exchange data.

However, the most ambitious project part of *A Europe fit for the digital age* is the compass for the next decade, which focuses on four main areas:

- **Skills**: Making sure the population has digital basic skills, with the target being at least 80% of the population, and making sure that more than 20 million **information and communications technology** (**ICT**) specialists have the right skills.

- **Secure and Sustainable Digital Infrastructures**: Using state-of-the-art communication technology such as 5G to avoid supply chain issues in semiconductors, thereby doubling EU production. There will be a particular focus on **quantum computing** and building more than 10,000 climate-neutral edge cloud nodes.

- **Digital Transformation on Business**: Ramping up technology to ensure that 75% of EU companies are using the cloud, **artificial intelligence** (**AI**), and big data. Financial instruments must be used to grow scale-ups and finance EU unicorns, as well as to push for a basic level of digital adoption for 90% of SMEs.

- **Digitalization of Public Services**: Have all the key public services 100% online, and have 100% of the citizens accessing their medical records digitally.

As you can see, it's quite an ambitious plan and needs to have security assurances. For example, the medical data of EU citizens must follow stringent security requirements to prevent breaches and misuse, hence why we will discuss cybersecurity next.

Cybersecurity

The EU has recognized that ICT is now pervasive and that the increased risks from these digital systems must be addressed. The *2019/881 regulation* established *ENISA* as a cybersecurity center to the European landscape that can help the EU draft new schemes and respond to cybersecurity matters.

In 2021, two essential candidate certification schemes were published by ENISA:

- **The EUCC Scheme (Common Criteria-Based European Candidate Cybersecurity Certification Scheme)**: This enables manufacturers or service providers to assess the security quality of their products. It provides evidence of the products and services to the end users, as well as for regulation and compliance purposes.

- **The EUCS Scheme (Cloud Services Scheme)**: Published in December 2020, this is a draft candidate scheme of the cybersecurity certification for cloud services.

The EUCS scheme has defined three assurances levels for the cloud providers. Their inspiration was taken from the german **BSI C5** scheme and the French **SecNumCloud** certification. For some reason, the CSPs were unable to achieve the French requirements.

The last piece of feedback they received, which was discussed on reference *OUT2021-00157*, was from the European data protection board asking to make this certification scheme compatible with *Schrems II*.

A European strategy for data

With the impact that digital technologies have had on citizens, organizations, and the public sector in the last few years, it is naïve to think that deceleration will never happen. The current rate of data production is increasing tremendously, from 33 zettabytes in 2018 to a forecast of 175 zettabytes in 2025. Data is not the new oil – data is the new uranium; it's very powerful, but when things go wrong, it lingers for a tremendous amount of time causing harm. Think about exposed patient records and the impact that those records would have throughout that patient's lifetime.

The EU understands that a few hyperscalers hold a large part of the world's data and want to ensure it succeeds in the new data economy. In that regard, it started to enact regulation that would protect personal data, in 2014 with the **General Data Protection Regulation** (**GDPR**), as well as others such as the **free flow of non-personal data** (**FFD**) regulation, the **Cybersecurity Act** (**CSA**), and the **Open Data Directive**. The EU also pushed for sector-specific rules regarding data, for example, the **Payment Services Directive Two** (**PSD2**) in finance.

The EU is leveraging four legal instruments, which started in November 2020 with the **Data Governance Act** to enable trust in terms of sharing data. In December of the same year, the EU launched the **Digital Market Act** to regulate the gatekeepers and large companies that hold most of the world's data.

In 2022, there will be a follow-up to the Open Data Directive that will define a high-volume dataset and make it freely available through APIs. It will be machine-readable so that it can be accessed by AI algorithms.

The last instrument, which is the **data act** to be enacted during 2022, ensures fairness in the data by facilitating business-to-business and business-to-government sharing of data.

As you can see, the EU has been planning and executing regulations to make sure data follows a unified strategy and can position itself strategically for the next few decades.

Mapping dataflows

As we discussed previously, the European Strategy for Data has recognized the strategic value of data and asked for a strategic analytical framework. This has resulted in a data flow monitoring tool being developed that allows cloud data flows to be quantified, mapped, and analyzed per sector across 31 countries in Europe.

This tool, which is located at `https://digital-strategy.ec.europa.eu/en/policies/european-data-flow-monitoring`, provides some interesting data, as shown in the following screenshot:

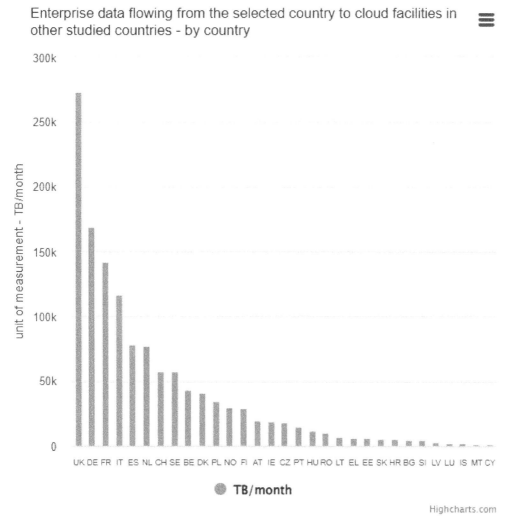

Figure 11.1 – Enterprise data flowing from countries to cloud facilities in another country

Using a projection for 2022, the UK ranks first in outflows at more than 250,000 TB/month. This is interesting, especially considering that the UK decided to pursue its own resilience and third-party risk regulations in financial organizations by saying that its *PS21/3* fulfills the **European banking authority's (EBA's)** requirements.

Nonetheless, you can select this sector in the visualization tool and check that the projections show the UK leading the data transfer effort with more than double the amount of exported data compared to its peers, followed by the big consumers of the cloud in the EU – that is, Germany and France.

Now, let's look at some of the regulations, groups, and guidelines that have been established by some regulators and countries.

Regulations

In this section, we will discuss some of the guidelines and regulations that cover the *A Europe fit for the digital age* program. We will focus on highly regulated industries with the DORA proposal and the *PS21/3* guideline.

NIS Directive

As part of the *A Europe fit for the digital age* program, the EU reviewed the NIS Directive as part of the cybersecurity strategy of the program. The reviewed directive is known as *NIS2*. NIS was proposed in 2016 as the first EU cybersecurity directive, with the goal being to improve cybersecurity across the member states, making sure three big themes were addressed:

- **Country Capabilities**: Requiring member states to have national cybersecurity capabilities, such as having a national **computer security incident response team (CSIRT)**, performing cyber exercises, and so on.

- **Collaborations Across Member States**: Creating information-sharing frameworks using the EU CSIRT network and defining cooperating groups.

- **Supervision of Critical Sectors**: EU members must supervise the cybersecurity of critical sectors, such as finance, energy, health, and more.

In summary, these themes provide cyber security capabilities that support how services operate and secure digital service providers. You can learn more about how each member state transposed the NIS Directive at `https://digital-strategy.ec.europa.eu/en/policies/nis-transposition`.

One of the issues with NIS was that its implementation was rather tricky and resulted in a non-harmonious implementation across the member states. *NIS2*, or the revised NIS, increases the scope to tackle supply chain issues by reporting obligations, more stringent supervisory measures, and penalties.

It also expands the coverage to 10 critical sectors – drinking water, public administration, health, wastewater, financial market infrastructures, digital infrastructure, banking, space, energy, and transport. The revised *NIS2* Directive is designed to improve cybersecurity in the EU and replace NIS.

The council approved the *NIS2* text in December 2021. This press release can be found at `https://www.consilium.europa.eu/en/press/press-releases/2021/12/03/strengthening-eu-wide-cybersecurity-and-resilience-council-agrees-its-position/`.

Besides this, the **Information Technology Industry Council (ITI)** also published a set of recommendations to help policymakers advance the *NIS2* trilogue, which can be consulted here: `https://www.itic.org/news-events/news-releases/iti-offers-recommendations-for-nis2-trilogue-negotiations`.

Since the parliament and council have reached their position on *NIS2*, the interinstitutional negotiations may begin. To adopt the *NIS2* directive, the parliament, council, and co-legislators (trilogue) will need to agree on the final text:

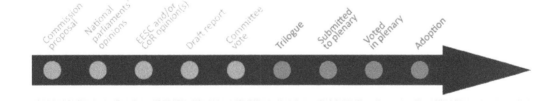

Figure 11.2 – NIS2 steps

One of the big pushes of this revised directive was harmonizing the requirements, reporting, and obligations across the member states, and *NIS2* will establish the baseline for risk across all sectors. Since sector-specific regulation should have precedence over *NIS2*, the response from Digital Europe was that the *NIS2* legislation should be promoted first.

For example, DORA, which we will discuss next, specifically for the finance sector, is factored into the *NIS2* proposal to guarantee its coherence as it helps prevent conflicts in the reporting structures.

DORA

The DORA is a proposal for regulatory bodies to address operational resilience in the EU financial sector. As we mentioned previously, *A Europe fit for the digital age* focuses on critical sectors such as banking; here, DORA is the sector-specific proposal.

Ever since the financial crisis in 2008, banks have made efforts to make sure risks are addressed, and there was enough liquidity to deal with an unforeseen event. The reality is that, since 2008, things have evolved, and financial organizations have relied on technology and ICT to modernize themselves. The challenge is that those same ICT systems, operating systems, and third-party service suppliers, such as CSPs, bring risk.

The **European Systemic Risk Board** (**ESRB**) has flagged cyber risk as a source of systemic risk to the European financial system due to the increase in cyberattacks, especially in the financial industry, which is 300 times more likely than other industries to be the target of cyberattacks.

Another source, the **International Monetary Fund** (**IMF**), has highlighted that cyber events can propagate risks through the entire financial system and cause systemic risks via three broad transmission channels: **risk concentration**, **risk contagion**, and **erosion of confidence**.

In the UK, regulators have flagged their concentration risk. The Bank of England highlighted the cloud as a concern in their stability reports in 2021, hence why the **Financial Conduct Authority** (**FCA**) launched its **PS21/3 - Building Operational Resilience** policy to address third-party risks from service and supply chain providers, as well as operational resilience, which the FCA highlighted as *the disruption caused by the coronavirus (COVID-19) pandemic, which has shown why it is critically important for firms to understand the services they provide and invest in their resilience.*

DORA goes a step beyond as you can see in the following sections:

- **ICT Governance and ICT Risk Management**: DORA uses a similar framework to **NIST CSF** and **Cyber Defense Matrix** as it groups the categories in terms of identification, protection and prevention, detection, response and recovery, learning and evolving, and communication.

- **ICT Incident Reporting**: While this will be harmonized with *NIS2*, the current proposal defines that financial organizations must submit initial, intermediate, and final reports and inform their users and clients where the incident has impacted or may impact their economic interests.

The current proposal states that the incident's details need to be communicated to the European supervisor authorities, the **European Central Bank** (**ECB**), and the point of contact defined under *NIS2*.

- **Digital Testing**: DORA will define digital operational resilience testing standards to ensure financial organizations are prepared for an incident. DORA goes beyond traditional testing and requires vulnerability assessments, open source analysis, network security assessments, penetration testing, and code reviews.

   DORA also recommends testing systems, tools, and processes via **threat-led penetration testing** (**TLPT**). The technical standards to support penetration testing haven't been defined at the time of writing, but the likelihood is that it will follow the **TIBER-EU** framework.

- **Information Sharing**: DORA encourages financial organizations to share threat intelligence and information within a community, much like the **Transaction Monitoring Netherlands** (**TMNL**) in the Netherlands for transaction monitoring.

- **Managing ICT Third-Party Risk**: With DORA, third-party providers will become subject to oversight to validate that they don't create operational risks. Guidelines on negotiating the contract will require locations where data is to be processed to be specified, full service-level descriptions accompanied by quantitative and qualitative performance targets, relevant provisions on accessibility, availability, integrity, security, and protecting personal data, and guarantees for access, recover, and return in case the ICT third-party service providers fail.

- **Tools and Processes to Impose Penalties and Remedial Measures**: Through a new harmonized legislative framework, DORA will ensure that the lead overseer for each critical ICT third-party service provider can impose penalties and that service providers such as CSPs are adequately monitored on a pan-European scale.

Programs such as **EU-HYBNET**, **ACCORDION**, **HORIZON2020**, and **DORA** will ensure Europe works as an entity by harmonizing the requirements to increase resilience, protect its citizens, and be digitally fit for the next decade.

Now that we've discussed a part of EU cybersecurity policy strategy, let's look at the capabilities of the CSPs to enforce coercive instruments.

CSP-specific

In the next few sections, we will discuss the different CSPs and the native capabilities they provide for someone to enforce coercive instruments. Here, we will talk about organizational policies and **Identity and Access Management** (**IAM**) policies. As we discussed in *Chapter 10*, *Policy as Code Tool Evaluation*, combining these two instruments creates effective policies.

Organizational policies

As we discussed briefly in *Chapter 10*, *Policy as Code Tool Evaluation*, organizational policies can be attached at the root level of the hierarchy. For example, in AWS, organizational policies can be enforced at the **organizational unit** (**OU**) level and the granularity on these policies is binary in that it allows or blocks access to a specific service.

For example, you would use organizational policies to restrict or constrain the usage of certain AI services due to data localization issues. In the following subsections, we will discuss each of the CSP organizational policy flavors.

IAM policies

IAM policies are more granular and apply to the resources of the cloud providers:

- **Cloud Accounts**: Cloud management consoles, billing consoles, and so on.
- **Cloud Services**: Databases, compute, storage, and networking services. These are the basis of any cloud provider.
- **Cloud Resources**: Files in either blob or block storage, virtual machines, containers in managed and unmanaged services, serverless infrastructure, and so on.

A good example of these can be seen in the following diagram:

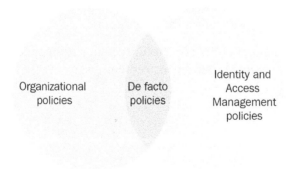

Figure 11.3 – De facto policies

To build these de facto policies in cloud environments, we can use a combination of IAM policies and organizational policies. The IAM policies would apply to users, groups, and roles in terms of what resources they can access, while the organizational policies would apply to accounts and what services they can offer.

AWS native policy offerings

Amazon Web Services (**AWS**) currently leads the cloud market and is also referred to as the 800-pound gorilla due to its plethora of services. In this section, we will discuss tools and services that allow to establish organizational policies in the AWS ecosystem.

Service control policies (SCPs)

SCPs are authorization policies that help create central control across the accounts in an organization. Think about establishing guardrails to make sure the accounts comply with the policies that have been applied. As we discussed in the previous section, SCPs on their own are not sufficient enough to grant permissions on the accounts. SCPs set the necessary limits and require an identity or resource policy to be attached to an IAM user, resource, or role.

Using AWS's words, you can see that it reflects what was shown in the preceding diagram:

"The effective permissions are the logical intersection between what is allowed by the SCP and what is allowed by the IAM and resource-based policies."

The basic premise of SCPs is that they can be configured either as a deny list that's allowed by default or as an allow list that's denied by default.

The example we looked at previously used an allow list, which meant that the other services were not denied. You can read more about SCPs here: `https://docs.aws.amazon.com/organizations/latest/userguide/orgs_manage_policies_scps.html`.

Organizational policies in AWS are known as AWS **Service Control Policies** (**SCPs**). They are applied to OUs, which is how AWS organizes its accounts:

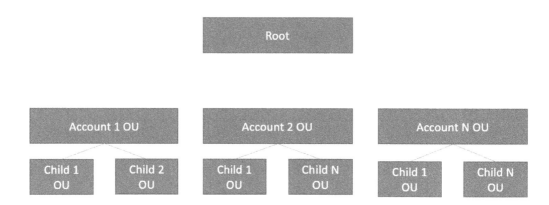

Figure 11.4 – AWS OUs

The preceding diagram shows an organization with different OUs. Here, SCPs would be applied to the account's OUs, and their children. Since there is inheritance, you could use policies at the parent level, and the child accounts would get them.

SCPs are very useful and can be used for different purposes, such as only allowing approved services, denying the creation of IAM access keys, establishing region enforcement, denying a VPC from being accessed from the internet, and so on. As we discussed in the previous chapter, the format is straightforward – for example, the following SCP would only allow lambda, EKS, and IAM services. Although this would not be useful as there are dependencies between the services, it highlights what you can achieve:

```
{
    "Version": "2012-10-17",
    "Statement": {
        "Sid": "AllowList",
        "Effect": "Allow",
        "Action": ["lambda:*","eks:*","iam:*"],
        "Resource": "*"
    }
}
```

Now, let's look at some of the services that AWS provides so that you can manage policies and have a governance plane of glass across all your accounts.

AWS Organizations

AWS Organizations is a service that allows someone to manage their accounts and apply policies from a central place in the AWS dashboard.

This allows you to create a single plane of policies that can be used to manually or programmatically add new accounts to the root account and ensure management policies are aligned across OUs and accounts.

AWS Organizations serves three key aspects:

- **Account Organization**: This provides a centralized place where you can manage your accounts, such as by nesting OUs or separate accounts. This is where you can associate your OUs with your billing account.

- **Policies**: This is a central place to establish policies. The policies that are supported in the AWS Organizations portal are opt out of AI services, implement backup policies, use SCPs, and tag enforcement. These basic policies are essential to improving an organization's resilience through the business continuity of the backups, SCPs to provide guardrails, and tag policies to offer accountability and identification.

- **Services**: In AWS Organizations, you can configure specific services to act as trusted services in your accounts on your behalf. This service would then use service-linked roles to perform actions on the accounts, making log alerts and auditing simpler. AWS Organizations contains four integrated services: access and permission, compliance and audit, resource management, and security.

These policies are known as management policies. Next, we will discuss authorization policies

AWS Policy Generator

At the time of writing, AWS has a tool called Policy Generator that can be used in a browser to generate policies on the fly. In the first few instances, the GUI asks about the type of policy since there's only a handful at the time of writing: **IAM Policy**, **S3 Bucket Policy**, **SNS Topic Policy**, **VPC Endpoint Policy**, and **SQS Queue Policy**:

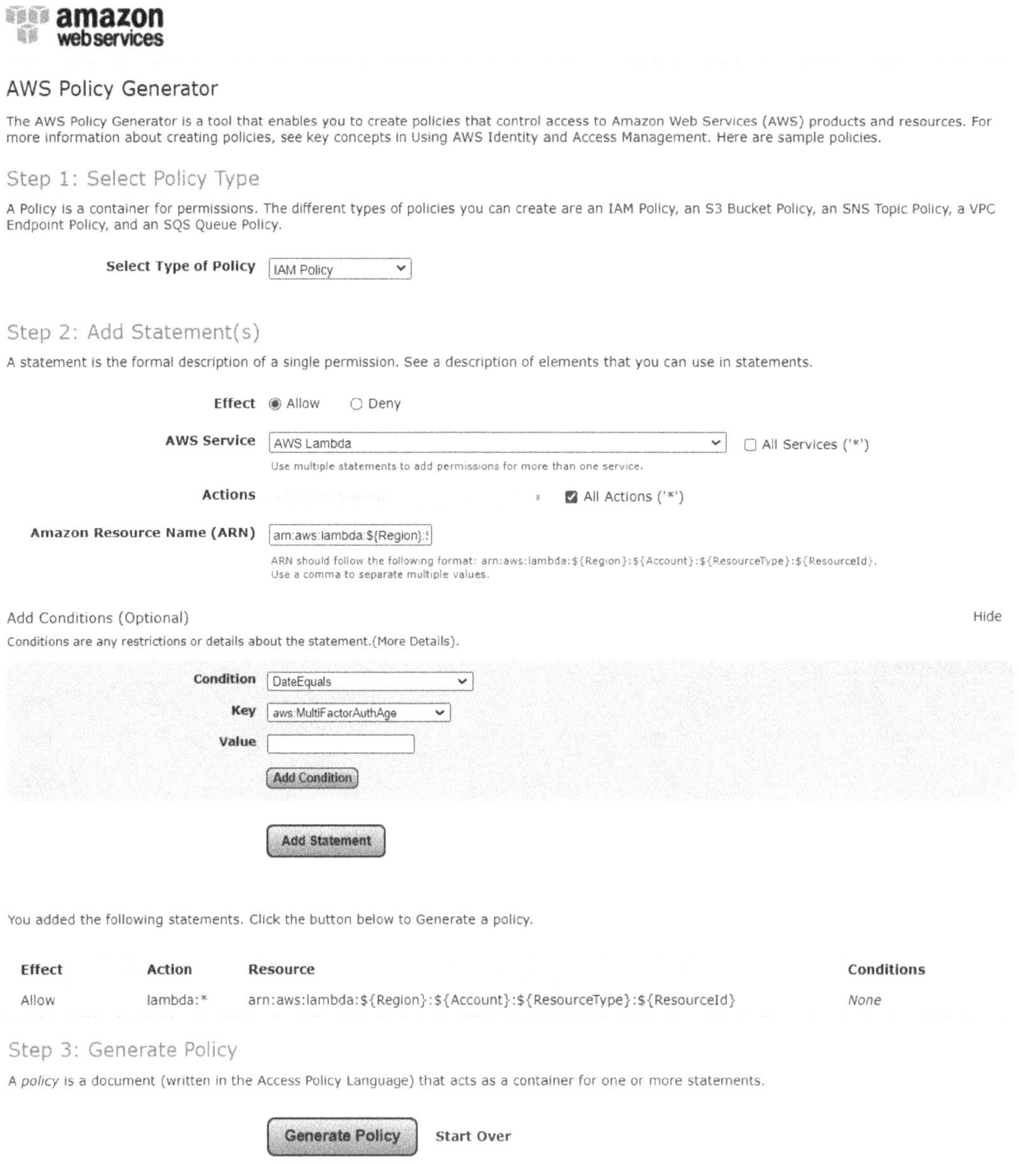

amazon
web services

AWS Policy Generator

The AWS Policy Generator is a tool that enables you to create policies that control access to Amazon Web Services (AWS) products and resources. For more information about creating policies, see key concepts in Using AWS Identity and Access Management. Here are sample policies.

Step 1: Select Policy Type

A Policy is a container for permissions. The different types of policies you can create are an IAM Policy, an S3 Bucket Policy, an SNS Topic Policy, a VPC Endpoint Policy, and an SQS Queue Policy.

Select Type of Policy   IAM Policy ⌄

Step 2: Add Statement(s)

A statement is the formal description of a single permission. See a description of elements that you can use in statements.

Effect   ◉ Allow   ○ Deny

AWS Service   AWS Lambda ⌄   ☐ All Services ('*')
Use multiple statements to add permissions for more than one service.

Actions   ☑ All Actions ('*')

Amazon Resource Name (ARN)   arn:aws:lambda:${Region}:$
ARN should follow the following format: arn:aws:lambda:${Region}:${Account}:${ResourceType}:${ResourceId}.
Use a comma to separate multiple values.

Add Conditions (Optional)   Hide
Conditions are any restrictions or details about the statement.(More Details).

Condition   DateEquals ⌄
Key   aws:MultiFactorAuthAge ⌄
Value   [   ]
[Add Condition]

[Add Statement]

You added the following statements. Click the button below to Generate a policy.

Effect	Action	Resource	Conditions
Allow	lambda:*	arn:aws:lambda:${Region}:${Account}:${ResourceType}:${ResourceId}	None

Step 3: Generate Policy

A *policy* is a document (written in the Access Policy Language) that acts as a container for one or more statements.

[Generate Policy]   Start Over

Figure 11.5 – AWS GUI for policy generation

Next, you must select the services and actions that have been permitted or denied. You can add conditionals such as time, making the policy only applicable after a specific date. Finally, you can press the **Generate Policy** button to generate the policy, which will produce the following JSON code:

Policy JSON Document   ✖

Click below to edit. To save the policy, copy the text below to a text editor.
Changes made below will **not be reflected in the policy generator tool.**

```
{
  "Version": "2012-10-17",
  "Statement": [
    {
      "Sid": "Stmt1645136177361",
      "Action": "lambda:*",
      "Effect": "Allow",
      "Resource": "arn:aws:lambda:${Region}:${Account}:${ResourceType}:${ResourceId}"
    }
  ]
}
```

This AWS Policy Generator is provided for informational purposes only, you are still responsible for your use of Amazon Web Services technologies and ensuring that your use is in compliance with all applicable terms and conditions. This AWS Policy Generator is provided as is without warranty of any kind, whether express, implied, or statutory. This AWS Policy Generator does not modify the applicable terms and conditions governing your use of Amazon Web Services technologies.

Figure 11.6 – Policy JSON Document

The JSON can then be applied programmatically or manually to the desired SCP.

You can find AWS Policy Generator at `https://awspolicygen.s3.amazonaws.com/policygen.html`.

AWS Control Tower

When organizations are migrating a project and establishing new target operating models for the cloud environments such as governance, security, and account management, is important to use best practices and have policies in place.

AWS Control Tower simplifies this process by providing an onboarding setup that's built on top of AWS organizations. This is called a **landing zone** and incorporates the best practices around account segregation and creation, such as a separate security account being responsible for log archiving and Auditing.

A good use case for Control Tower is the ability to prohibit access to AWS services based on a region by marking it **non-governed**. Useful for compliance with specific regulations requiring more strict data localization rules.

AWS Security Hub

One of the significant advantages of using Control Tower is that security and compliance can be accessed from the AWS Security Hub, allowing automation of security checks but also integration with key AWS services, such as the following:

- **Amazon GuardDuty**: This scans your AWS accounts looking for malicious activity.

- **Amazon Inspector**: This searches for vulnerabilities in your AWS environment resources.

- **Amazon Macie**: This leverages machine learning to discover and protect sensitive data in AWS environments.

This makes the usage of AWS Security Hub an effective service to integrate with Control Tower. A post that discusses the automation capabilities of these two services can be found here: `https://aws.amazon.com/blogs/mt/automating-aws-security-hub-alerts-with-aws-control-tower-lifecycle-events/`.

AWS Blueprints

AWS Blueprints leverages Control Tower or AWS organizations to be able to deploy a portfolio of applications and AWS services that were tested and validated.

These blueprints allow a small organization to get started quickly by leveraging pre-packaged portfolios to deploy them automatically. The following GitHub link provides an example and high-level architecture: `https://github.com/awslabs/aws-blueprints`.

AWS Systems Manager

Because most deployments in large organizations will have a legacy component, AWS Systems Manager allows the effective management of hybrid resources. Resources in AWS, but also in other Cloud or premises environments.

It provides resource grouping capabilities and automation to patch and manage servers and applications from a single plane.

AWS Systems Manager is handy during the process of workload migration. It allow you to manage both on-premises and cloud resources during migration, aggregate resources per project or workload, and run commands in different groups of servers.

An AWS blog post that discusses the usage of **CloudEndure** and the role that AWS Systems Manager can play can be found here: `https://aws.amazon.com/blogs/mt/how-to-take-advantage-of-aws-control-tower-and-cloudendure-to-migrate-workloads-to-aws/`.

Now that we have discussed some of the most important AWS services for managing policies and creating adequate guardrails, let's look at the Azure offering.

Azure native policy offerings

Azure has evolved quite a bit over the few last years regarding governance and policies, with some services that differ across cloud providers. In this section, we will discuss the services that Azure provides to its users for governance and policy management purposes.

Azure management groups

In Azure, an account unit is called a subscription, and you can put different subscriptions into containers called **management groups**. Similar to AWS OUs, these management groups can have policies, and the principle of inheritance applies to their child resource, which is either a subscription or a management group:

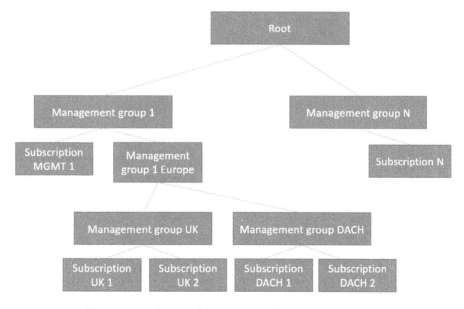

Figure 11.7 – Azure subscriptions and management groups

These management groups allow someone to apply policies with Azure Policy, as discussed in the next section, or Azure **role-based access control** (**RBAC**).

Azure Policy

One of the main differences compared to other CSPs is that Azure Policy allows you to assess compliance at scale from a centralized point. It also comes with a built-in dashboard to help you visualize the overall state of the environment and query individual resources.

The dashboard is straightforward but flexible as policies can be imported from JSON code.

Similar to AWS, in Microsoft's own words, *"The combination of Azure RBAC and Azure Policy provides full-scope control in Azure."*

Let's look at the **Azure Policy** blade:

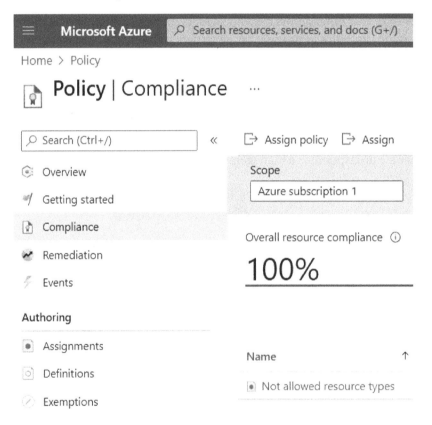

Figure 11.8 – The Azure Policy blade

As you can see, on the left-hand side, there's the **Compliance** menu, where you can assign policies and initiatives. Initiatives are a group of policies. For example, if you are trying to implement *NIST 800-53*, you could search for that specific initiative. Many preconfigured initiatives are available, such as CIS, CSP, UK OFFICIAL, PCI, HIPAA, and more.

The **Remediation** menu allows you to address non-compliant resources. For example, imagine that, at a certain point, you will need to be compliant with a specific policy. You can use remediation to review resources, subscriptions, and management groups. You can also create tasks that enable logs in virtual machines or delete unencrypted disks to make sure you will be back in a compliant state, as defined by the policy.

The **Policy** event menu allows us to subscribe to state changes in resources. For example, if we want to monitor a resource group and have it alert us when a specific change occurs, it will do that with a serverless function.

After that, we have the main **Authoring** menu, which contains the assignments. We can assign policies and initiatives and see how many have been assigned to the specific scopes.

The **Definitions** menu allows you to customize how policies and initiatives are created since you can create them from scratch using JSON or by reusing JSON constructs from the Azure Policy's GitHub repository, which can be found at `https://github.com/Azure/azure-policy`.

Finally, we have the **Exemptions** menu, where you can exempt either a resource or a management group from the policies or initiatives. This item only shows the current exemptions as they are made when you apply a policy in the **Assign Policy** menu.

As an example, I wanted to create a policy to prevent anyone from making a resource – in this case, a virtual machine.

I can go to **Assign Policy** in the **Compliance** or **Assignments** menu and choose **Assign Policy**. Once you've selected the policy definition based on **Not allowed resource type**, select the list of resources. For example, if you choose **microsoft.compute**, you will see the following screen:

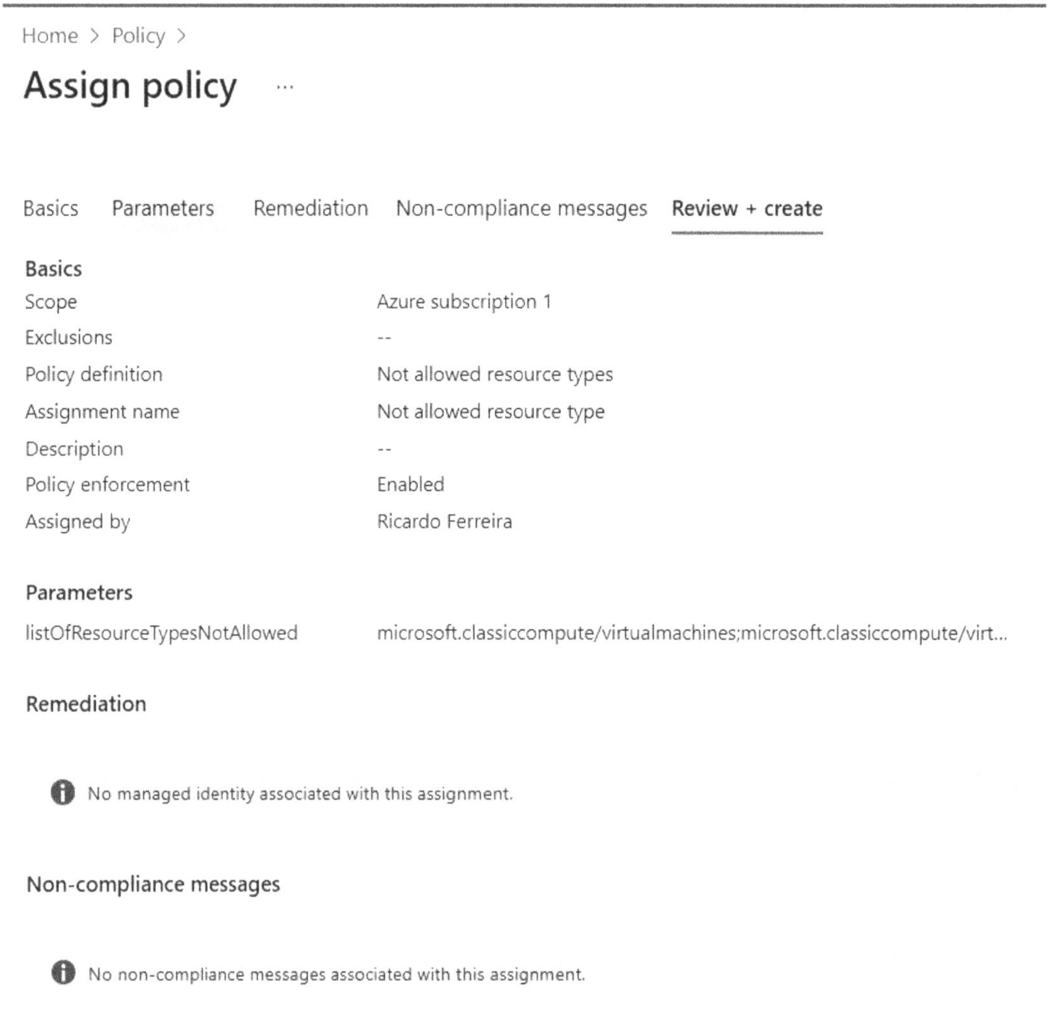

Home > Policy >

Assign policy   ...

| Basics | Parameters | Remediation | Non-compliance messages | **Review + create** |

Basics

Scope	Azure subscription 1
Exclusions	--
Policy definition	Not allowed resource types
Assignment name	Not allowed resource type
Description	--
Policy enforcement	Enabled
Assigned by	Ricardo Ferreira

Parameters

listOfResourceTypesNotAllowed	microsoft.classiccompute/virtualmachines;microsoft.classiccompute/virt...

Remediation

ⓘ No managed identity associated with this assignment.

Non-compliance messages

ⓘ No non-compliance messages associated with this assignment.

Figure 11.9 – Assign policy – Review + create

Once the policy has been enabled and we've validated that its compliance state has a green tick next to it, we are good to go, as shown in the following screenshot:

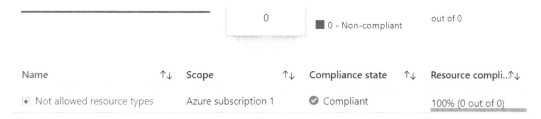

Figure 11.10 – Azure Policy compliance dashboard

Now, it's time to test that it works. If we try to create a virtual machine, we will get the following error, which tells us that the deployment failed due to a policy violation:

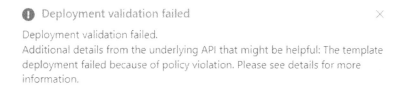

Figure 11.11 – Policy violation deployment warning

As you can see, Azure Policy is quite powerful and a clear differentiator from other CSPs as it contains everything you will need to perform policy and initiative assignments, manage them, and, if required, extend them through custom JSON code.

We also get an integrated remediation menu, which brings value as most environments will enable a specific policy after the resources have been created, which means they need to be reviewed and tracked to be remediated.

Azure Blueprints

While this service is in preview, it is quite helpful. **Azure Blueprints** allows artifacts such as policies, role assignments, and Azure Resource Manager templates to be combined into bundles that can then be repeated across multiple subscriptions. Since we are only focusing on one policy, we will use a simple policy example. However, the usefulness of Blueprints comes from being able to combine different artifacts into a single bundle.

For example, let's say that I want all the subscriptions in a specific management group that contain Europe as a region to have a policy that restricts the creation of AI-enabled services. Here, Azure Blueprints would allow me to create that particular guardrail, apply it to a scope, and track and manage its deployment.

Let's look at a simple example where we will use an existing blueprint to assign policies to the NIST 800-171 address.

Let's start by creating a blueprint and searching for NIST:

Home > Blueprints >

Create blueprint   ...

Choose a blueprint sample

You can start with a blank blueprint or pick one of our pre-defined samples to help you get started quickly

Blank Blueprint

An empty blueprint with no initial properties or artifacts.

Start with blank blueprint

Other Samples

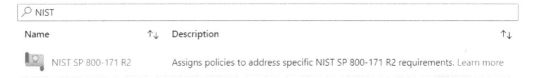

🔎 NIST

Name	↑↓	Description	↑↓
🏴 NIST SP 800-171 R2		Assigns policies to address specific NIST SP 800-171 R2 requirements. Learn more	

Figure 11.12 – Creating the NIST 800-171 blueprint

Then, we must select some artifacts. In this case, they are based on NIST SP 800-171 and deal with things such as the version of a specific programming language, the version of TLS for Windows servers, the log workspace's ID, which will collect all the information from the virtual machines, and so on:

Figure 11.13 – A list of parameters for the NIST 800-171 artifact

Once we've saved the policy, it's time to publish it and have a versioning number to roll back and upgrade.

Now that the blueprint is ready to be assigned to a subscription, we can select its location and lock assignment:

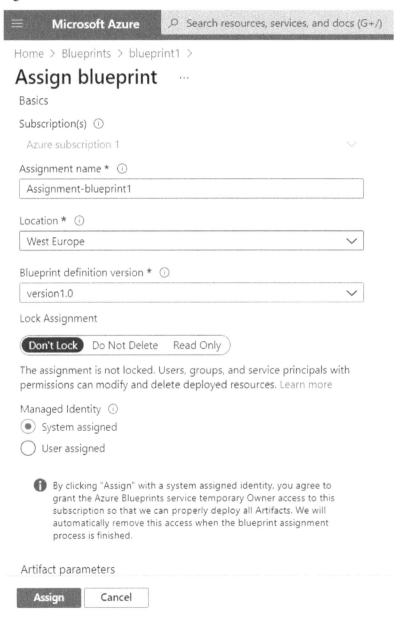

Figure 11.14 – Applying a blueprint to a subscription

The most important aspect of this process is the lock assignment aspect, where you can choose from three types:

- **Don't lock**: This allows users and groups to modify the deployed resources. Here, the blueprint is not being enforced.

- **Do not delete**: This allows resources to be altered but not deleted.

- **Read-only**: Here, the deployed resources cannot be changed or deleted, even by the subscription owner.

Blueprints allow us to gain consistency and standardization when managing an organization in Microsoft Azure as subscriptions and accounts will follow the established governance policy rules. Regarding policies, Azure provides a simple dashboard that integrates the governance of the cloud environment. In contrast, other CSPs may have more capabilities and flexible tools. Still, in the end, I believe that UX is almost as important as good service or instrumentation.

Google Cloud native policy offerings

Google Cloud is one of the major cloud providers and despite being late to the cloud game, it has grown a lot in the last few years. Google Cloud has similar concepts to AWS and Azure regarding policies, organizational policies, and IAM policies.

In this section, we will learn how Google uses policy services and how we can use them.

Organizational policies

Similar to AWS, Google Cloud uses projects as the basic units of an account. Projects can be part of a folder, folders can be nested, and the root account is called an organizational node. The following diagram depicts this hierarchy:

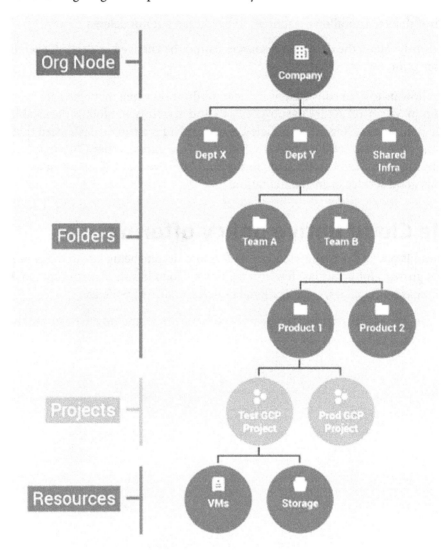

Figure 11.15 – Google Cloud hierarchy

This layout provides flexibility when you're planning to apply policies. In Google Cloud, the policies in the organization are called **organization policies**, and compared to the other providers, there is no dashboard. This layout can be seen in the following screenshot:

Figure 11.16 – Google Cloud organization policies

On the left-hand side, we can see a very comprehensive list of policies, which Google Cloud calls constraints. Constraints can be used to enforce resource configurations, limit feature access, or even modify the default behavior of Google Cloud. The entire list, can be found here: `https://cloud.google.com/resource-manager/docs/organization-policy/org-policy-constraints`.

They work very similarly to AWS SCPs with one key difference – propagating policies down the hierarchy. Google Cloud `allow` type rules apply merges. In AWS, intersections are used instead.

The `allow` type rules in AWS can be argued to be safer as you can be sure that `allow` rules never expand as they go down the hierarchy. In Google Cloud, there is the option to disable inheritance by setting `inheritFromParent` set to `FALSE`. In that case, the organization policy will not propagate.

All of these policies can also be used from an **Infrastructure as Code (IaC)** perspective, as you can see in the Terraform module documentation: `https://registry.terraform.io/providers/hashicorp/google/latest/docs/resources/google_organization_policy`

Suppose you want to see a real-world example that highlights how to set up a Google Cloud foundation using security best practices in Terraform. In that case, you can take a look at the following Github repo: `https://github.com/terraform-google-modules/terraform-example-foundation/tree/da6f860e6b9bb0b11d442458c5eaa900e4a87781/1-org`

Its structure is divided into different parts, as you can see in the following image:

Figure 11.17 – Google Cloud terraform foundation example

The previous link highlights the organizational aspect, but if you want to learn more about the constraints and how to use them in Terraform, then the following folder in the same GitHub repo contains policies in YAML that can also be used in Kubernetes by Open Policy Agent: `https://github.com/terraform-google-modules/terraform-example-foundation/tree/master/policy-library/policies`

The same Google Cloud Foundation can be built using Google Cloud UI instead of Terraform, as shown in the next section.

Google Cloud Foundation

Google Cloud Foundation works similarly to Azure Blueprints and AWS Control Tower. It creates an organizational structure so that you can manage your organization. Once this has been established, we can apply the policies across the entire organization.

To use this feature, you must have an organization. The setup phase covers many aspects such as users, administrative access, billing, defining the hierarchy, networks, monitoring, and security, as shown in the **Set up your foundation** blade:

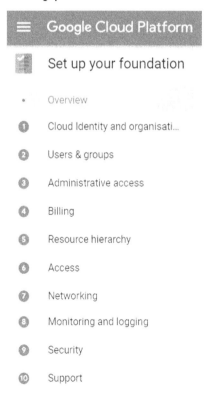

Figure 11.18 – The set up your foundation UI blade

Next, let's talk about a service that is particular to Google Cloud – Policy Analyzer.

Policy Analyzer

Policy Analyzer uses **Google Cloud BigQuery** to determine which identities, users, groups, domains, and service accounts have access to specific Google Cloud resources.

As in any cloud environment, questions such as who can access service X, who can access this file at a specific time and date, or who has permission to impersonate service accounts in my organization are very common security and compliance questions.

These questions, as well as many more, can be created in Google Cloud Policy Analyzer, which is simple to use.

The following screenshot shows the service's main page, which contains some templates. You can also create a custom query here:

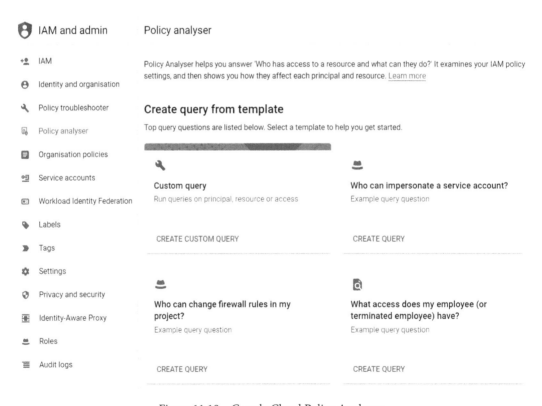

Figure 11.19 – Google Cloud Policy Analyzer

Let's say that we select the first option, **Custom query**, and select the scope of the query. In this example, we will select the **axiomatic-137** project. Next, we need to define the query parameters. In this case, I want to find its owner, so I will choose the resource and add another parameter to choose the role:

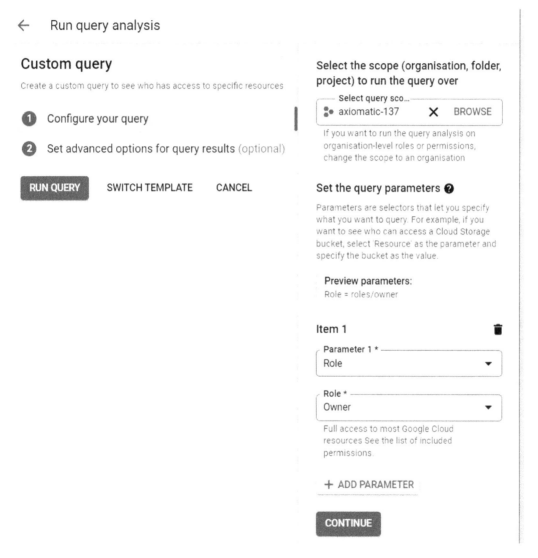

Figure 11.20 – Google Cloud Policy Analyzer – the Run query analysis screen

Once all the parameters have been filled in, we can run the query. This will show some results. At the top, we will see the query URL:

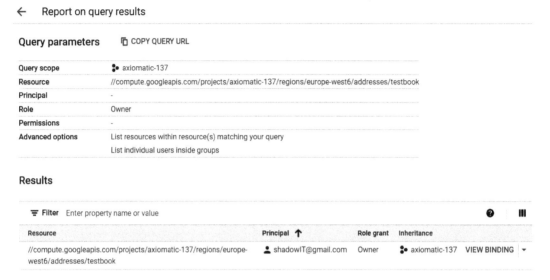

Figure 11.21 – Google Cloud Policy Analyzer – the Report on query results screen

As you can see, Google Cloud shines in terms of how they build and integrate services with their products – in this case, BigQuery. While Google Cloud is not as mature as Azure in this regard, it has other capabilities, such as **Policy Linter**, which find semantic errors, any use of legacy types, or ineffective conditions.

Policy Linter can be used either through the portal, the command line, or via the REST API:

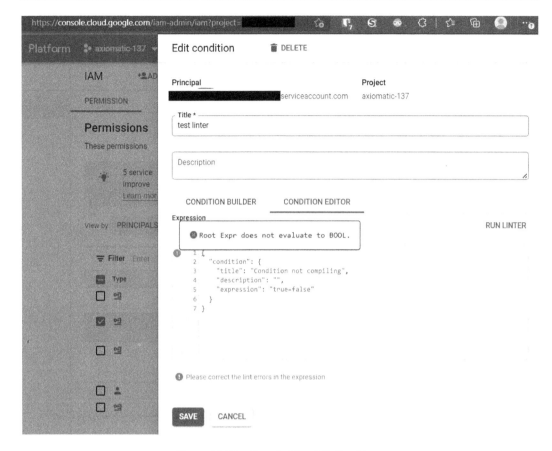

Figure 11.22 – Google Cloud Policy Linter

The other interesting feature is **Policy Simulator**, which lets you see how an IAM policy change could be impacted and use the simulator to ensure there won't be any disruptions.

Summary

In this chapter, we discussed the digital policies that the EU is using and how it uses regulations to advance its digital agenda. Most of the regulations directly target cloud providers as they hold much of the EU's enterprise data. The fact that the EU created a framework and tool to highlight how much data flows out of the originating countries shows us how much these hyperscalers threaten the sovereignty of EU data.

In the next chapter, we will learn how to integrate with existing workflows while focusing on the process side of things. Here, we'll learn how to integrate the Policy as Code toolset with workflows such as Jenkins and ServiceNow, as well as how to build guardrails within these workflows.

12
Integrating Policy as Code with Enterprise Workflows

When trying to leverage **Policy as Code** across organizations, we need to integrate automation, tools, and platforms with existing processes to achieve cohesion, generating value bigger than the sum of its parts.

One way that governance and management of IT are done is by using frameworks such as **Information Technology Infrastructure Library** (**ITIL**) or **Control Objectives for Information and Related Technologies** (**COBIT**). We will introduce these frameworks and how we can leverage software to enforce the framework governance structure. These IT service management tools are widespread in enterprises. We will cover them here and integrate them with our **Policy Engines** (**PEs**).

Finally, we will cover **Continuous Integration and Continuous Delivery** (**CI/CD**), some of the most popular tools, such as **Jenkins**, **Spinnaker**, and **GitHub Actions**, and we will highlight an example of testing our policies in an automated pipeline using GitHub Actions.

Finally, we will cover an architecture to highlight integrating these systems for a PolicyOps function.

In this chapter, we'll cover the following topics:

- Integration with existing enterprise workflow software
- Policy as Code automated life cycle
- Designing for automated policy enforcement across the enterprise

Technical requirements

A basic understanding of IT service management enterprise frameworks such as ITIL will be required to follow along with the chapter.

Integration with existing enterprise workflow software

As we have seen up until now, having policies implemented in an organization requires technology that is integrated, automated, and capable of being orchestrated. This is due to the organizational context as organizations adopt best-of-breed solutions, leaving them with many loose products and platforms, requiring platforms that can be integrated into these best-of-breed but loose solutions.

Since policies and their tools and frameworks should be horizontal, we need to make sure integration is vital. This section will discuss the significant enterprise workflow technologies and detail how we could integrate **Open Policy Agent** (**OPA**) or any **Policy Engine** (**PE**) within the organizational workflow.

Most of the tools we will discuss in this section are **IT Service Management** (**ITSM**), which deals with the processes regarding design, implementation, and operation of IT services.

These ITSM systems overlap with some of the most common ITSM frameworks, which some of you might be familiar with, such as ITIL, COBIT, and ISO.

Enterprise frameworks

Most organizations will want to have a standard to align themselves and ensure the proper processes are in place. From my experience, **The Open Group Architecture Framework** (**TOGAF**), ITIL, COBIT, or some variation thereof are used throughout the most prominent companies. While some of these frameworks clash with the rapid development of software and the agile manifesto, they have been updating their models to adapt to DevOps and the requirement of agility.

ITIL

ITIL is a framework that guides organizations regarding service management. In its latest iteration, **ITILv4** defines four dimensions of service management, representing the different perspectives required to create products and services with value to customers. The four dimensions are as follows:

- **Organizations and people**: ITIL in this dimension is concerned about making an organizational culture that will create value. People in this dimension go beyond the workforce. It encompasses customers, suppliers, or any other stakeholders.

  Reskilling, upskilling, and training all are part of this dimension. The purpose is also for the workforce to understand the core business and how their role drives value.

  Roles, responsibilities, organizational structure, and competencies are all related to the organizational value.

- **Information and technology**: This dimension is the one that is concerned with the tools, communication systems, inventory systems, and management systems such as the ones we will be talking about in this section.

  Some of these tools and services may include artificial intelligence, low-code platforms, and cloud platforms. This dimension cares about how these services will be managed, what information and processes need to be delivered to facilitate the management of these services, and how the information in these systems is protected, managed, and disposed of.

  Ensure that information systems are compliant with specific regulations and the data passing through those systems in regulated industries.

  As we have addressed throughout this book, people and their culture are an integral part of IT behavior. Some organizations will be more resistant to change than others. Some will adopt disruptive technologies.

- **Partners and suppliers**: The 2020 pandemic has shown us all that supply chains are integral to any business and can cause a massive impact worldwide when disrupted. The partners and suppliers dimension focuses on the contract between organizations to supply goods, deliver a service, or a service partnership; for example, providing teleconference hardware and software, providing cloud computing platforms and services, and finally, providing workforce training.

The factors that influence the choice of these suppliers are dealt with in this dimension and can be, for example, a strategic focus where the company decides whether it should outsource non-core competencies. Cost concerns will involve making choices based on pricing. Subject matter experts use partners to help in areas where the organization does not possess the know-how.

- **Value streams and processes**: The last dimension in ITIL focuses on the activities, procedures, policies, and workflows required to achieve a specific objective. The definition of *value stream* from ITIL is as follows: *A series of steps an organization undertakes to create and deliver products and services to consumers.*

COBIT

As we highlighted in this chapter, having frameworks to establish governance and the management of IT is essential. COBIT is another framework that helps establish the management and governance of information systems.

The top five principles in COBIT are designed to achieve the following:

- **Meeting stakeholders' needs**: Since stakeholders are influenced by many factors, either internal or external, this principle tries to understand the needs of stakeholders, and COBIT maps their needs into different types of goals, such as enterprise- and IT-related goals.

- **Covering the enterprise end to end**: COBIT understands that enterprises are complex. Thus, it tries to cover the entirety of the governance layer, such as the governance objective, governance scope, and governance enabler.

- **Applying a single integrated framework**: COBIT integrates the **Information Systems Audit and Control Association (ISACA)** with other governance frameworks to act as a single consistent overlay that is agnostic and technology-independent.

- **Enabling a holistic approach**: COBIT achieves this by using the enablers. The enablers represent people, processes, culture, services, information, and structures. COBIT understands that these enablers are interconnected and can only work as input or output to another. You can read more on the COBIT enablers here: `https://www.isaca.org/resources/news-and-trends/industry-news/2015/cobit-5-principles-and-enablers-applied-to-strategic-planning`.

- **Spearing governance from management**: The final principle discusses the need to separate governance from management. COBIT differentiates by assigning governance at the board level and the management of day-to-day activities performed by executive management.

The need for these frameworks is to establish processes and governance within the organization. So now, let's look at ITSM tools that enable us to develop those guidelines. This is important because to apply the policies at the organization level, we need to make sure we integrate with the tools described here.

Vendor ITSM

This section will discuss the most popular ITSM tools and how to integrate with them. Their integration can be from a technical perspective, for example, using a REST API or Webhook, or more processes oriented to achieve a policy goal.

ServiceNow

ServiceNow is a **Software as a Service** (**SaaS**) ITSM platform that provides support to business processes. It is advantageous when trying to implement some of the governance and management best practices from the frameworks discussed in the previous section as well as any other process such as our policies.

ServiceNow can be a tremendous tool for implementing processes. Let's look at some examples.

ServiceNow integration points

ServiceNow supports integrations through their native store, which has a lot of partners such as Microsoft Azure in the DevOps class. Still, it also has a lot of other classes, such as policy and compliance management, risk management, and the traditional IT business, IT operations, and IT service management.

ServiceNow provides a REST API that enables us to interact with it. You can use the API to retrieve different information, such as account information, data from **Advanced Work Assignment** (**AWA**) work items, and import data from tables.

An interesting API that we can integrate with our PEs is the DevOps API. You can check orchestration tasks, create callbacks, search commits, and repositories. This capability allows us to understand the development cycle risk assessment, impact, unit test coverage, security test passed, and integrate with our PE. More information on the ServiceNow DevOps API can be found here: `https://docs.servicenow.com/bundle/rome-application-development/page/integrate/inbound-rest/concept/devops-api.html#devops-api`.

Another useful API is the CI/CD API. While not as flexible as the DevOps API, it can integrate with the most common CI/CD systems, such as Jenkins, GitHub Actions, and GitLab. More information can be found here: `https://docs.servicenow.com/bundle/rome-application-development/page/integrate/inbound-rest/concept/cicd-api.html#cicd-api`.

These two APIs allow us to build some exciting workflows. For example, if the risk assessment of the code is flagged up, ServiceNow can instruct a PE such as OPA to deny authorization to that specific microservice that has a categorization of high risk, and establish the proper workflow to alert the security team and the SOC that a component with an increased risk is in production.

From an IT management perspective, ServiceNow can integrate different data types to provide organizational context for the PE decision.

JIRA Service Management

While ServiceNow was more ITIL-oriented, JIRA has been providing **JIRA Service Desk**. In 2020, Atlassian decided to go the extra mile with ITSM and **launched JIRA Service Management**. JIRA Service Management is a tool for IT support and customer service operations. JIRA Service Management's new capabilities integrate incident management, change management, and better integration with the Atlassian ecosystem.

JIRA integration points

JIRA, just as ServiceNow, also has a very mature REST API that can be used for our integration purposes. You can read more here: `https://developer.atlassian.com/cloud/jira/platform/rest/v3/intro/#about`.

These ITSM tools are essential as they allow the following:

- **Collaboration**: DevOps, PolicyOps, and other collaboration frameworks require deep integration between the different team workflows, such as to request, incident, problem, change, and configuration management. ITSM tools can abstract the workflows between those teams and serve as an overlay glue for the organization.

- **Risk management**: Depending on the type of industry, and especially on highly regulated verticals, a change advisory board requires a review of the risks associated with deploying to production. Traditionally, IT teams must submit documentation, compliance testing, security risks, and dependencies. Having an ITSM automate the change approval of our PE rules or policies is vital for enabling PolicyOps teams to become agile.

- **Prioritization**: Having a centralized repository of tickets detailing issues from users, teams, and so on allows responsible teams to prioritize the problems that are having the most significant impact. This is especially useful for triage issues from our PE or for detecting when rule changes impact a service.

Now, let's look at how we can create an integrated Policy as Code life cycle resorting to CI/CD pipelines.

Policy as Code automated life cycle

To increase the speed of adoption and the release speed of the policy rules, using the same toolset and frameworks of DevSecOps can be a good thing as it goes hand in hand with the mantra *Eat your own dog food*.

To build pipelines that can validate and deploy our rulesets, we can resort to CI/CD. These tools integrate the current **software development life cycle** (**SDLC**) but with broader organization through ITSM, as we saw in the previous section.

In this section, we will discuss some of the tools and concepts we might use to achieve automated life cycle management for the policies-as-code

CI/CD

If you have been in the agile field for a while, you must have come across *Martin Fowler*. Martin has a good definition for CI, which is:

> *"A software development practice where members of a team integrate*
> *their work frequently, usually each person integrates at least daily,*
> *leading to multiple integrations per day. Each integration is verified by an*
> *automated build (including test) to detect integration errors as quickly as*
> *possible. Many teams find that this approach leads to significantly reduced*
> *integration problems and allows a team to develop cohesive software*
> *more rapidly."*

As we saw in *Chapter 7, Building a Culture of PolicyOps*, for any organization that uses DevOps, one of the key tenants is automation. To start building an automated CI system, **source code management** (**SCM**) needs to be used as a **single source of truth** (**SSOT**) throughout the organization. All the team commits the changes to this SSOT, database configurations, scripts, policies, and so on.

An automated process is used to build the artifacts and check for issues. For example, in OPA policies, we might use **Conftest** to test whether the policies are valid before deploying them to production.

As we discussed throughout the book, it's more than just tech; even a CI system needs to be integrated to alert and provide notification of broken builds. The previous section allows us to integrate with ITSM systems to make sure we get a risk ranking on each build, along with a centralized ticketing system in case there are issues so they can be fixed as soon as possible.

In CI/CD, there is also the elevator pattern. Once the artifact is built, it gets tested in a QA environment before being promoted to production. Nowadays, testing should also be done directly in production with a canary release to catch issues. This is only possible in an organization with substantial CI maturity and rollback capabilities

There is also CD for completeness, but because CI activities are interlinked with CD, we usually refer to CI as CI/CD.

CD is about the processes and tools that deploy the artifacts built by CI systems, hence the reason why CD is a natural extension of CI. You want to deploy the artifacts somewhere; that's why they were made in the first place.

You can see a visual representation of the process here:

Figure 12.1 – CI/CD pipeline

The preceding diagram highlights the pipeline. It shows how we can test our artifacts when they are being built. Now, I would like to cover some of the most popular tools to do CI/CD.

Jenkins

Jenkins is one of the most popular CI/CD tools on the market. It can run in multiple operating systems, has an easy configuration through a simple and modernized GUI, and it has a massive amount of plugins. All these factors make it one of the most successful CI/CD systems. Jenkins can automate the pipeline described in *Figure 12.1* from starting to build the artifacts to deployment. The extensibility nature of Jenkins allows it to integrate with the majority of IT tools and IT systems.

You can learn more about Jenkins at the following URL: `https://www.jenkins.io/doc/book/pipeline/`.

Spinnaker

Spinnaker is a cloud native continuous delivery tool focused on CD. While Jenkins can support the CI and CD requirements, it does not have advanced features for CD. One of the most common patterns is that organizations choose Jenkins to build the artifact, the integration part (CI). Then they use Spinnaker to deliver the artifacts, which is the delivery process (CD).

Spinnaker, by itself, does not support the building of any artifacts. Its strength lies in integrating with cloud environments and the ability to execute release management. For example, the canary release of Spinnaker allows you to partially roll out a change and evaluate it against the existing deployment to assess its stability, performance, and risk.

In the following diagram, we can see a high-level representation of how Spinnaker can be used to push policies into OPA to support dynamic authorization, a compliance requirement, or any other policy need:

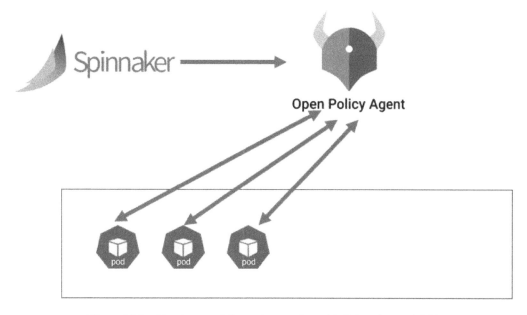

Figure 12.2 – Continuous delivery integration with Spinnaker and OPA

Armory, an organization that specializes in CD, has a blog post where they talk about deploying policies using Spinnaker. You can read more here: `https://www.armory.io/blog/deployment-policies-with-spinnaker/`.

The blog post talks about some possible use cases using CD and OPA, such as conforming to best practices, validating IaC, blacklisting (accounts, services, and resources), and enforcing compliance standards (ISO27002, PCI, and CSA).

GitHub Actions

GitHub, which is the most used SCM globally, has GitHub Actions that enable the creation of a build, test, and deployment pipeline. The most powerful feature is that it can integrate nicely with events on the repository, such as building every time there is a pull request or deploying stable branches to production. Owing to the deep integration with GitHub, GitHub Actions can create workflows on any event such as issues, labels, pull requests, and reviews. GitHub Actions also provides all flavors of virtual machines to run the workflows.

You can read more on GitHub Actions here: `https://docs.github.com/en/actions`.

Now that we have covered some of the tools you can use for your CI/CD purposes, let's look at how you can test your policies in a CI/CD pipeline.

Policy testing

As seen in the previous section, testing is essential for building our artifacts. In this section, we will learn how to do policy tests against OPA Rego files during the build.

We will create a GitHub action and test our OPA policies for this example. We will be using a container, and most of the information can be found on the GitHub documentation here: `https://docs.github.com/en/actions/creating-actions/creating-a-docker-container-action`.

So first, we need our repository. Once we have that, we create our Dockerfile in the repository root as follows:

```
FROM ubuntu:latest
RUN apt-get update && apt-get install -y curl
RUN curl -L -o /opa https://openpolicyagent.org/downloads/latest/opa_linux_amd64
RUN chmod +x /opa
RUN /opa version
COPY entrypoint.sh /
RUN chmod +x /entrypoint.sh
ENTRYPOINT ["/entrypoint.sh"]
```

These instructions are similar to what we have seen in *Chapter 9, A Primer on Open Policy Agent*. At this stage, we are just building our container with the OPA binary.

As you can see, we will also need an entry point Bash file, the `entrypoint.sh` file in the repository root where the OPA commands are constructed, as you can see here:

```bash
#!/bin/bash
IFS=';'
mapfile -t lines < <(echo "$INPUT_TESTS" | grep -v "^$")
e_code=0
for line in "${lines[@]}"; do
  read -r -a args <<< "$line"
  cmd="/opa test ${args[@]} $INPUT_OPTIONS"
  echo " Running: $cmd"
  eval "$cmd" || e_code=1
done
exit $e_code
```

The last part involves building the code on the `action.yml` file in the repository root:

```yaml
name: "OPA"
description: "OPA tests"
branding:
  icon: check-square
  color: green
inputs:
  tests:
    description: "Rego file or directory path."
    required: false
    default: ./
  options:
    required: false
runs:
  using: docker
  image: Dockerfile
```

Once we have these three files, we can create a release and assign a tag.

We can then proceed to the last step with the release and tag, which is building the GitHub actions.

In the repository, create a file called `main.yml` under `.github/worflows` as follows:

```
on: [push]
jobs:
  hello_world_job:
    runs-on: ubuntu-latest
    name: A job to test policies
    steps:
      - name: Test
        uses: ricard0ff/opabooktest@v1.1
```

What this is snippet is going to do is that on the push action, every time a change happens in our repository, it will run our action, which, in our case, is called `opabooktest@v1.1`.

Once a push or a commit is done, GitHub Actions will run automatically. You can check the status of actions, which will show the different steps, as you can see in the following screenshot:

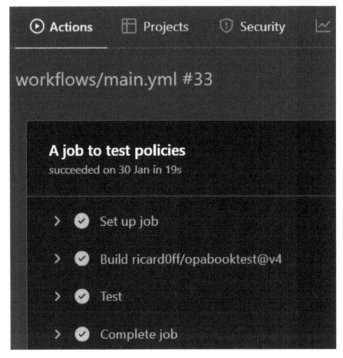

Figure 12.3 – GitHub Actions logs

GitHub Actions can be used to quickly add policy testing to our pipeline.

The sample policies were taken from the OPA policy testing web page, which you can find here: `https://www.openpolicyagent.org/docs/latest/policy-testing/`. You should also look at Conftest as well.

Open Policy Agent testing

One of the features you can use to test policies is available within OPA, as the framework to write tests for policies is built in.

First, we want to create two files, as shown:

```
example@xps:~/opa_test$ ls
book.rego  book_test.rego  opa
```

We create a file called `book.rego` with the following contents. It is a simple policy example that only allows the URI to be `sales` and the method to be `GET`:

```
example@xps:~/opa_test$ cat book.rego
package authz
allow {
    input.uri == ["sales"]
    input.method == "GET"
}
```

In a separate file, we create the test cases. In this example, we will use two policy testing cases: one that tests allowing `GET` methods and another, `test_get_wrong`, testing the blocking of `POST` methods:

```
example@xps:~/opa_test$ cat book_test.rego
package authz
test_get_correct {
    allow with input as {"uri": ["sales"], "method": "GET"}
}
test_get_wrong {
    not allow with input as {"uri": ["sales"], "method":
"POST"}
}
```

Once we have those files in the same directory, we can run the OPA binary with the test flag. We are also using the verbose flag:

```
example@xps:~/opa_test$ ./opa test . -v
data.authz.test_get_correct: PASS (443ns)
data.authz.test_get_wrong: PASS (294ns)
-----------------------------------------------------------------
-----------------
PASS: 2/2
```

Running the test validated that all of the policy test cases would succeed. If we used OPA as a policy enforcement point, we would not be able to POST to the service but would be able to GET against the sales URI as intended.

OPA coverage reports

We can also run OPA in **coverage mode** to define metrics on how many tests were performed. In this case, OPA shows that the coverage was 100, and it highlights both files, book.rego and book_example.rego.

There is no lack of coverage in this small example, but if there were, OPA would pinpoint the offending line, and the final metric would be different:

```
example@xps:~/opa_test$ ./opa test --coverage . -v
{
  "files": {
    "book.rego": {
      "covered": [
        {
          "start": {
            "row": 3
          },
          "end": {
            "row": 5
          }
        }
      ],
      "coverage": 100
    },
    "book_test.rego": {
```

```
        "covered": [
          {
            "start": {
              "row": 3
            },
            "end": {
              "row": 4
            }
          },
          {
            "start": {
              "row": 7
            },
            "end": {
              "row": 8
            }
          }
        ],
        "coverage": 100
      }
    },
    "coverage": 100
}
```

Let's now modify the policy test use case only to allow requests for the IT URI:

```
example@xps:~/opa_test$  cat book_test.rego
package authz

test_get_correct {
    allow with input as {"uri": ["IT"], "method": "GET"}
}

test_get_wrong {
    not allow with input as {"uri": ["sales"], "method":
"POST"}
}
```

If we now run the tests, we get the following:

```
example@xps:~/opa_test$ ./opa test . -v
FAILURES
------------------------------------------------------------------
-----------------
data.authz.test_get_correct: FAIL (427ns)

  Enter data.authz.test_get_correct = _
  | Eval data.authz.test_get_correct = _
  | Index data.authz.test_get_correct = _  (matched 1 rule)
  | Enter data.authz.test_get_correct
  | | Eval data.authz.allow with input as {"method": "GET",
"uri": ["IT"]}
  | | Index data.authz.allow with input as {"method": "GET",
"uri": ["IT"]} (matched 0 rules)
  | | Fail data.authz.allow with input as {"method": "GET",
"uri": ["IT"]}
  | Fail data.authz.test_get_correct = _


SUMMARY
------------------------------------------------------------------
-----------------
data.authz.test_get_correct: FAIL (427ns)
data.authz.test_get_wrong: PASS (323ns)
------------------------------------------------------------------
-----------------
PASS: 1/2
FAIL: 1/2
```

The example now failed as the Rego policy did not match the allow statement. This shows how easy it is to use the OPA built-in engine to do unit testing on Rego policies and be able to create coverage reports.

You can read more about policy testing at https://www.openpolicyagent.org/docs/latest/policy-testing/.

Now that we covered how to do policy testing, let's discuss an enterprise integrated architecture.

Designing for automated policy enforcement across the enterprise

This chapter has covered ITSM frameworks and tools and CI/CD to build automated pipelines. This last section will discuss an architecture that will discuss the different integration points and how we can leverage policies to affect the entirety of the organization.

The following diagram represents the architectural diagram of the relationship between the different components of an organization that leverage policy enforcement. Let's look at this and then detail every aspect.

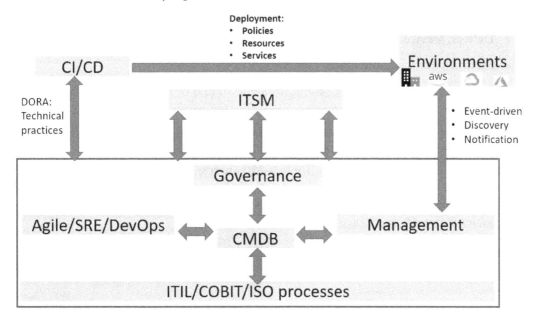

Figure 12.4 – Enterprise architecture deployment workflow

The bottom part inside the rectangle is governed by the ITSM principles that we discussed earlier. ITSM in this respect represents the good practices from ITIL or COBIT that get reflected in the rectangle and comprise the following five areas:

- **Governance**: This layer represents the policies that will be put in place, such as the coercive instruments that we can use PEs for, and the rules and guidelines for the organization to provide and manage its services.

- **Management**: These are the management principles that we apply, such as ensuring the services, platforms, and resources get cataloged, and the inventory gets updated in the CMDB. This layer is also responsible for making sure we discover resources that get spawned.

- **CMDB**: The configuration management database serves as a source of truth regarding the configuration of items within an organization. This helps to track the relationships between resources, but also the history of changes.

- **ITIL/COBIT/ISO processes**: The processes defined by the frameworks support the management of resources. Each of the frameworks has its own similar processes; for example, COBIT specifies five processes:

  - **Evaluate, direct, and monitor (EDM)**

  - **Align, plan, and organize (APO)**

  - **Build, acquire, and implement (BAI)**

  - **Deliver, service, and support (DSS)**

  - **Monitor, evaluate, and assess (MEA)**

  All these processes support the framework and should be integrated with the PolicyOps function. You can find an interesting infographic at the following URL: `https://www.infotech.com/browse/management-and-governance`.

- **Agile / SRE / DevOps / PolicyOps**: These methodologies support policy enforcement in the organization. These teams are responsible for the coding that create automated services and Policy as Code to support the organizational requirements. They should use the **DevOps Research and Assessment (DORA)** metrics to provide metrics to the organization.

All these functions and pieces work together to provide a basis for an organization using PolicyOps to excel at its digital adoption.

Summary

This chapter highlighted some of the frameworks that enterprises use for their ITSM, while also introducing the most popular frameworks, such as ITIL and COBIT, that try to bridge the gap between technical, business, and the requirements in between.

We also discussed some of the most common tools that allow those IT processes centered around IT business management, IT operations management, IT service management, infrastructure management, and so on, to be established through tools such as ServiceNow and JIRA. We discussed the APIs these tools offer and that integration with our workflows is critical.

We covered CI/CD, the most popular tools, the differences between CI and CD, and why they are critical. We created an example of leveraging GitHub Actions to have an automated pipeline to check and test OPA policies.

Finally, we discussed an enterprise architecture and how all parts work together to make sure we can create detective, corrective, and preventative controls in an automated fashion.

In the next chapter, we will be discussing cloud-native policy capabilities. Building from *Chapter 10*, *Policy as Code Tool Evaluation*, we will expand on organizational policies, leverage them, and use them in the major cloud providers.

13
Real-World Scenarios and Architectures

As we reach the end of this book, we will be looking at some real-world scenarios and architectures. We will choose four examples and apply the policy framework we introduced. This allows us to consolidate our knowledge and understand how to use the framework to design policies and architectures that support our goals.

In this chapter, we will discuss several policies. The first use case will show how to tackle costs through a policy. The second example will cover authorization, focusing on supply chain security and highlighting the benefits of attestation. The third example will cover a service migration policy where we will focus on the people aspect to support a transformation effort. Finally, we will cover a compliance enforcement scenario with **Open Policy Agent** (**OPA**).

For this chapter, we will use the framework established in *Chapter 4*, *Framework for Digital Policies*. Every section will use it to discuss the design and implementation. We will use the four stages of the framework to assess the challenges based on the use case, choose the appropriate instruments that align with the goal, and evaluate the effectiveness based on the questions detailed in *Chapter 4*, *Framework for Digital Policies*.

In this chapter, we'll cover the following policies:

- A cost policy scenario

- An authorization policy scenario

- A service migration policy scenario

- A compliance enforcement scenario

Technical requirements

A basic understanding of the framework discussed in *Chapter 4*, *Framework for Digital Policies*, architecture design, basic YAML, and coding is required to follow along with this chapter.

A cost policy scenario

An organization has adopted cloud computing services to migrate some of their existing services and provide more flexibility for teams to develop services using managed solutions such as EKS as they move into containers. The development and infrastructure teams have limited experience using OpenStack, but they have never used a public cloud provider.

Due to security concerns, NAT gateways provide connectivity to virtual machines in private networks. Some services have been set up in different regions to provide redundancy and business continuities. As time progressed, costs from the **Cloud Service Provider** (**CSP**) became concerning, and the **Chief Financial Officer** (**CFO**) got involved to control the rise of expenses.

Framework analysis

This section uses the digital policy framework defined in *Chapter 4, Framework for Digital Policies*, to identify the challenges, establish a goal, and define the instruments to support the policy. The last part is the evaluation, where we will answer some questions to evaluate the effectiveness of the policy.

Challenge identification

The challenges in this organization exist in different domains. First, there is a clear lack of experience when dealing with public cloud providers and the best practices associated with the management of cloud computing infrastructures. The organization hasn't established any best practices that consider onboarding, change of process, and reskilling. The organization does not have a robust process to attributes cost centers to teams and projects, lacking the necessary granularity in terms of spending per project. Technology-wise, the teams are not using anything to control or manage the costs. This can be summarized as follows:

- **People**: There is no FinOps function to control costs. There is a lack of know-how of enterprise architecture and cloud environments.

- **Process**: There is no defined onboarding process to new cloud environments. There also isn't a clear attribution of projects to the specific cost center, which worries the CFO as they cannot track spending across projects.

- **Technology**: There aren't any tools to help track spending. There is no know-how on leveraging the native functionalities of AWS, such as reserved instances, using the billing dashboard, and more.

Now that we have identified the challenges within the organization, let's see what we can do from a policy design perspective.

Policy design

The organization can implement a policy to address the spiraling costs. Let's suppose the policy is rolled out across different groups. In that case, we can leverage a catchy code name that has a psychological effect. For example, *A cost-conscious agile organization*. The policy will aim to reduce the spending of the **cloud environment**.

The instruments used for this policy will be a mix. We will use suasion, coercive, and financial instruments to address the people, processes, and technology.

First, we will address the people side. We will use suasion instruments to launch a certification program that gives employees badges and email signatures to show their accomplishments in achieving certifications in a specific domain. We can couple it with financial instruments to reward employees who earn specific certifications in critical areas of the organization's digital domain, such as analytics, the cloud, big data, and more.

Regarding coercion instruments, we will use **service control policies** (**SCPs**) to enforce controls to avoid the usage of specific resources, especially in development environments where we can limit the type of resources.

Additionally, we will implement a governance structure based on a control tower to ensure new services are onboarded according to the specification.

Policy implementation

This section will define the instruments with real examples that tie to the *Policy design* section. In this section, we will split the format of the instruments into three big pillars: **people**, **processes**, and **technology**.

People

Here, we will subscribe to an e-learning platform such as **Coursera** to launch and implement an impactful learning program for key areas identified in the organization; in this case, we will focus on FinOps, the cloud, and analytics.

Having dashboards that measure the skill level allows us to track proficiency across the different teams, as shown in the following screenshot:

Figure 13.1 – The e-learning platform dashboard

As you can see, the dashboard allows easy tracking across teams to understand the mastery and the number of learners. These e-learning platforms have robust management tools coupled with a **Learning Management Solution** (**LMS**), and they provide all the building blocks to implement learning programs within an organization.

Let's look at the technology and process-linked instruments to support the goal of reducing costs.

Technology

To reduce costs, we will use **AWS Control Tower** to establish a governance layer, with SCPs added to new accounts. Control Tower allows us to have a tag strategy policy to enforce cost centers and be able to track spending across different projects while also being able to use SCPs to prevent expensive resources from being spun up.

The architecture is defined in the following screenshot. It highlights how we can apply a tagging policy, along with SCPs, at the organization level so that new onboarded accounts will have tagging and service control policies applied:

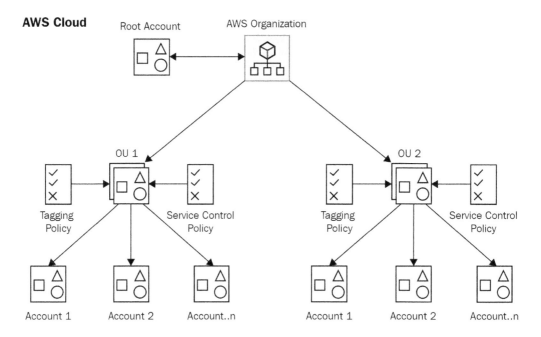

Figure 13.2 – The Control Tower cost policy architecture

The tag strategy will enforce a cost center on every new account. With Control Tower, it is easy to create this policy that will mark resources as being compliant when a tag is used.

The tag policy that we can import into Control Tower will be something similar to the following snippet:

```
{
    "tags": {
        "CostCenter": {
            "tag_key": {
                "@@assign": "CostCenter"
```

```
        },
        "tag_value": {
            "@@assign": [
                "ProjectX",
                "ProjectY"
            ]
        },
        "enforced_for": {
            "@@assign": [
                "ec2:instance"
            ]
        }
    }
  }
}
```

The preceding snippet shows different stanzas. The first is `tag_key`, where we will specify that `CostCenter` needs to be present. The second is `tag_value` to define the existing projects, which, in this case, is two, `ProjectX` and `ProjectY`. Finally, we specify the types of resources with which this tag will be enforced. In this example, we use the `enforced_for` keyword to select where the enforcement is going to happen, we choose `ec2:instance` as the resources.

More information can be found at the following link, which is a lab for Control Tower regarding tag policies: `https://controltower.aws-management.tools/ops/tag/`.

Now, let's look at how we can implement a budget notification associated with the cloud accounts to alert the FinOps teams. We can define it in the YAML code and apply it to the Control Tower dashboard. The following snippet demonstrates how to do this:

```
Description: "Budget Example PAC Book"
Resources:
  BudgetBase:
    Type: "AWS::Budgets::Budget"
    Properties:
      Budget:
        BudgetLimit:
          Amount: 1000
```

```yaml
        Unit: USD
      TimeUnit: MONTHLY
      TimePeriod:
        Start: 1643840542
        End: 1993501342
      BudgetType: COST
    NotificationsWithSubscribers:
      - Notification:
          NotificationType: ACTUAL
          ComparisonOperator: GREATER_THAN
          Threshold: 98
        Subscribers:
          - SubscriptionType: EMAIL
            Address: <finops@org.com>
      - Notification:
          NotificationType: ACTUAL
          ComparisonOperator: GREATER_THAN
          Threshold: 75
        Subscribers:
          - SubscriptionType: EMAIL
            Address: <finops@org.com>
Outputs:
  BudgetId:
    Value: !Ref BudgetBase
```

The preceding snippet uses `AWS::Budgets::Budget`, as defined in the YAML code with the budget limit. In this example, this is `1000USD` for a monthly period, and the period needs to be defined in the **Unix epoch** with a start date and an end date. Finally, we specify alerts at 75% and 98% of the budget; this is so we can alert the FinOps teams once the budget crosses the defined threshold.

The snippet can be used as a **Customization for AWS Control Tower** (**CFCT**) solution. For more information, please visit `https://docs.aws.amazon.com/solutions/latest/customizations-for-aws-control-tower/welcome.html`.

The last instrument that we can use is the restriction of resources via SCPs. In the following snippet, we will enforce the restriction of resources associated with NAT gateways, as they were identified as a cost issue in the development environments. The SCP for it would be as follows:

```
{
    "Version": "2012-10-17",
    "Statement": [
        {
            "Action": [
                "ec2:CreateNatGateway",
                "ec2:CreateInternetGateway",
                "ec2:DeleteNatGateway",
                "ec2:AttachInternetGateway",
                "ec2:DeleteInternetGateway",
                "ec2:DetachInternetGateway"
            ],
            "Resource": "*",
            "Effect": "Deny"
        }
    ]
}
```

The preceding snippet builds upon the SCPs from previous chapters. But in summary, it uses a DENY statement, which can be seen after Effect, to block the resources defined in Action.

As you can see, we used and mixed different types of instruments to achieve the goal of cost-saving. Next, we will touch on the evaluation part, where we will evaluate the effect of the policy, which can serve as a feedback loop if we want to iterate on the policy design phase.

Evaluation

This section will review some of the evaluation questions defined in *Chapter 4*, *Framework for Digital Policies*. This step is crucial as it allows you to gather feedback and adjust the instruments or goals in future revisions. Consider the following list of questions:

- What effect did the policy have on the actors?

  The policy increased the teams' knowledge by supporting certifications in the organization. Also, it created the proper guardrails and governance structure so that teams could focus on delivering value.

- Were there any side effects of applying the policy?

  One of the side effects was that people in non-IT roles also wanted to take part in the learning platform, which improved the know-how of the organization.

- What is the effect of this policy on the organization groups?

  The CFO is now able to track spending from the IT teams. The policy had the effect of preventing spiraling costs, allowing teams to spend those savings in other parts of the business.

- Was the policy implemented in the agreed timelines?

  There was a delay in setting up the Control Tower instruments due to the engineering effort. Currently, the KPIs on digital inclusion are also being monitored.

As you can see, in this example, there was a mix of policies using suasion instruments to create an e-learning environment and financial instruments to increase the adoption of the learning platforms. Additionally, we used coercive instruments to enact the guardrails by using the tagging policy and the SCPs.

Now, let's look at an authorization policy scenario that deals with supply chain issues.

An authorization policy scenario

An organization that develops software in-house has recently found that they were vulnerable due to using an open source library in their code. As supply chain attacks have been increasing tremendously over the last few years, *Sonatype* states in their 2021 study that **open source software** (**OSS**) supply chain attacks have increased by 650% compared to 2020. Additionally, open source downloads are growing, with last year hitting 2.2 trillion, highlighting the impact third-party dependencies and packages might have on the organization.

The organization wants to prevent any supply chain issues by the development teams during the **Software Development Life Cycle (SDLC)**.

Framework analysis

This section uses the digital policy framework defined in *Chapter 4, Framework for Digital Policies*, to identify the challenges, establish a goal, and define the instruments to support the policy. The last part is the evaluation, where we will answer some questions to evaluate the effectiveness of the policy.

Challenge identification

The organization uses DevOps pipelines to test, validate, and package the software in an automated fashion. Currently, there is no verification in the supply chain to check whether the steps were intended or whether the right actor performed the action.

The challenge is that the organization requires a way to secure the integrity of the software supply chain. Let's look at what we can design to help address this challenge.

Policy design

This example will design a policy to secure the supply chain based on secure computing. The attestation policy will be around providing instruments that can provide verifiable proof of the quality of the software. The design will be based on the **in-toto** specification. In-toto is a specification to build a system for securing the SDLC (for instance, the development, the build, the testing, the packaging, and more). Using the in-toto specification allows you to attest the integrity and verifiability of all the actions performed in the pipeline:

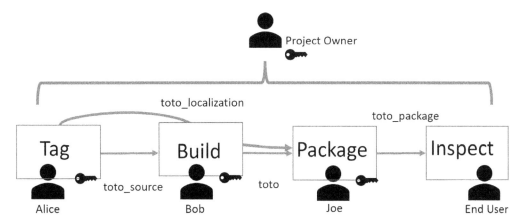

Figure 13.3 – In-toto usage in the supply chain

In the preceding diagram, a project owner has created the layout to describe the supply chain structure that the client can use to verify.

Underneath the project owner, Alice, Bob, and Joe carry out their functions, and have an extra step, linking metadata to ensure the operations can be verified in the future. We call this being able to **attest** to their operations. Finally, the end user can use the final product, metadata links, and layout to verify the integrity of the products and the entire chain.

To create a visual layout of your supply chain, you can use the following website, which has a GUI that simplifies the creation of supply chain layouts: `https://in-toto.engineering.nyu.edu/`:

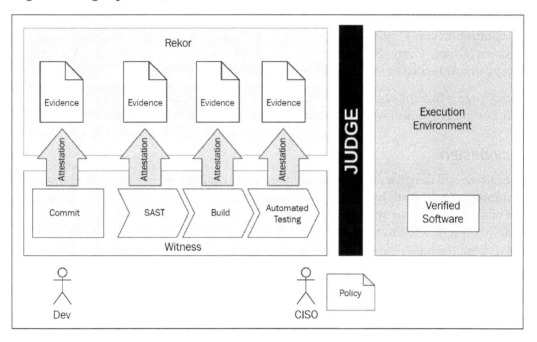

Figure 13.4 – Software life cycle, from a commit to verified software, a pipeline in TestifySec

In *Figure 13.4*, we can see the flow from the developer to the final stage, which is verified software. Let's see the various steps.

First, the developer makes a commit that triggers an automated **Continuous Integration** (**CI**) pipeline. Each step of the CI pipeline outputs evidence; this evidence is *linked* to the artifact and signed with a trusted key.

The **Chief Information Security Officer** (**CISO**) distills the organizational policy into a witness policy and signs it using a private key. This policy is configured in an admission controller that utilizes the witness verification library of **Judge** (an open source project that can be found at `https://github.com/testifysec/judge-k8s`) along with the corresponding public key.

When a new artifact is scheduled in the execution environment, it is evaluated against the policy for admission.

Policy implementation

For this implementation, since we are focused on the organization's supply chain issues, we will use Witness.

Witness is an implementation of the **in-toto** specification. It is licensed under Apache 2.0 and has commercial support available. You can find more information about it at `https://www.testifysec.com/`.

 The following example will walk you through the following activities:

1.   Creating and signing a witness policy
2.   Creating attestations linked to an artifact
3.   Verifying that the artifacts were developed in compliance with the policy

Now, let's talk about Basic Witness Demo.

Basic Witness Demo

First, make sure you clone the repository at `https://github.com/testifysec/witness-examples`.

Next, you will need to download the Witness binaries and place them in the root repository. You can download them at `https://github.com/testifysec/witness/releases`.

Then, move them into the cloned repo:

```
$ cd witness-examples
```

Next, you will need to create a keypair to sign the attestations and extract the public key:

```
$ openssl genrsa -out buildkey.pem 2048
```

Now you can extract the public key:

```
$ openssl rsa -in buildkey.pem -outform PEM -pubout -out
buildpublic.pem
```

Now that we have the public key, let's construct the policy template.

Policy template

Next, we will build the Witness policy template, allowing users to make assertions and test attestation collections generated during the Witness run. You can read more about Witness policies at https://github.com/testifysec/witness/blob/main/docs/policy.md:

---

policy-template.yaml

```
expires: "2035-12-17T23:57:40-05:00"
steps:
  build:
      name: build
      attestations:
          - type: https://witness.dev/attestations/material/v0.1
          - type: https://witness.dev/attestations/product/v0.1
          - type: https://witness.dev/attestations/command-run/
v0.1
          regoPolicies:
          - name:  "exitcode"
            module: "{{CMD_MODULE}}"
      functionaries:
          - type: publickey
            publickeyid: "{{KEYID}}"
publickeys:
  "{{KEYID}}":
    keyid: "{{KEYID}}"
    key:
```

There is also a **Rego policy** to ensure that the commands are what we expect:

cmd.rego

```
package commandrun
deny[msg] {
    input.exitcode != 0
    msg := "exitcode not 0"
}
deny[msg] {
    input.cmd[2] != "echo 'hello' > hello.txt"
    msg := "cmd not correct"
}
```

Once we have those building blocks in place, we can template the policy. You can use the `template_policy.sh` script on the repository or copy it from the following snippet. This script does the following:

- It generates a key ID by taking the sha256 hash of the public key used to sign attestations.

- Base64 encodes the PEM-encoded public key.

- Base64 encodes the Rego policy.

- It replaces the {{KEYID}} and {{KEY}} placeholders in the template with the generated values.

- It transforms the YAML into JSON

You will also require yq. You can execute the following command, which will get the latest binary for Linux x64:

```
$ wget https://github.com/mikefarah/yq/releases/download/
v4.23.1/yq_linux_amd64 -O /usr/bin/yq && chmod +x /usr/bin/yq
```

template_policy.sh

```
#!/bin/sh
#requires yq v4.2.0
cmd_b64="$(openssl base64 -A <"cmd.rego")"
pubkey_b64="$(openssl base64 -A <"buildpublic.pem")"
```

```
cp policy-template.yaml policy.tmp.yaml
keyid=$(sha256sum buildpublic.pem | awk '{print $1}')
sed -i "s/{{KEYID}}/$keyid/g" policy.tmp.yaml
yq eval ".publickeys.${keyid}.key = \"${pubkey_b64}\""
--inplace policy.tmp.yaml
sed -i "s/{{CMD_MODULE}}/$cmd_b64/g" policy.tmp.yaml
yq e -o=json policy.tmp.yaml > policy.json
```

Now we can create a keypair to sign the policy:

```
$ openssl genrsa -out policykey.pem 2048
```

Extract the public key as follows:

```
$ openssl rsa -in policykey.pem -outform PEM -pubout -out
policypublic.pem
```

Now we can sign the policy with Witness:

```
$ ./witness sign -k policykey.pem -f policy.json -o policy.
signed.json
```

Creating the attestations

At this stage, we are ready to generate the attestations. Let's try it with hello.txt (make sure it is not in the root repository):

```
$ ./witness run -s build -k buildkey.pem -o build-attestation.
json -- \
bash -c "echo 'hello' > hello.txt"
```

You can use the following command to view the attestation:

```
$ cat build-attestation.json | jq -r .payload | base64 -d | jq
.
```

We can now verify the attestation from the file output of hello.txt to see whether it satisfies our policy.

Using the corresponding public key, we validate whether the policy is trustworthy:

```
$ ./witness verify -k policypublic.pem -p policy.signed.json -a
\
build-attestation.json -f hello.txt
```

The output should be similar to the following:

```
INFO      Verification succeeded
INFO      Evidence:
INFO      0:
sha256:a2dccb3ce3b54310cfec2d339493fa62dbc24d3c4c5b961efe7
d030704bded42   build-attestation.json
```

But let's go ahead and change the product name to `hello.fail.txt`:

```
$ ./witness run -s build -k buildkey.pem -o build-attestation.
json -- \
bash -c "echo 'hello' > hello.fail.txt"
```

We verify it as follows:

```
$ ./witness verify -k policypublic.pem -p policy.signed.json \
-a build-attestation.json -f hello.fail.txt`
```

And now we get an error:

```
ERROR     failed to verify policy: failed to verify policy:
attestations for step build could not be used due to:
policy was denied due to:
cmd not correct
```

As you can see, Witness can secure the supply chains of organizations and fulfill the need identified for this organization, being able to attest to the software produced.

In the next example, we will break the mold of what we have been doing so far in this chapter. Instead, we will focus on **FedRAMP Vulnerability Scanning Requirements for Containers** by mapping the requirements to the policy that has been implemented.

Evaluation

This section will compare the policy implemented against the FedRAMP Vulnerability Scanning Requirements for Containers. You can access the document at `https://www.fedramp.gov/assets/resources/documents/Vulnerability_Scanning_requirements_for_Containers.pdf`.

Let's go through the different requirements next.

Hardened images

Judge, an attestation validator, as shown in *Figure 13.4*, can enforce a policy that ensures only hardened baseline images are deployed to production environments. This policy enables the necessary requirements for hardened images in specific environments. You can read more on Judge and a proof of concept Kubernetes admission controller using the witness attestation verification library here:

```
https://github.com/testifysec/judge-k8s
```

Container build, test, and orchestration pipelines

Witness validates cryptographic material issued by **continuous integration (CI)** providers. This material can be validated before deploying it into production systems. This makes it easier to integrate with the container pipeline as per the FedRAMP requirements.

Vulnerability scanning

Judge scans every artifact when it is scheduled. A policy can be created to ensure that all workloads meet the 30-day scan window. This requirement should be adopted in any container environment.

A good practice is to maintain short container uptimes by tracking the **reverse uptime** and **golden image freshness**.

Registry monitoring

Judge enforces the Witness policy to ensure containers that do not meet FedRAMP policy cannot be deployed in production environments. It works with any container registry or sideloading method, including air gap deployments.

Asset management and inventory reporting for deployed containers

Judge injects a reference into the entire audit trail of the deployed container, including all signatures, approvals, scans, **Software Bill of Materials (SBOM)**, and attestations.

Security sensors

Judge can act as a security sensor. It can be deployed and integrated with **Endpoint detection and response (EDR)** technologies. This makes it a good integration point with other toolsets present in the organization.

FedRAMP Vulnerability Scanning Requirements for Containers can be fulfilled using the policy implementation discussed in this section.

Now, let's move on to another scenario that will be less technical and more from a people management perspective.

A service migration policy scenario

An organization is undergoing a modernization effort to become more competitive. The areas identified as critical for their roadmap include cloud computing consumption and workload migration.

The existing development teams are offshored, and there is no in-house knowledge. The organization would like to migrate some of its monolithic services to microservices and serverless and create a local development team.

Framework analysis

This section uses the digital policy framework defined in *Chapter 4, Framework for Digital Policies*, to identify the challenges, establish a goal, and define the instruments to support the policy. The last part is the evaluation, where we will answer some questions to evaluate the effectiveness of the policy.

Challenge identification

In this scenario, the challenge is more related to the people side than the technological side. As such, the policies should be designed to support the people aspect, similar to what we used in the cost policy scenario.

Another critical challenge is that there is currently no in-house development team, which means that crucial business processes should be carefully thought out in the new environments to avoid losing business IP and support for those systems.

Policy design

Define a policy to support the onboarding and retention of talent in key areas, such as cloud migration, microservices, and serverless. Create an LMS system to support new and existing employees.

Define a reward policy for newly onboarded employees to receive rewards if they complete specific courses and implement a retrain policy for existing workers.

Policy implementation

This policy will primarily implement an LMS system, making it accessible to new and existing employees. However, the policy could also go a step further in terms of financial instruments. For example, McKinsey stated that a one-off investment of 50 million in financial incentives could generate 1 billion in recurring value.

This economic incentive aims to link it to transformation outcomes within the controls of teams, for example, the number of decomposed services or workloads migrated to microservices. There should be more than a linear performance bonus by celebrating and rewarding overachievement.

Finally, tailor the program to the organization's culture. For example, a small organization could cap the financial instruments to 90% of their annual salary, but a large organization could tie the financial instruments with the value provided, such that employees would get 1.5% of the value generated by the initiative (in some instances, for example, achieving a 200 million benefit, would mean a bonus many times the annual salary).

Now, let's check the evaluation of this policy

Evaluation

Since the organization has implemented several instruments to retain and retrain employees, we will now check the evaluation of the policy:

- Is the policy respecting **Consistency, Congruency, Coherency (3Cs)?**

  Yes; from a **consistency** perspective, the instruments are aligned. We have the suasion instruments with nudges to help people onboard the LMS and the financial instruments to help drive more knowledge into specific areas and support the transformation. From a **congruency** perspective, all instruments are aligned to support the goals. And finally, it is **coherent** as the goals are aligned. The policy exists to support the organization's transformation.

  What is the effect of this policy on your organization groups?

  The effect of the policy was to accelerate the transformation, bring new talent, and solidify know-how in critical areas.

- What were the costs of implementing this policy?

  From a cost perspective, the financial incentives were a one-off cost, and the subscription to the LMS system was a recurring cost. Operational costs also increased due to the hiring of new employees with expertise in the identified key areas.

This example was less technical but still crucial, as sometimes, the goal does not require software usage but only the implementation and adaptation of existing processes.

In the last scenario, we will look at compliance enforcement.

A compliance enforcement scenario

In this scenario, a highly regulated organization wants to adopt CIS and PCI DSS 3.2 standards to ensure their microservices cloud environments are compliant.

One of the issues they have is that, due to their environment being operated in a CSP, they don't know how to access compliance or use a **policy enforcement point** to delegate authorization and access to their services.

There's also been friction between the IT and compliance teams, and the project has been paused many times due to a lack of compliance in some of the payment services.

Framework analysis

This section uses the digital policy framework defined in *Chapter 4, Framework for Digital Policies*, to identify the challenges, establish a goal, and define the instruments to support the policy. The last part is the evaluation, where we will answer some questions to evaluate the effectiveness of the policy.

Challenge identification

The challenge of this organization is in the way it deals with compliance. There is no alignment between the teams, and there is no technology to provide near real-time compliance assessment. Therefore, this makes the role of both teams very hard. On one hand, the IT team gets a decrease in agility and release velocity, while on the other hand, the compliance team never gets an accurate representation of the state of the environment.

Policy design

In this case, there is a need to implement a compliance monitoring system to have a dashboard representing the necessary regulations, industry standards, and governance policies.

This would allow the organization to be on top of any regulation changes and check the up-to-date standard. A compliance culture that can be fostered would ensure transparent processes regarding adherence to specific standards, the responsible stakeholder, guidance documentation, and any penalties.

Since most of the requirements are in Kubernetes and microservices, there is a need to accelerate the compliance and provide cloud-native capabilities and integration with the existing services and systems.

Policy implementation

We will use Styra **Declarative Authorization Service** (**DAS**) from the original creators of OPA to implement this policy. Styra DAS is built for cloud-native environments, making moving to the cloud more accessible and faster by using existing centralized **Identity and Access Management** (**IAM**) systems.

One of the functionalities of Styra DAS that can fulfill this policy is the ability to use `compliance packs.`

The Styra DAS compliance packs are the fastest and most straightforward way to deploy OPA Policy as Code to meet regulatory requirements. Let's check it out.

Once we have added our system to the Styra environment, we can activate the specific compliance packs by navigating to the **Compliance** blade, as shown in the following screenshot:

Figure 13.5 – Activating compliance packs in Styra

Once the compliance pack has been activated, we can see the individual rules and change or add custom rules.

For example, we can configure the rules in **ignore** mode, **monitor** mode, or **enforce** mode. In this scenario, we will show two rules.

The first rule is to restrict containers to specific ports. In the rule we stated that only ports from `1024` to `1224` should be accessed. The second rule prevents pods from accessing the host network, including the host loopback device. We will activate this one in **monitor** mode:

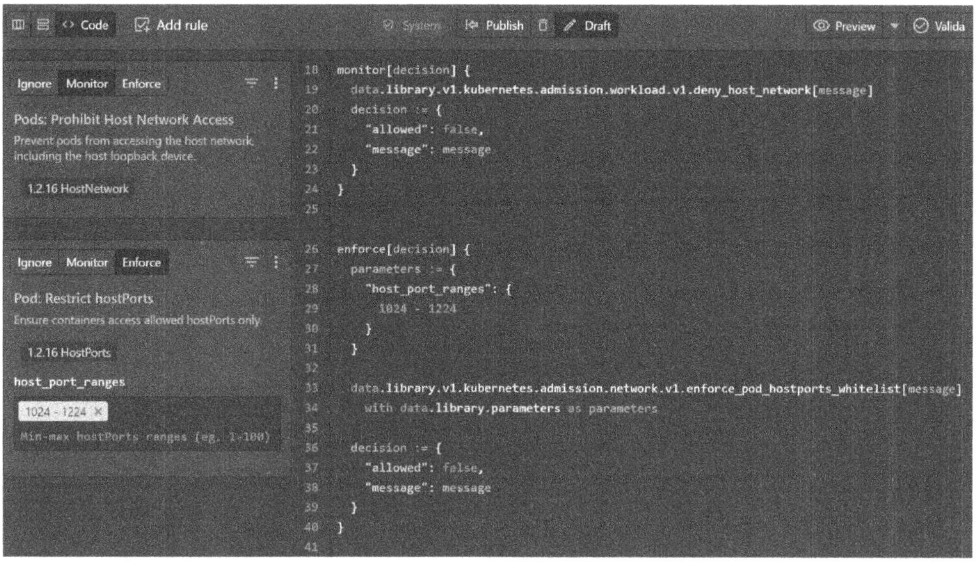

Figure 13.6 – Styra DAS CIS Benchmarks rule editing

As you can see, the use of compliance packs is straightforward, with the possibility of customizing the rules and going beyond the traditional controls.

Since Styra provides a compliance dashboard, it can serve as a single plane for both IT and compliance teams to share and see what is happening in near real time from a compliance perspective.

Another possibility is the usage of **RegScale**, which is a platform to provide the organization with real-time reporting and analytics of the compliance tasks. This means that the old, traditional methods of manual risk reporting can be overcome. RegScale delivers the ability to discard paper and move into digital compliance assessment, meet regulatory needs, and track them in real time, achieving continuous compliance.

Evaluation

This section will evaluate the policy's purpose within the different teams. This is to understand what can be improved in future implementations of this policy. Take a look at the following list of questions:

- What effect did the policy have on the actors?

  The compliance teams worked more closely with the development teams to ensure the organization was compliant. The dashboard was shared by the different teams and allowed them to quickly see how their services and actions would impact the compliance of the organization in near real time.

- Was the baseline defined?

  The baseline was defined after a period of experimentation where only notifications were used before enforcing any corrective actions. This allowed the teams to adjust to the buffer period and understand how to adapt their processes without impacting their velocity too much.

- Was the baseline explained during the implementation?

  No. The baseline requires an adaptive period. In this period the rules work in monitor mode. As such, the baseline could only be explained after the monitor phase. Styra supported the baseline explanation by monitoring the compliance rules and then enforcing them.

Summary

This chapter analyzed different scenarios within the framework defined in *Chapter 4, Framework for Digital Policies*. Most of these scenarios were based on real-world use cases and highlighted different policies.

The first case regarding cost is a very prevalent case and one that used a mixture of process policies, along with **Policy as Code**. It made the best use of mixing instruments, one to support the guardrails and the other to persuade people to take training.

The second use case focused on an authorization policy that focused on supply chain security issues, which is top of the agenda in organization boards. The example mostly used Policy as Code using the TestifySec software of Judge and Witness to highlight how attestation can be done.

The section on migration was more process-oriented. As such, you did not see many tools or Policy as Code implementations. But it is essential to highlight how people are the fundamental piece of any organization.

Finally, we covered a compliance use case. In that use case, we focused on commercial tools such as **Styra DAS**, which could quickly be used in conjunction with compliance packs to provide the necessary best practices. This, used in conjunction with **RegScale**, drives the organization toward shared ownership with the compliance and IT teams working hand in hand to drive the organization's goals further.

This chapter helped you understand the framework for digital policies when applied to real-world scenarios and how the framework can be used in your organization to establish digital policies.

Index

`Packt.com`

Subscribe to our online digital library for full access to over 7,000 books and videos, as well as industry leading tools to help you plan your personal development and advance your career. For more information, please visit our website.

Why subscribe?

- Spend less time learning and more time coding with practical eBooks and Videos from over 4,000 industry professionals

- Improve your learning with Skill Plans built especially for you

- Get a free eBook or video every month

- Fully searchable for easy access to vital information

- Copy and paste, print, and bookmark content

Did you know that Packt offers eBook versions of every book published, with PDF and ePub files available? You can upgrade to the eBook version at `packt.com` and as a print book customer, you are entitled to a discount on the eBook copy. Get in touch with us at `customercare@packtpub.com` for more details.

At `www.packt.com`, you can also read a collection of free technical articles, sign up for a range of free newsletters, and receive exclusive discounts and offers on Packt books and eBooks.

Other Books You May Enjoy

If you enjoyed this book, you may be interested in these other books by Packt:

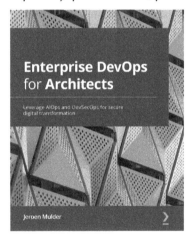

Enterprise DevOps for Architects

Jeroen Mulder

ISBN: 9781801812153

- Create DevOps architecture and integrate it with the enterprise architecture
- Discover how DevOps can add value to the quality of IT delivery
- Explore strategies to scale DevOps for an enterprise
- Architect SRE for an enterprise as next-level DevOps
- Understand AIOps and what value it can bring to an enterprise
- Create your AIOps architecture and integrate it into DevOps
- Create your DevSecOps architecture and integrate it with the existing DevOps setup
- Apply zero-trust principles and industry security frameworks to DevOps

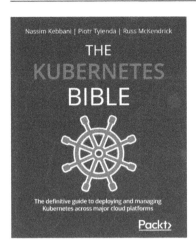

The Kubernetes Bible

Nassim Kebbani, Piotr Tylenda, Russ McKendrick

ISBN: 9781838827694

- Manage containerized applications with Kubernetes
- Understand Kubernetes architecture and the responsibilities of each component
- Set up Kubernetes on Amazon Elastic Kubernetes Service, Google Kubernetes Engine, and Microsoft Azure Kubernetes Service
- Deploy cloud applications such as Prometheus and Elasticsearch using Helm charts
- Discover advanced techniques for Pod scheduling and auto-scaling the cluster
- Understand possible approaches to traffic routing in Kubernetes

Packt is searching for authors like you

If you're interested in becoming an author for Packt, please visit `authors.packtpub.com` and apply today. We have worked with thousands of developers and tech professionals, just like you, to help them share their insight with the global tech community. You can make a general application, apply for a specific hot topic that we are recruiting an author for, or submit your own idea.

Share your thoughts

Now you've finished *Policy design in the age of digital adoption*, we'd love to hear your thoughts! Scan the QR code below to go straight to the Amazon review page for this book and share your feedback or leave a review on the site that you purchased it from.

https://packt.link/r/1-801-81174-1

Your review is important to us and the tech community and will help us make sure we're delivering excellent quality content.